S0-ARN-434

The Best
AMERICAN
ESSAYS
2008

GUEST EDITORS OF
THE BEST AMERICAN ESSAYS

The Best AMERICAN ESSAYS® 2008

Edited and with an Introduction
by ADAM GOPNIK

Robert Atwan, Series Editor

HOUGHTON MIFFLIN COMPANY
BOSTON · NEW YORK   2008

Copyright © 2008 Houghton Mifflin Harcourt Publishing Company
Introduction copyright © 2008 by Adam Gopnik
ALL RIGHTS RESERVED

The Best American Series and *The Best American Essays* are registered trademarks of
Houghton Mifflin Harcourt Publishing Company.

No part of this work may be reproduced or transmitted in any form or by any
means, electronic or mechanical, including photocopying and recording, or by any
information storage or retrieval system without the proper written permission of
the copyright owner unless such copying is expressly permitted by federal copyright
law. With the exception of nonprofit transcription in Braille, Houghton Mifflin is
not authorized to grant permission for further uses of copyrighted selections reprinted in this book without the permission of their owners. Permission must be ob-
tained from the individual copyright owners as identified herein. Address requests
for permission to make copies of Houghton Mifflin material to Permissions,
Houghton Mifflin Company, 215 Park Avenue South, New York, New York 10003.

www.houghtonmifflinbooks.com

ISSN 0888-3742
ISBN 978-0-618-98331-5
ISBN 978-0-618-98322-3 (PBK.)

Printed in the United States of America

VB 10 9 8 7 6 5 4 3 2 1

Patricia Brieschke, "Cracking Open," from *PMS*, no. 1, 2007. Copyright © 2007
by Patricia Brieschke. Reprinted by permission of the author.

Rich Cohen, "Becoming Adolf," from *Vanity Fair*, November 2007. Copyright ©
2007 by Rich Cohen. Reprinted by permission of the Wylie Agency, Inc.

Bernard Cooper, "The Constant Gardener," from *Los Angeles Magazine*, October
2007. Copyright © 2007 by Bernard Cooper. Reprinted by permission of the author.

Atul Gawande, "The Way We Age Now," from *The New Yorker*, April 30, 2007.
Copyright © 2007 by Atul Gawande. Reprinted by permission of the author.

Albert Goldbarth, "Everybody's Nickname," from the *Georgia Review*. Copyright
© 2007 by the University of Georgia. Reprinted by permission of the author.

Emily R. Grosholz, "On Necklaces," from *Prairie Schooner*, Summer 2007. Copyright © 2007 by Emily R. Grosholz. Reprinted by permission of the author.

Anthony Lane, "Candid Camera," from *The New Yorker*, September 24, 2007.
Copyright © 2007 by Anthony Lane. Reprinted by permission of International Creative Management, Inc. Elliot Erwitt photograph reprinted by permission of Magnum Photos.

Jonathan Lethem, "The Ecstasy of Influence," from *Harper's Magazine*, February
2007. Copyright © 2007 by Jonathan Lethem. Reprinted by permission of the Richard Parks Agency. "In My Room" by Brian Wilson and Gary Usher. Copyright ©
1964 Irving Music, Inc. (BMI). Copyright renewed. Used by permission. All rights
reserved.

Ariel Levy, "The Lesbian Bride's Handbook," from *New York,* April 30, 2007. Copyright © 2007 by Ariel Levy. Reprinted by permission of the author.

Jamal Mahjoub, "Salamanca," from *Transition,* no. 97, 2007. Copyright © 2007 by Jamal Mahjoub. Reprinted by permission of the author.

Louis Menand, "Notable Quotables," from *The New Yorker,* February 19 and 26, 2007. Copyright © 2007 by Louis Menand. Reprinted by permission of the Wylie Agency, Inc.

Ander Monson, "Solipsism," from *Pinch,* Fall 2007. Copyright © 2007 by Ander Monson. Reprinted by permission of Ander Monson and *Pinch.*

Rick Moody, "On Celestial Music," from *Salmagundi,* Winter/Spring 2007. Copyright © 2007 by Rick Moody. Reprinted by permission of the author. "Try a Little Tenderness," words and music by Harry Woods, Jimmy Campbell, and Reg Connelly. Copyright © 1932 (Renewed) Campbell, Connelly & Co., Ltd. All rights in the United States and Canada administered by EMI Robbins Catalog Inc. (publishing) and Alfred Publishing Co., Inc. (print). All rights reserved.

Hugh Raffles, "Cricket Fighting," from *Granta,* no. 98, Summer 2007. Copyright © 2007 by Hugh Raffles. Reprinted by permission of Denise Shannon Literary Agency Inc.

David Sedaris, "This Old House," from *The New Yorker,* July 9 and 16, 2007. Copyright © 2007 by David Sedaris. Reprinted by permission of the author.

Sam Shaw, "Run Like Fire Once More," from *Harper's Magazine,* August 2007. Copyright © 2007 by Sam Shaw. Reprinted by permission of the author. Lyrics by Sri Chinmoy are reprinted by kind permission of the Sri Chinmoy Marathon Team.

Charles Simic, "The Renegade," from the *New York Review of Books,* December 20, 2007. Copyright © 2007 by Charles Simic. Reprinted by permission of the author.

Lauren Slater, "Tripp Lake," from *Swink,* no. 3, 2007. Copyright © 2007 by Lauren Slater. Reprinted by permission of the author.

John Updike, "Extreme Dinosaurs," from *National Geographic,* December 2007. Copyright © 2007 by National Geographic Society. Reprinted by permission of National Geographic Society and John Updike.

Joe Wenderoth, "Where God Is Glad," from *Open City,* no. 23, 2007. Copyright © 2007 by Joe Wenderoth. All rights reserved. Reprinted by arrangement with Mary Evans, Inc.

Lee Zacharias, "Buzzards," from *Southern Humanities Review,* Spring 2007. Copyright © 2007 by Auburn University. Reprinted by permission of *Southern Humanities Review* and Lee Zacharias.

Contents

Foreword

"Essays end up in books" — like this one — "but they start their lives in magazines," wrote Susan Sontag in her introduction to *The Best American Essays 1992*. That's what I see first, year after year: the magazines.

Hundreds of them. Some so slick they slip from my hands and slide off each other when I try to construct neat piles. Some of the satiny and scented fashion magazines display so much commercialized fetishism — high-gloss models brought to erotic ecstasy by luxurious handbags — that I feel, as I dutifully flip through the clingy pages searching for content, I must be a creature from a different planet, a terribly deprived and disadvantaged one. Still, that doesn't prevent me from sniffing the perfume ads along the way, and for an intoxicating moment sample a world where reading and writing essays seems not just a marginal occupation, but decidedly déclassé.

From the commodity-porn of the fashion magazines, it's a relief to turn to the *Nation,* the *New Republic,* the *American Prospect,* the *Weekly Standard,* the *Progressive, Mother Jones* — solid, politically oriented magazines with little glitz and gloss (and user-friendly tables of contents) that earnestly bring me back to the planet I inhabit, with all its urgent problems and noisy differences of opinion. Here the difficulty isn't in attempting to locate an essay buried among pages of ads for fashion designers, cosmetics, jewelry, and five-thousand-dollar spike heels, but in finding essays that have a good chance of surviving past their moment of publication. These durable essays are more likely found in such prestigious magazines as

The New Yorker, Atlantic Monthly, and *Harper's,* or some of the Sunday magazines (the *New York Times* and *Washington Post* supplements being among the best), where true essays appear along with commentary, criticism, and top-flight reporting.

But even the general weeklies and monthlies are stingy when it comes to personal essays; their bread and butter still depends on timely topics, information, and public controversy. So if you want to find literary essays by the cartload, you need to turn to the literary periodicals, where much of the best nonfiction is being published. These "little magazines," with their low budgets and high aspirations, are usually, but not always, published with the cooperation of university English departments across the nation. Although sometimes the affiliation is clear (*Antioch Review, Kenyon Review, Harvard Review, Notre Dame Review, Gettysburg Review*), most often it isn't: *Salmagundi* (Skidmore), *Raritan* (Rutgers), *Agni* (Boston University), *Epoch* (Cornell), *Prairie Schooner* (Nebraska), *Southern Review* (Louisiana State), *PMS* (University of Alabama, Birmingham).

PMS is an interesting case. The punning initials stand for *poemmemoirstory.* The periodical, superbly edited by Linda Frost, has been published once a year since 2001. Yet with only seven issues printed up to now, the magazine has been featured in this series three times, a rate of success that no other periodical has approached. Susan Orlean selected Holly Welker's "Satin Worship" for the 2005 volume, David Foster Wallace chose Molly Peacock's "Passion Flowers in Winter" for 2007, and this year's book opens with another remarkable *PMS* essay, Patricia Brieschke's "Cracking Open."

Lately, a number of eye-catching literary periodicals are appearing independently, without the typical university support. Magazines like *Open City, Tin House, N+1,* and *McSweeney's* are hipper, intellectually edgier, and are quickly becoming required reading for anyone who wants to feel a vital part of today's urban literary scene. Some of the latest arrivals are also physically dazzling, reminding us that writing — however we conceptualize it — is also a form of graphic art. To see what's happening in periodical production, readers should take a look at one of the most impressively designed magazines available, *Ninth Letter,* a literary/art journal that comes out semiannually from the University of Illinois, Urbana-Champaign. As its clever title suggests, *Ninth Letter* also features a great deal of personal writing.

So, for me, each year, the essays remain at first encounter an inseparable part of the particular magazines that I am holding in my hands. If I consider the essay a good candidate for the collection, I literally take physical possession of it by ripping it out of the periodical and thus starting it along its path of de-contextualization as it wends its way from (as Sontag says) magazine to book, from one sort of paper existence to another. And now, as you might be thinking, an inescapable question arises: what if, as we repeatedly hear, the age of printed magazines is coming to an end? What if, in the twenty-first century's next decade, we will be reading our familiar magazines only online? From so much of what I read and see, this forecast is not far-fetched.

If we tweak John Lennon's words and "imagine there's no paper," how do we then imagine imaginative literature? Right now, the Internet does not appear overly hospitable to originally published literary works: most writers are still happier to see their words first published on paper than on a screen, even if those words originally appeared on a computer screen and were transmitted to a publisher electronically. Paper still carries prestige. But that can quickly change as a younger generation grows increasingly wedded to electronic media. My twenty-four-year-old son finds it ludicrous that I still read several morning newspapers. So how long will it be before we regularly find serious literary works — a Mary Oliver poem, a Don DeLillo story, a Louis Menand essay — only online? Or, as Adam Gopnik suggests in his introduction, are there now emerging talents, literary bloggers, posting significant works intended only for electronic consumption? "But though I am persuaded beyond argument," he notes, "that there must be an Emily Dickinson or an Agnes Repplier of the Internet out there somewhere, blogging away for her life, and ours, I haven't found her, at least not yet."

This isn't to say that there aren't a few promising online magazines publishing literary works (as opposed to the overwhelming amount of opinion and commentary found among the bloggers). A few of these magazines appear in this year's Notable list, and next year may see more, though if readers want to explore a number of older titles, they will quickly discover a dismal life expectancy, with many archived issues dating back only four or five years. On the other hand, finding literary material in the blogosphere is so far a hit-or-miss venture, with so-called "best blogs" sites (yes, thank Kate MacLean and Beth Newberry for their kind assistance in helping me track down material for this year's book. As always, the Houghton Mifflin staff did everything possible to bring so many moving parts together in so short a time, and I once again appreciate the efforts of Deanne Urmy, Nicole Angeloro, Larry Cooper, and Megan Wilson. It was a delightful experience to collaborate on this year's volume with one of my favorite writers, Adam Gopnik, whose own essays have frequently appeared in these pages. This collection wonderfully reflects his wide-ranging tastes and receptivity to the varieties of prose experience.

R. A.

Introduction

THE ESSAYIST, like his friend the hangman, is expected to apologize for his profession even as he practices it. (Apologize to the more detached spectators, that is. The immediate victims — the essayist's are his editors — are too tied up to say much.) Alone among writers, he is assigned the self-deprecatory cough, the defensive cringe, the Mister Modesty shrug. The hangman's apology is for being too murderous; the essayist's for not being murderous enough. The form is too small, too minor, too self-indulgent, too ephemeral, rooted in old book reviews and held in collections of ancient journalism. The language of littleness and self-deprecation rises even from masters like Max Beerbohm and E. B. White, who practice competitive self-disparagement the way novelists practice competitive self-praise. I'm but a wee thing with a wee craft, the essayist says. Look to the novelists for largeness.

Well . . . the hell with that, at least for the next few minutes. The mouse roars, or tries to. The essay, in truth, is a strong form, a beautiful form, a living form, one that counts, and one that is as likely to produce material that goes rocketing on through time as its more boastful near-relations. The essay is a living genre, in the simple sense that people write them for money when they are not being at all "literary." Science essays, food essays, parenting essays — editors who wear hazmat suits to deal with the crush of short stories coming through the transom still commission essays, although they often don't call them that. The essays of our time, taking them in the wide role of what writers actually call "pieces" (as in "Can you give us a piece on . . .") to distinguish them from straight reviews, are as likely to hang on and make history as any novel or play or poem, maybe more. There is more of life in the essay, less art and more matter, fewer workshop wiles and more real manners — the sound of people talking about what interests them instead of writing what they think will impress — than in almost any other form. Coming across an essay, however finely wrought, by a novelist, we expect, and usually get, something more heartfelt and direct — an opinion, a testament, even an endorsement, something ingenuous and passionate — than we find in his novels. (The novel is becoming in our time, the essayist enlivened by his new fighting spirit thinks, what the verse tragedy was in Dr. Johnson's: one of those things that everyone was honor bound to try and honor bound to praise if it worked at all, but not honor bound, or naturally compelled, to actually remember. Dr. J praises Congreve's tragedies, but you don't have the feeling he *read* them much.)

And then the essay is strong because it is varied, a mixed genre without being a mixed-up one. Uniquely among all the kinds of writing, it splices the argument and the anecdote, thoughts and feelings, ideas and emotions, the way it feels and the way it thinks. A sudden flight of abstract reflection gets ruled right out of the classic Flaubert-James novel, and even in the pre- or postmodern novel, where a certain amount of digression is okay, too many drive-by editorials are disallowed. In the same way, in scholarly criticism a sustained run of winning anecdotes is frowned upon, and when an "I" can be smuggled into scholarship, it must be a quizzical, meta-ish "I." But an essay without a bit of both abstract reflection and winning anecdote — without a tear to raise and a point to score, without an unimpeded argument and an obvious "I" — isn't quite an essay. The ideal essay has facts and feelings, emotions and thoughts, an argument about and an anecdote from, parallel and then crisscrossing, all over it. It is a classical form for short-winded romantics, a way of turning a newborn feeling back into a series of pregnant sentences.

The essay is made strong by being grafted, hybrid, not too pale and purebred, even, at times, parasitic. There are three chief kinds of essays being written these days (says an anthologist who has just read what feels like a few thousand of them), and each grafts the essay onto another genre: there are review essays, memoir essays, and odd-object essays. The review essay is maybe the most common, or at least the easiest to get published, and marks the leap from an opportunity into an arabesque. Find me an occasion to write about X, the reviewer asks his editor, and, occasion found, X marks the spot, and the point. (And here may be a good place to second Clive James's insistence that collections of review essays — a nice forgotten Wolcott Gibbs, an early overlooked Kenneth Tynan — are among the real prizes of secondhand bookstores, and, far from being dated, are as alive with judgment and observation as any novel of their time. We reconstruct the writer's objects from their insults.)

The memoir essay takes the common form of the reminiscence, the personal anecdote, a story, What Happened to Me Once, but sets itself off from the pure memoir by adding a reflection, a lesson, even a moral. Hugely popular among readers, and what most people mean by "essays" — they form the backbone of every magazine, from Oprah's out — they therefore get both the anger directed at the memoir and the resentment aimed at the essay. Their popularity, like the popularity once held by short stories — back when they were the commercial form, and Scott Fitzgerald had to resist writing too many of them just for money! — suggests that they must be doing some kind of necessary labor.

Certainly people attack the memoir, and the memoir essay, in exactly the way people once attacked the novel when *it* was doing all the work of communication, moving emotions from one mind to another, as vulgar and above all as self-indulgent. But "self-indulgent," fairly offered, means that expression is in too great an ascendance over communication — that the urge to shape an emotion has overwhelmed the urge to share a thought. In truth, the impulse to argument that is part of the essay's inheritance, the constant felt demand for a point, makes the memoir essay, even of the mushiest sort, the *least* self-indulgent of forms, the one where the smallest display of self for self's sake is practical. A novelist can muse motionlessly for pages on the ebb and flow of life, but if an essayist hasn't arrived at the point by the top of page three, her editors kill the piece and put in something about What Is to Be Done Over There, wherever *there* is this week. If the leap into a higher general case, from the specific "I" to the almost universal "you," doesn't take place quickly, the essay won't work. When Katha Pollitt tells of her lost love and her new driving lessons — or when, in this collection, Lauren Slater tells of her first horse — the driving lesson or the pony is there to make a point that a novelist might have softened or obscured, been reluctant to underline. No essay can be written without at least the ghost of a moral at the end. Virginia Woolf can float emotions and sensation in lulling solution, but *A Room of One's Own,* for all its beautiful hesitations and scrupulous personal voice, is one of the most strenuously *argued* pieces of writing in English. Memoir essays move us not because they are self-indulgent, but because they are other-indulgent, and the other they indulge is us, with our own parallel inner stories of loss and confusion and mixed emotions about even the people (and animals) we love.

The third kind of essay, the odd-object essay, is perhaps the, well, oddest of the essay forms, but one that thrives in strange places. This is the kind that takes a small, specific object, a bit of material minutia — the old science-fiction paperback, a toothbrush mustache, a Leica lens — and finds in it a path not just to a larger point but also to an entirely different subject. In one way the oldest of all essay forms — for Addison and Swift loved small objects for large subjects too — it has had a new life recently, partly because it works so well pedagogically, helps to teach things, especially something scientific or historical. (Stephen Jay Gould became a master of the essay while writing nothing but odd-object essays — the odd objects in his case being all of the tiny improvisations of nature, pandas' thumbs and prime-number cicadas, which exemplify a broader idea about Darwinism.)

The odd-object essay also works because, in a material-minded time, our lives are filled with things waiting to be made into metaphors. Working as well as it does for the teaching mind, it's also the form beloved of the reluctant memoirist: you can smuggle a lot of Self into an essay on Something Obviously Else. (In this collection, Albert Goldbarth and Anthony Lane write disguised autobiographies of that kind.) Just as the memoir essayist has always been kicked around for being "self-indulgent," the odd-object essayist gets spat at for being "precious" or "sentimental" or "pretentious," but these, like the others, are reviewers' words long ago robbed of meaning. Sentimental or precious things are those made in deliberate ignorance of the facts: no one weeps as widely as did a Dickens reader, but then no one dies as picturesquely as Little Nell. By true standards, Quentin Tarantino is a sentimental artist; in his panting glorification of violence, he asks us to separate thrills from facts. Louisa May Alcott, on the other hand, is not sentimental at all. She gives to fictional death the emotions proper to it. Normal feelings of tenderness and love are part of life, and a literature made in ignorance of them is a literature condemned to aridity and alien to human experience. "Pretentious," meanwhile, is a good word only for something that is willed to impress — the test is not density of allusion, which is a good thing, but evidence of effort. If it feels as though the writer stopped to think about the allusion before making it, it's a form of pretense; the other is just a form of thought. (In any case, Vincent van Gogh was the most sentimental — i.e., concerned with common and homely emotion; the most self-indulgent — wrapped up in what it felt like to him, and how he looked; and the most pretentious — read his letters on the books he read, a name dropped on every page! — of all painters. And still the best.)

What all three genres have in common — and keep in common with such now largely vanished essay types as the sermon essay, the literary-visit essay, and the essay on a classical text — is a certain double focus. They have text and inner text, personal story and the larger point, the thing you're supposed to be paying attention to and some other thing you're really interested in — the Leica in the amateur photographer's hands points at a lady, and the lens's focal length is placed in counterpoint with the visions of love in his mind. So the essay, in partial definition, is simply that: a shortish prose form in which the apparent object of the piece is different from its real subject, and the writer thinks he knows what the difference is. The three things together — small object, big subject, and knowing author — are about equally important to its effect. The essay takes as its objects vultures and crickets and chemotherapy; from these it makes for subjects education and China and modern medicine. Even when the essay seems most attached to its object, the kind that begins in journalism, a larger subject peeks out: the description of aging teeth leads to a meditation on how the whole body creaks, the molars become our mortality. The essay begins with an ordinary object — a goldfish dies — and ends, the essayist hopes, with an unexpected subject: what is death?

The essay differs from the lyric poem (which does the same kind of thing) by being in prose, but also by being funny and by being clear — the essay is rarely ambiguous in itself, as the poem might have to be; the lucidity of philosophical prose, not the ambiguity of lyrical verse, is the effect most often sought. It is closer to philosophy and psychology than to poetry and polemic. It shows something in order to prove something or argue something, and the proof it offers is the effect the thing had on you. Poems have an object right here, an urn or the autumn, and a subject over there, but we don't mind if the poet feels his way through these things, intuits their connections rather than explaining them. If a poet knows too exactly what the small object means for a big subject, in fact, it doesn't feel sufficiently poetic. (And if he knows exactly what the relation is, with clear Cartesian vision, then he writes poems called "An Essay on Criticism" or "An Essay on Man.")

The essay is hybrid to be durable, and this also means that it's as varied as the weeds: there are polemical essays, point-scoring essays, descriptive essays — as many kinds as there are writers to write them. But the part of the essay tradition that has its own quiddity, its own special vibration, is the tradition of Lamb and Hazlitt, White and Thurber, Beerbohm and Agnes Repplier (dig her!) and Wolcott Gibbs. And though all of them are allergic to rhetoric, and in favor of what Sydney Smith calls short views, the immediate vision, this doesn't mean that the essay as its masters have given it to us is without a worldly role or a consistent politics of its own. The role of the essay, and the consistent contribution of the great essayists, has been to try and drain the hysteria from the world's religious wars, or at least to drain the melodrama from some overwrought debate, and replace it with common sense and comedy. The satirist's point is to ridicule the absurdities of the other side; the essayist's is that there is often something silly about the business of taking sides. The essayist's end is achieved not so much by argument as by asserting the facts of actual experience: this is what it feels like to be alive right now, whatever it's supposed to feel like, or however nice it would be to feel some other way.

Michel de Montaigne, the inventor of the modern essay, doesn't have a view on all the subjects he turns around, and he can therefore seem bewildering. But he makes that doubleness humane: "We are, I know not how, double within ourselves, with the result that we do not believe what we believe, and we cannot rid ourselves of what we condemn," he writes, a motto for every essayist since.

Writing at the end of the sixteenth century, at a time when religious wars were ripping apart France and all of Europe with a violence still horrible to contemplate, Montaigne insisted on the value not just of doubt but of what one might call comic doubt: not just an uncertainty about who's right, but about whether being right is worth all the pain it causes — the same doubt that Falstaff has, or Hamlet. (It is this comic skepticism, along with his all-pervasive curiosity, that makes Montaigne Shakespeare's secret sharer, the writer with whom he is in constant conversation. Hamlet is Essay Man, with his curiosities, breaking through the wall of Dynastic Man, with his revenge vendettas.) Montaigne was an accidental philosopher, as one of his new biographers rightly says, and the accident was part of the philosophy: he knew that you never know where or when you're going to bang your shins against a truth. His essays are a history of his bruises.

Hazlitt, who founded the romantic essay at the beginning of the nineteenth century, plays a similar role in the overheated arguments of his time. In his letters and love diaries Hazlitt is an archromantic, full of radical love and revolutionary fervor. But in his essays he is an anti-romantic, an explorer of minute effects, trying to understand odd objects like the juggler's balls or the newspaper's loft or the lift of a boxer's fist. His essays are unsublime, radical in their pointillism, and it was this reportorial, even detached, but always anti-ideological quality that this often ideologically minded man loved in the tradition of the essay: "It does not treat of minerals or fossils, of the virtues of plants, or the influence of planets," he writes of the essay; "it does not meddle with forms of belief, or systems of philosophy, nor launch into the world of spiritual existences; but it makes familiar with the world of men and women, records their actions, assigns their motives, exhibits their whims, characterises their pursuits in all their singular and endless variety, ridicules their absurdities, exposes their inconsistencies, takes minutes of our dress, air, looks, words, thoughts, and actions; shews us what we are, and what we are not; plays the whole game of human life over before us, and by making us enlightened Spectators of its many-coloured scenes, enables us (if possible) to become tolerably reasonable agents in the one in which we have to perform a part."

Max Beerbohm (still supreme among English essayists to this reader), at the end of the same century, plays that sympathetic skeptic's role for the aesthetes who surrounded him — sharing their affections while seeing their absurdities. He drains aestheticism of its silliness as Hazlitt drained romanticism of its sublimity. An aesthete himself, Beerbohm sees the absurdity of the aesthetic position, and is to Wilde's passion what Montaigne is to Pascal's passion: the man who gets it and doubts it all at once. Beerbohm's best essays mock the idea that the world will go on getting better, or that the world was once a more beautiful place. They make fun of the fatuous progressivism that was the main line of thought in his day, and of the unreal medievalism that was its answer. He parodies Shaw and Wells, Chesterton and Belloc, all fondly, and all for the sin of saying untrue things about existence, which is lovely enough as it is to be worth singing without adding something extra. He is disabused of their illusions without being disintoxicated with their longings.

Even James Thurber and E. B. White, who remade the American essay in the 1930s — though we don't often think of them as even mildly contentious, much less "political" — wrote beautifully against the grain, and the hysteria, of their time. At a moment in the worried 1930s when "commitment" was the insistent theme, and a choice of master plans demanded, White's voice, with its admixture of vinegary New England plainspokenness and honeyed Manhattan twilight lyricism, suggested that there were more hopes, and tones, for liberalism than it might have seemed, while Thurber's parodies of popular determinism — in his "Let Your Mind Alone!" taking on the vulgar drippings of Freud and Marx — are as bracing and invigorating as they are funny. The world is a messy place, Thurber says, and the mind a messy keeper of it. The essayist's time, he tells us, "is his own personal time, circumscribed by the short boundaries of his pain and his embarrassment, in which what happens to his digestion, the rear axle of his car, and the confused flow of his relationship with six or eight persons and two or three buildings is of greater importance than what goes on in the nation or the universe. He knows vaguely that the nation is not much good any more; he has read that the crust of the earth is shrinking alarmingly, and that the universe is growing steadily colder, but he does not believe that any of the three is in half as bad shape as he is." The voice is modest and real, at a time that demands pomposity and the conventional lie.

The essay has always, as this slightly breathless survey suggests, acted as an antidote to whatever the available hysteria around. When the essayist goes wrong, it's with too long a trip down the highway of ideas; White's essays on world government are a less convincing argument than his writing on a farm in Maine, which makes the case for a peaceable kingdom more persuasively, more politically, and you come away convinced that different entities can live in a permanent ornery truce.

An essayist wouldn't be an essayist if he couldn't follow a vindication with a sigh, or at least a cough. The essay is not without its clichés, its enforced narrators. The essayist's tone of wistful regret, plaintive longing, high-hearted beaming regard, is seductive but partial, and the essayist's face can at moments twist into a look of permanent feigned sensitivity, like that of British mandarins whose eyes were fixed in smile lines from a lifetime of insincere smiling. Poisonous anger, irrational lust, permanent grief — they are part of anyone's life too. Manners are the surfacing of morality, but morality is not all manners. The space between a great essayist like Beerbohm and a major writer like Marcel Proust, who began as an essayist too, and whom Beerbohm resembles in gifts, is real, and arrives not because Proust outgrew his essayistic material — long sections of *Recherche* are essays, on memory, appetite, desire — but because he sobered up his essayist's manner, and wrote as well about the shameful appetite of lust and lies as about the deliciousness and light of life. We must reform our minds and hearts to grasp for greater matter too.

And, while the essay may be a living form for the moment, like all living things it may be ailing even as it thrives. With the decline of places where the essay once ran into coterie political journals, or group blogs, the place for the essay proper grows smaller. The blogger, newly born, might be, should be, an essayist manqué, but the first thing about the blog form is that its units are short. It has already taken its place as part of the history of the pamphlet, the polemic, the pointed epistle — but doesn't yet build up enough acceleration to take a left turn into anything else. Blogs play a terrific role as makers of solidarity, community, and network — as builders of social capital. But though I am persuaded beyond argument that there must be an Emily Dickinson or an Agnes Repplier of the Internet out there somewhere, blogging away for her life, and ours, I haven't found her, at least not yet.

As with all art, the answer to an uncertain future is a repledged allegiance to the truth of things, however strange they may be. In a culture given over to malice and noise, the essay is still a place for shared jokes and confidential whispers and the occasional ill-advised and tipsy confidence. For the time being, here are all these good essays, some from the heart of commercial publishing, some from the edge where the small reviews still fight the good fight. All are essayists in Hazlitt's sense: they record actions, assign motives, exhibit whims, take minutes of dress, air, looks, words, thoughts, and actions. Some review, some remember, some contemplate their own odd object, but each one of these essayists asks the essayist's essential question, which is not the preacher's or polemicist's question — how shall we live? — but Montaigne's question: what does it feel like to be alive? How does it feel to grow old, help a friend with AIDS, arrange a lesbian wedding, go to a strip club, walk down the street with a toothbrush mustache that echoes evil, forget a familiar quotation, wear a necklace, be a bird watcher, be a Serbian American, run a New Age ultramarathon in an Old World borough, remember an old love? The breath of things as they are, I think, runs through these pages, and all of the writers included achieve what Dr. Johnson said was the essayists' only real ambition: to be masters of our common life.

ADAM GOPNIK

The Best
AMERICAN
ESSAYS
2008

Cracking Open

FROM *PMS*

FOUR DECADES AGO, when I was young and stupid and didn't know a baby from a wormy *kapusta*, according to my Polish mother, I gave birth to a tiny damaged boy on my kitchen table. Just out of high school, I was working in a fertilizer factory, going to night school, and writing frantically in my spare time to reshape myself in the image and likeness of George Eliot. But she never had children. Nevertheless, I figured since an infant is small and portable, it wouldn't interfere with my plan for the contemplative literary life. The day I decided to go off the pill, John Lennon and Yoko Ono staged a bed-in for peace in Amsterdam. One thing I knew with missionary clarity: this baby was my olive branch to the universe. Unlike my mother, who produced misfits who could only hobble and crawl, my child would be so loved he would soar. Our bond would heal every rift, every schism, every abuse. My husband, Matthew, an Irish boy who had been dismissed from his religious order at age twenty for chugging brandy in the Christian Brothers winery, was another hobbler and crawler. He wrote me poems, I gave him sex — an elegant but sparse compromise.

I registered at the local maternity center for prenatal care: two rooms over a store facing the Maxwell Street Market. Toward the end of the pregnancy, I made weekly bus trips to the center, where a volunteer palpated my belly to the crooning of Muddy Waters. I prepared my supplies for the time of delivery: a two-foot-high stack of newspapers, a large plastic sheet, a dime for calling the maternity center, a strong electric light, and a kettle for boiling water.

Giving birth was like my first accordion lesson. When they put the bellowy instrument in my lap, I didn't know where to put my hands, how to hold it. I had no idea how to have a baby, so I sat on the beat-up couch in our third-floor flat on Ainslie Avenue, crossed my legs, and asked Bernie, a pink-faced intern, "Okay, what do I do?"

"Maybe we should have read a book," Matthew said, gathering up empty beer cans from the coffee table.

Bernie took one of Matthew's poems that I had framed from the wall. I read a few lines before he hung a makeshift IV from the nail. *A small bright delighting thing / A dark deep beckoning / Embodied twilight turning day to night.* My baby, a small bright delighting thing, felt huge inside me: a nuclear fission ready to break upon the world. I pressed my thighs together to hold back the dribble of green water that had been leaking for a couple of days. The baby was still head up and had no intention of turning and preparing for descent.

Oxytocin dripped into my veins. Bernie's partner, a small Filipino woman, boiled water, spread my stack of *Chicago Tribunes* over the kitchen table and floor, and swung a 100-watt bulb from an extension cord above the table. Matthew tamped his pipe, composing a poem in his head. "Change into something comfortable and crawl up on the table," Bernie said as he unpacked his doctor's bag on the kitchen sink, clanging shiny tools on paper towels. I grabbed an oversize Beatles T-shirt. The Filipino woman helped me maneuver the IV tubing as I hoisted myself up on the table. Earlier, I had been paying bills there, flipping a penny to decide who would get paid — Con Ed or Ma Bell. Envelopes scattered on the floor. Would Bernie and the Filipino woman ask for money?

Perfect control. Nobody will see me flinch. I lay on newsprint, naked from the waist down. Not a telltale sound or revealing grunt. My belly heaved. Muscles closed around the baby like a slow glacier. I controlled the pain by imagining an advertisement for a Burberry raincoat permanently affixed to my back thigh. Finally, I began to crack open: one centimeter, two centimeters . . . six, seven. After several hours and a few choruses of "don't push, don't push, don't push, okay push," two little legs dangled out of me. "Where's his head?" The kitchen was eerily quiet. I heard the baby cry inside me. He didn't want to be born.

"You must move bowels in twenty-four hours," the Filipino woman said, lecturing me about hemorrhoids and sitz baths. Bernie called for backup to figure out how to get the rest of the baby out.

My son wasn't exactly what I had expected. A blob of proto-plasm, shiny and translucent. But he was my first wonder of the world, my Grand Canyon. When Bernie cleaned him off, his skinny legs twisted around themselves like Gumby. He looked more poul-try than baby but was the most exquisite chicken I had ever seen. For a moment, I thought there must be something wrong with him. But what did I know? The only baby I remembered clearly was my youngest brother, and I never really looked at him, just plotted how to dispose of him. My baby was perfect, if a bit crooked.

In the days that followed, I became sweet with curiosity about this new little being, in the larger scheme of things nothing but a speck of dust on the earth, but for me, a reason for living. I nuzzled his swollen belly against mine, cooed over his soft crown and doll fingers, drank in the perfume of yellow diapers. *Little caterpillar.* It was now my life's work to protect, honor, and celebrate this deli-cate creature. *Snail without a shell.* After two weeks, I was in love. We were a team: I gave him life, he gave me breasts.

The name on his birth certificate was Beckett. Matthew rejected my choice, which was Oliver. Reminded him of olives or liver. But it didn't matter what anybody else called him. Ollie and I formed a secret bond. At night in bed when he whimpered, I whispered his name. His fish mouth, heat-seeking and hungry, clamped on to me. My mother called in her blessing: "Now you'll know heartache. May your child do to you what you did to me." *You had only weak tea in your breasts; mine are filled with crème fraîche.* I would do mother-hood right, and love my Ollie better than all the Polish mothers of the old neighborhood, stuffed into their Goldblatt housedresses.

During our two-week checkup at the maternity center, I ran into Debbie, whose prenatal visits had coincided with mine. "He's beau-tiful," she said.

"You don't think he looks like a chicken?" Ollie and I were so tightly swaddled in my Madonna and Baby Jesus fantasy that I half wanted a reality check.

"All babies look like chickens."

When the doctor held him up, his legs didn't uncurl. "Dislo-cated hips." *There's nothing wrong with my baby. Maybe he looks a little funny, but Matthew and I aren't exactly centerfolds.* A common mixed-breed girl: Irish milk skin dinged with acne, Germanic chin, and Polish thighs, too lavish for their petite frame. A dreamy Irish boy, bone-skinny and delicate. *Ollie's one of us.* "Take him over to the pediatric hospital," the doctor said. "They'll snap his hips into place, and he'll be good as new."

I zipped Ollie inside my jacket, snuggling his tiny ear to my heart, as the bus dodged potholes down Lincoln Avenue. My mother cautioned me: "When I was eight, Pa took me for my first streetcar ride. I woke up in Cook County Hospital without my tonsils. My sister Josie was supposed to get the operation, but she run away." A few years out of Poland, they believed they'd be kicked off relief if someone didn't show up. *Does Ollie's doctor need to fill a spot on his docket? Get a grip, you're not an immigrant.* I was clumsy at nurture. He was my practice case, and I might as well have been in a foreign land.

Ollie became a file number: 127164. Snapping his baby hips back into place took more than a flick of the orthopedist's wrist. "Leave him here, come back in a week, maybe two, he'll be fine," the doctor said. Like taking a car in for service. His femurs were deformed, and they put him in traction, hanging a five-pound weight from eight-pound Ollie. *Do it to me, hang me upside down, pack me in concrete, but don't touch my baby.* Only two weeks old, he was so new to the world, my little pot roast, fresh from my kitchen table.

I left the hospital without Ollie, escorted by a burly security guard who smelled like fried carp and who offered me a Lucky Strike. "Don't go gettin' all hot and bothered, honey, visiting hours is over, and you can't stay here no more." But where was I to go? Ollie couldn't live without me. They'd ignore him, starve him, experiment on him. I was his milk, my arms were his skin. It was as if they had taken one of my organs and left it, disconnected and bleeding, to die. "Go get yourself some broasted chicken," the guard said.

I sat with Matthew in the coffee shop across the street from the hospital until it closed at midnight. Do something! Kill the guard, storm the hospital, file a lawsuit, kidnap our baby. Didn't he see that I was coming apart? Why had I married him anyway? He had wooed me with his poems, so light and airy that the groaning breath of the world seemed to stand still. The poems held me tight, and I clung to them the way Matthew clung to me. Before we got married, my father had been calling at three in the morning, dawn, noon. "Whore, I know you're on drugs! No good Catholic girl runs away from home and shacks up with a man. Where you getting them drugs? Give yourself up." He said the narcotics squad had surrounded my apartment and would take me away in a white coat and lock me up. After months of intermittent calls, and the silence of my mother, who drew the shades and told everyone I was dead, I said to Matthew, "Let's get married. Maybe it'll stop."

"Sure," he said. I picked out two rings at Woolworth's, ninety-nine cents each, and when it was my turn to say I do, I started to laugh. The county magistrate, Myriam Whitley, said stop cackling or leave the courthouse. *But it's not in the plan. I'm not supposed to get married. Not supposed to be my mother.* I tried to think of one thing I liked about Matthew: even his poems couldn't save me now. Myriam stamped our marriage certificate: E 7766. The next day, my father called: "Now you're a legitimate whore." My mother broke her silence and took the telephone: "Father Bernard says now you're excommunicated. You didn't get married in the Church." A week later, Matthew received a telegram from his parents: IF YOU MARRY THAT POLISH GIRL WE NEVER WANT TO SEE YOU AGAIN.

During Ollie's second week in the hospital, I rented a breast pump. I couldn't hold him or nurse him because it would interfere with his traction. So he lay in his steel crib at night, under the weight of a Rube Goldberg contraption, while I lay in my bed with rubber suction cups over my nipples, trying to keep the nectar flowing between us. Matthew drank at his desk until the apartment was dark and the only poetry he could get out was a grunt. Mornings, I waited at the hospital with my Styrofoam cooler filled with plastic bottles of breast milk, peering through the glass door, counting minutes on the clock above the lobby desk until, at ten o'clock, the security guard released the latches and a stampede of mothers were let loose to find their babies. I gave my bottles of milk to the nurse, small offerings to let Ollie know that I was still the source of good things. But when shifts changed, the bottles were lost or emptied down the sink.

With Ollie's legs still crooked after ten days in traction, the doctor attached a heavier weight to loosen his hips. His body slid across the sheet, jamming against the steel bars of the crib. They strapped him to a board to hold him in place, but the straps tore his skin. "We have to get serious, mother," the doctor said. In the cast room, he drove a metal pin through Ollie's femur, drilling through bone without anesthesia. Matthew and I stood at the window watching Ollie's body stiffen and turn scarlet as the doctor hammered the pin through his leg. Ollie gasped, and I pounded on the window. His fists opened and closed like fish gills sucking in air, and I lunged for the door. He screamed, I answered, and for the only time since his birth, we were in complete synchrony: an aria of mother-and-child wailing. When the pin was in place, the doctor stopped drilling, wiped beads of sweat from his brow, and looked quizzical. "What's all the fuss about, mother? Babies don't feel pain."

I kept vigil at Ollie's bed. I would leave the apartment in the morning, mostly unwashed, often in the same clothes from the night before. Circling the hospital, I searched for the window to his room. From the moment the lobby doors opened until a polite voice on the loudspeaker informed all visitors to leave, I was at his side, petting the downy hairs of his head through the metal bars as he lay on his board. He cried all the time, even in sleep. Matthew sat on the other side of Ollie's bed, no longer able to write an unslurred word, hiding whatever he found to drink in a brown bag. I circled the hospital again at night when the security guard forced me from his room. Sometimes I didn't go home at all but lived on Halsted Street, watching for light in his window. Late into the night, I sat on the curb feeling milk leak through my shirt. One day I took the last breast pump bottle and filled it with found objects from my daily circling: a bottle cap, a rusted paper clip, an expired bus transfer, half a holy card with the Blessed Virgin's head ripped in two. I sent it floating away in the melting snow. Soon there was no more milk, and my breasts disappeared. Ollie and I were no longer a team.

A social worker came to see me. "I'm Miss Bennett. Could I ask you a few questions?" She was neat and pretty, like June Cleaver, the *Leave It to Beaver* mother.

What a relief to talk to someone who didn't want to poke or probe Ollie.

"We like to get a complete history whenever a family presents with birth defects. Is this your first child?" I shook my head yes. "Former miscarriages or abortions?" I shook no. "Did you ever take drugs?"

"You mean like aspirin?"

"No, I mean illegal substances."

I didn't even take Midol when I got cramps. I had tried marijuana, long before I was pregnant, but didn't like the burning in my throat so never smoked again. *They all have this thing about drugs. Does she know my father?* Miss Bennett explained that congenital malformations of the hips occur between the sixth and eighth week of fetal development. What was I doing back then? Later, I turned back the pages in my daybook to March, April, the beginning of spring. Shakespeare paper due. Boss on vacation. Matthew sold his blood to buy beer. What else? Malathion, scribbled in the margin of the calendar next to the daylight-saving time reminder. White fly! The begonia had white fly, and I had sprayed it with a weak mixture of Malathion. Could I have poisoned myself? The bottle did have a skull and crossbones on the warning label. Did I do anything else to cause Ollie's birth defects? Sex, masturbation, impure thoughts? Was the Church right after all? Was this punishment, retribution? Or was it something I ate? Too much red licorice? What about that time I ate the whole package of cupcakes with the pink frosting? Food dye! Could I blame the Food and Drug Administration?

During teaching rounds, doctors gathered around Ollie's crib and talked while he whimpered. If he cried too loud, the wall of white coats moved to the hall. The urologists were the worst. One doctor in particular poked and probed with analytic glee, as if my baby were a specimen for dissection. Ollie screamed long after the doctor left. I put gin in his milk to help him sleep. If it silenced my husband, it might soothe my baby. But he threw it up. I could have killed him. I wanted to kill him. He was a tiny, quivering, imperfect baby whom I was helpless to protect.

Dr. Merman, the chief urologist, said that there was something wrong with Ollie's kidneys. He wanted to explore surgically. "Only one kidney showed up on x-ray, and even that one doesn't function as it should." I got on the Halsted bus and kept riding: through Greektown, through the Cabrini-Green housing project, past Ernie's Guns and Ammo. I returned to the hospital with a

soft blue blanket and a fleecy white dog, small penances to tuck
around my Buddha baby. Ollie's file had been left in the room.
The first thing I saw when I opened it was the social worker's report: *Mother admitted to taking drugs during pregnancy.*

Surgery took place just before Christmas. The snow was heavy,
and Matthew and I argued all the way to the hospital. Borrowing
money from his parents had put him in a bad mood. "Couldn't
they offer up ten dollars for their grandson?" We could get more
mileage out of ten dollars than ten Hail Marys. They'd reminded
him that he wouldn't have these problems if he hadn't married the
Polish girl.

We waited in a room for five hours with a dozen other parents
on plaid couches. One woman worked a rosary, her fingertips cal-
lused, waiting out her four-year-old's sixth surgery. Another passed
out donuts while her daughter, Carmen, had a shunt planted in
her skull. Alone in the corner, under a painting of the Himalayas,
Matthew sucked Guinness from a brown bag. Halfway through
Ollie's surgery, a doctor emerged from the operating room with a
progress report: "Everything's fine. We want you to know that we
removed his appendix as a bonus."

In the morning, we learned about ureterostomies. During surgery, Dr. Merman had decided to cut Ollie's ureter and create an
opening in his right side to take stress off his baby plumbing. The
chair next to Ollie's bed was laden with dirty sheets. He was throwing up. "We came here for crooked legs." *They've butchered my son.*

"Your baby has a rare kidney condition," the doctor said. "He
probably won't live to be a year old."

How will he pee? The raw pink hole in Ollie's side leaked drops of
urine.

"The urine bypasses the ureter and bladder altogether now.
He'll wear a bag. An elegant surgery. We've never done one of
these on a baby."

"He'll pee in a bag?" *Whip out his bag when the other boys are compar-
ing notes in the boys' bathroom?*

"This'll buy him some time." Then it hit me. There would be no
life. In the spring or the fall, we'd put Ollie in a tiny coffin and say
goodbye.

I dug out the diary from my Friends of the Library tote, but
words were caked in me like scum on the oatmeal pot. I was under

the porch stairs again, where I went as a child to examine my bloody welts. Crouching in the musty space, my back against the third step and my head bowed under the fourth, I killed my mother, my SS officer, Scary Sophia, over and over in a spiral Raggedy Ann notebook. By eighth grade I had killed her 107 times, the Blessed Virgin 13 times, and God twice. Now there was no one to kill.

On Christmas Eve, the five other cribs in the hospital nursery were empty, the lights dim. Ollie had a 105-degree fever. The nurse packed him in ice and hung a red Santa on his bed. I leaned over his crib, lips close to his face, tasting his baby breath. *Feel my warmth and take me in.* I had nothing to give him. Not my milk, not my arms. I was like my cat, licking her stillborn kitten back to life. But I didn't know how to protect him. "Let me stay." The voice came over the loudspeaker for the end of visiting hours.

"You can't. Against policy," the nurse said. "We don't have room for parents. If you stay, all the other parents will want to stay."

I looked around the empty room. "What other parents? Please, please, I won't take up any space, just let me stay with my baby. You can have my leather jacket. I'll do anything. Sweep the floor, file. Please. I'll hide in the closet if security comes. Please, please, he's so little, so scared. Let me stay with him."

A few days of traction turned into a month, then two. Not long after Ollie's kidney surgery, the orthopedist came to see me. Matthew was at school trying to persuade a professor not to fail him, even though he had not written his *Tale of Genji* paper, and had gone to class so seldom that when he showed up, the professor thought he had come to repair the leaky radiator. Having quit work and dropped out of school, I was a permanent fixture next to the steel crib. I never showed up again anywhere after Ollie was born. Nobody knew where I was, except my parents, who offered up a Mass for Ollie's soul. I had damned him by not baptizing him. "The kidney is punishment," my father said. "God don't abide no pigheadedness." "*Nerka, nerka, nerka,*" SS lamented. "The baby's damaged because his mother thinks she knows things."

"He seems to be doing better," the doctor said when Ollie was out of traction. "Healing nicely." Drops of pale urine dripped from Ollie's side, and I dabbed them with gauze. His skin was too raw for an adhesive bag to stick. Everything was clear now. We'd take him home where he belonged, home where he began and where nothing would hurt him again. He'd have a sweet time on earth, however short. I was already preparing my arms for him to die.

"I've scheduled surgery for Thursday," the orthopedist said.

"He *had* surgery." Couldn't he keep his patients straight?

"No, orthopedic surgery. The traction didn't accomplish what we had hoped, so we'll go in surgically now and repair his left hip. He'll have to wear a body cast for a few months. Then we'll do the other hip."

"Why?" Was I missing something?

"So he can walk when he grows up."

"Don't you guys talk to each other?" I pulled down the crib bars and started to dress Ollie. The doctor put his hand on my arm. As if by signal, two nurses and an aide swooped down on me like a SWAT team. "I'm taking him home. Get away!" A scrimmage for my baby.

"You can't do that." He squeezed my arm harder. "I'll get a court order."

"But he's going to die."

"Maybe. Then again, he may not. In medicine, nothing's certain. At least give him the chance to walk. Without surgery, he'll never stand up. He deserves that much. Don't make me get a court order."

Did we take Ollie home to die peacefully, defying medical advice, or leave him in the hospital for further repairs, on the off chance that he might live? Was the glass half empty or half full? Was there some unifying principle holding all this together? I chewed my nails and bit the skin until it bled. I had taken to snitching Ollie's chart to see what the doctors were planning. The orthopedist had scribbled in red ink: *Mother repeatedly thwarts doctors' efforts to help baby.*

Two surgeries later, wrapped in plaster from his ankles to his underarms, Ollie came home to an apartment littered with empty beer bottles and open books. I put him on a soft pillow in his crib. He lay stiff, legs splayed in the full spica cast, unable to move anything but his head and arms.

It was spring, and I opened all the windows so Ollie could hear the sounds of the neighborhood and watch the dance of the origami animals on the ceiling. Matthew folded them at night while he drank. I tried to hold Ollie, maneuvering his bulky cast to bring his face close to me, but he arched his neck and pulled away, refusing my touch. He held his own bottle, as if he needed no one. I spent my days sitting by his side, mourning for my baby. Or deep in the rabbit hole of my diary, trying to write my way out of the maze. Or wandering from room to room, eating whatever I could find, thinking of things to amuse Ollie, ashamed of not loving him enough.

I stood over him, singing "You Are My Sunshine," daydreaming about the other babies at the hospital: the tiny Mexican girl with cleft palate, the Hasidic baby with cerebral palsy, and the one with the bowling-ball head and the shunt for draining it. The mother of the four-year-old gave me her rosary with aurora borealis beads when her boy died. I had used it to distract Ollie when the doctor cut a circle in the side of his cast and the nurse showed me how to put Kotex over the hole in his body to soak up the pee. He whipped the rosary across my face, nicking my cornea with the edge of the crucifix. His skin was raw now. Urine leaked into the layers of plaster, burning sores into his back and wetting his cast. I fanned him with a Chinese fan, shooing away flies that landed on his toes and buzzed around his head. One day I poked my finger into the doughy plaster and noticed tiny translucent larvae wriggling in the soft spots of his cast. Flies had laid their eggs in the crevices that were soggy with urine. I put my head out the window and screamed. I put a pillow over Ollie's head and wished he would die. He was mine to protect, and I couldn't keep the maggots away.

One evening, as we were listening to *The Midnight Special*, I asked Matthew, "What are we going to do for money?" Rent was past due, and the superintendent of our building, a no-nonsense guy from West Virginia in an undershirt, had been at the door twice with threats and a shotgun. My father tried to get Matthew a job driving a truck or washing windows, like him. But even my father knew that some men are not made for work. Matthew had hands like a Florentine Jesus. His body was gaunt and stylized, nourished on tobacco and spirits. "Money's the root of all evil," Matthew said.

"Is that why you sell your blood?" Money was driving us apart.

When Debbie, my acquaintance from the maternity center, and her husband, Sam, came to visit, we had no food to offer them. Sam couldn't bear to be around Ollie. "Man, look at that poor little thing. It breaks me up. I can't take it. Shit, Debbie, we gotta go, honey."

"Maybe if we had some cheese or a cake to offer Debbie and Sam, they would have stayed," I told Matthew.

"Yeah, and maybe if I returned Sam's kisses when he followed me into the bathroom they would have moved in." And maybe if we had a healthy boy with plump legs and perfect kidneys, the world would be different. In the night, Matthew woke me up to describe a trip to Mars, and I knew he was on acid. Purple microdot had replaced poetry.

Every day I planned how Ollie would die. The details changed — in the morning, in the night, after a spring rain, during a storm — but in my fantasies, he was nestled between Matthew and me, our three hearts beating together until Ollie's stopped and there was only the two of us. That's the part that scared me. But Ollie thrived. When he didn't die by the end of his first year, I drew a tiny Grim Reaper in a birthday hat in the margin of my diary. Dr. Merman said, "These things are unpredictable. Your boy surprised us." Then he said Ollie wouldn't make it to his teenage years. But I stopped listening. "He has thirty percent function of one kidney," the doctor said. "I'm sorry, but no kidney with that damage can withstand the raging hormones and systemic changes of adolescence." From then on, I pretended that the glass was half full. Together we would look for the rest of the nectar.

One day, when Ollie was almost three, I sat on the stoop in front of our flat, watching him play on the sidewalk. He fed ants lumps of bread, then put the ants, along with a damaged grasshopper, into his pocket. "My friends, Mommy." Everything seemed right with the world. Matthew had a job working in a preschool, and the rent was paid. I had completed my bachelor's degree, squeezing in courses piecemeal between Ollie's hospital stays; I wasn't even sure what my degree was in. Ollie's hips were held together with steel, and he had learned to walk. He could even pee. Dr. Merman had decided to sew up his ureter. "The truth is, we don't really know what's wrong with his kidney, but thirty percent function is enough to get by, for *now*." Ollie dumped more crumbs on the sidewalk, some for the ants, some for him, and I looked up from my book. I was reading about the life of Isadora Duncan, the part where she waves goodbye to her small children, Deirdre and Patrick, and watches their rolling car plunge into the Seine, killing them. I read her words aloud, accompanied by the Spanish dance music blaring from a window across the street: "Only twice comes that cry of the mother," Duncan wrote, "at birth and at death." One the cry of joy and the other of sorrow. And they were the same. Ollie asked what I was mumbling. When he started to run, his long stick legs pumping awkwardly beneath his checkered shorts, I decided to have another baby. I would name her Isadora, and she would dance for us, teaching Ollie to move his legs with freedom and teaching me to open my heart.

RICH COHEN

Becoming Adolf

FROM *Vanity Fair*

I decided to grow a Toothbrush mustache. Well, that's not what I called it. Until I started this story, I had only one name for the thing in mind: a Hitler mustache. An inch of hair that speaks of bottomless evil. A few nights earlier, I had seen Richard Dawkins, the author of *The God Delusion,* interviewed by Bill O'Reilly, who, citing Stalin and Hitler, said he thought atheists, because of their lack of restraining faith, were more susceptible to evil. To which Dawkins (in essence) replied: both Stalin and Hitler wore mustaches — do we therefore think the mustache was the cause of their behavior? I experienced this as an epiphany: *By Jove!* I said to myself. *It was the mustache!* From that moment, I stopped shaving. From that moment, I started reading. From that moment, I became wrapped up in facial hair and the role it has played in politics. The Toothbrush mustache offered a new way to look at the past. It was a pinprick through which I could see the old scene from a fresh angle. It was the history of our time retold as the story of the 'stache.

The Toothbrush mustache is the most powerful configuration of facial hair the world has ever known. It overpowers whoever touches it. By merely doodling a Toothbrush mustache on a poster, you make a political statement. Actually wearing a Hitler mustache, as I planned to do — well, that is like yelling racial epithets in a crowded subway. Wasn't Hitler amazing? Whatever he touched turned to ice. His life ended the long and fabled career of the name Adolf, which had included the stories of Adolph Zukor, Adolphe Menjou, Adolph Ochs, and Adolph Coors. Never again will a pregnant mother innocently consider the name for her son, or imagine shouting it across a teeming playground. As for the

Toothbrush mustache, it did not only die with the Führer — it was embalmed with him. It was his essence, and so it has been relegated to the black book of history.

This is the part where I am supposed to explain just why I decided to write this story now. I might talk about the reemergence of facial hair on the world stage, or the rise of the "new anti-Semitism," or Holocaust denial in Iran, but the fact is, my interest in the Hitler mustache never started and never ends. It is always. If you're a Jew, the Hitler mustache exists in the eternal present. I grew it for the same reason Richard Pryor said the word "nigger." I wanted to defuse it. I wanted to own it. I wanted to reclaim it for America and for the Jews. My name is Rich Cohen, and I wear a Hitler mustache.

The Imperial, the Walrus, the Stromboli, the Handlebar, the Horseshoe, the Mustachio (also called the Nosebeard or the Fantastico), the Pencil, also called (by idiots) the Mouthbrow — the catalog is illustrious. (The history of the razor is longer than the history of the mustache, but only by a few minutes.) Most mustaches lie waiting for some Clark Gable or Tom Selleck to fix them in the mind. The greatest are identified with a single man, a bad man, usually, who so wrapped his identity with a particular configuration of facial hair that the two became inseparable. Like the Fu Manchu, in which long tresses hang to the chin, where they can be stroked as the madman laughs. It is named for Sax Rohmer's (racist) villain from the golden age of Hollywood, the bad guy from the B movies who became a symbol for the creeping Asian menace. Or think of the long, droopy Pancho Villa. It was worn by the pistol-flashing Mexican bandito as he chased gringos through the border towns along the Rio Grande. These days, you see it only on Halloween, or at reunion shows of Crosby, Stills & Nash.

The Toothbrush mustache was first introduced in Germany by Americans, who turned up with it at the end of the nineteenth century the way Americans would turn up with ducktails in the 1950s. It was a bit of modern efficiency, an answer to the ornate mustaches of Europe — pop effluvia that fell into the grip of a bad, bad man.* Before that, the most popular mustache in Germany

---

* Of course, some brave, foolhardy man must have been the first — must have asked himself, while trimming his 'stache, "Why stop?" This man, this lost precursor, lived and died without ever knowing his effect on the style of modern tyranny.

and Austria had been the sort worn by the royals. It was called the Kaiser, and it was elaborate. It was perfumed, styled, teased, and trained. It turned up at the ends. It was the old, monarchical world that was about to be crushed by the rising tide of assembly-line America. In other words, in the case of Hitler and his 'stache, America faced an extreme case of blowback.

By the beginning of the century, it had been taken up by enough Germans to draw notice in the foreign press. In 1907, the *New York Times* chronicled a growing distaste for the import under the headline "TOOTHBRUSH" MUSTACHE: GERMAN WOMEN RESENT ITS USURPATION OF THE "KAISERBART."

In the years before the First World War, the Toothbrush was taken up by a German folk hero, which is the moment it became a craze. Before that, it had been an elite fashion shared by the dandies and swells of Berlin and Vienna. After that, it was worn by every yokel who dreamed of greatness. I am imagining young Hitler poring over newspapers in search of any mention of Hans Koeppen, a Prussian lieutenant who had become a pop star in the manner of the solo aviator, the illusionist, or the tightrope walker. Here is how he was described in the *New York Times:* "Lieut. Koeppen is 31 years old and unmarried. Six feet in height, slim and athletic, with a toothbrush mustache characteristic of his class."

The moment he appeared in the press with the Toothbrush mustache is like the moment Michael Jordan appeared on the basketball court in Bermuda-length shorts, changing the look of the game forever. In early 1908, Koeppen was given leave from the Prussian army to cover a New York–to–Paris motor race for *Zeitung am Mittag,* a German newspaper. When I think of the Hitler who must have followed this race, because it was followed by everyone, I think of the Hitler who loved cars and built the autobahn (as opposed to the Hitler who killed the Gypsies and the Jews).

After a disagreement with the German drivers, Koeppen took over. By the time he left Vladivostok, he was a star. The *Times:* "When he dashes across the German frontier from Russia . . . the tall, trim young infantry officer" — with the Toothbrush mustache — "may count upon a greeting hardly less joyful than if he were returning from victorious battle."

By the end of the war, the Toothbrush mustache was being

sported even by the defeated royals. A last image of the Old World is captured in pictures taken in November 1918, when William Hohenzollern Jr., the son of the Kaiser, the heir to an office that had ceased to exist, was sent into exile. He stands on the deck of an imperial steamer. He wears shiny boots, a greatcoat, a military cap, and a Toothbrush mustache. When he turns to look at the people crowding the shore, showing them only his Toothbrush mustache, he is showing them a picture of their future.

I search the photos that survive of Hitler before Hitler was famous for the moment the 'stache appears. Because that is the moment the Devil gets his horns. In early photos, he is barefaced. The first shot that captures Hitler being Hitler was taken in August 1914, at the Odeonsplatz in Munich. It was photographed from high above the square and shows thousands of people. Hitler, who was nothing and nobody, is no bigger than a cigarette burn, yet he jumps out. Once you see him, you can't stop seeing him. He wears the sort of grand mustache you expect to see on a barkeep. His eyes glow. A speaker has just read the declaration of war. I shudder when I see this photo, and remind myself he is dead and I am alive.

Experts disagree on the exact year Hitler began wearing the Toothbrush. Ron Rosenbaum, perhaps the only historian to give the mustache its proper due, fixes its appearance with confidence. "It was Chaplin's first, before Hitler's," he writes in an essay from *The Secret Parts of Fortune.* "Chaplin adopted a little black crepe blot beneath the nose for his Mack Sennett silent comedies after 1915, Hitler didn't adopt his until late 1919, and there's no evidence (though some speculation) that Hitler modeled his 'stache on that other actor's."

But some suggest Hitler began wearing it earlier. According to a recently rediscovered essay by Alexander Moritz Frey, who served with Hitler in the First World War, Hitler wore the mustache in the trenches. Because he had been ordered to. The old bushy mustache did not fit under his equipment. In other words, the mustache that defines Hitler was cut in a shape to fit a gas mask. Which is perfect. Because Hitler was the bastard son of the Great War, conceived in the trenches, born in defeat. He inhaled mustard gas and exhaled Zyklon B. In another memoir, dismissed by some as a fraud, Hitler's sister-in-law Bridget claims she was the cause of the

mustache. Bridget Hitler was Irish and lived in Liverpool, where,
according to the memoir, the young Adolf spent a lost winter.
Bridget (or whoever) says she often bickered with her brother-in-
law. Because he was disagreeable, but mostly because she could not
stand his unruly 'stache. In one of the great inadvertent summaries
of historical character, she writes that in this, as in everything, he
went too far.

He was wearing the Toothbrush at the first Nazi meetings, when
there were just a few people in a room full of empty chairs. One
day, an early financial supporter of the Nazi Party advised Hitler to
grow out his mustache. He did this delicately but firmly, in the
manner of a man trying to protect an investment. The mustache
made the Nazi look freakish. Hitler was advised to grow it at least
"to the end of the lips." Hitler was a vain man, and you can almost
feel him bristle. Here's what Hitler said: "If it is not the fashion
now, it will be later because I wear it."

In the coming years, the Toothbrush mustache would belong to
just two men, Chaplin and Hitler. The funniest and the scariest.
The dialectic of history. For many people, the Toothbrush mustache became no less a symbol of evil than the cloven hoof.

But here's the big question: Did the mustache affect history, or
was it just a matter of style? Did it attach itself to a person and drive
him crazy? Was the man in charge, or was the mustache calling the
shots? Ron Rosenbaum argues that the presence of Chaplin's
'stache on Hitler's face encouraged Western leaders to underesti-
mate the Führer. "Chaplin's mustache became a *lens* through
which to look at Hitler," he writes. "A glass in which Hitler became
merely Chaplinesque: a figure to be mocked more than feared, a
comic villain whose pretensions would collapse of his own disproportionate weight like the Little Tramp collapsing on his cane.
Someone to be ridiculed rather than resisted."

In 1942, Vidkun Quisling, the premier of Norway, whose name,
because of his sellout to the Nazis, became synonymous with
treachery, forbade Norwegian actors from mustache-wearing. Because thespians had been donning the 'stache to parody the Führer.
"The purpose of this singular ordinance is . . . to halt 'actor-
pranks' that have been 'stopping the show' by affecting a Hitler
mustache," the *New York Times* reported. Note how, in this story, the
Toothbrush mustache is not identified as the Toothbrush mus-

tache but as the Hitler mustache. From then on, the Toothbrush would belong only to Adolf. Not just a symbol but a totem of the dictator. A voodoo doll. It's not hard to see how you go from here to the plan cooked up by officers of the Office of Strategic Services, the precursor to the CIA, to inject estrogen into Hitler's food — female hormone that would make Hitler grow weepy, make Hitler grow breasts, and, crucially, destroy his mustache. A smooth-faced Adolf would lose confidence and fall from power. I mean, without the mustache, is Hitler even Hitler?

When Hitler died, he took his mustache with him. Not even the most cutting-edge stylist can pry them apart. If you dress like Chaplin, you run the risk of being mistaken for Hitler, as, if you dress like Evel Knievel, as I do when it rains, you run the risk of being mistaken for Elvis. The Vandyke, the Goatee, the Soul Patch, these things can become the objects of nostalgia, but the Hitler mustache is never coming back.

You could not wear a Toothbrush mustache after World War II, obviously. Because if you did, you were Hitler. In fact, you could not wear any kind of mustache after the war, because, running from Hitler, you might run into Stalin. Hitler plus Stalin ended the career of the mustache in Western political life. Before the war, all kinds of American presidents wore a mustache and/or beard. You had John Quincy Adams with his muttonchops. You had Abe Lincoln, whose facial hair, like his politics, was the opposite of Hitler's: beard full, lip bare. You had James Garfield, who had the sort of vast rabbinical beard into which whole pages of legislation could vanish. You had Rutherford B. Hayes, Grover Cleveland, and Teddy Roosevelt, whose asthma and elephant gun were just a frame for his mustache. You had William Howard Taft — *the man wore a Walrus!*

After the war, the few American politicians who still wore a mustache were those who had made their name before Hitler and so had been grandfathered in. Like Thomas Dewey. Dewey was Eliot Spitzer. He was a prosecutor in New York in the 1930s (and later governor), the only guy with the guts to take on the Mob. For Dewey, the rise of Hitler was a fashion disaster. Because Dewey wore a neat little mustache. Dewey ran for president twice — losing to FDR, losing to Truman. In my opinion, without the mustache, the headline in the *Chicago Daily Tribune* (DEWEY DEFEATS TRUMAN) turns true. One of the few prominent American politicians to wear facial hair in recent memory is Al Gore, who grew a Grizzly Adams beard after he lost to George Bush, in 2000. The appearance of this beard was taken to mean either (1) Gore would never again run for office, or (2) Gore had gone completely mental. The decision to grow a mustache or a beard is all by itself reason to keep a man away from the nuclear trigger.

As a player in political life, the mustache lives on only in the Third World — a conclusion drawn not from any statistical analysis but from my own travels. You see the mustache on politicians in such lands the way you see old Peugeots in the French Antilles. It is the past. It is what we left behind. In the Third World, a portion of voters still go for the sort of hair-growing display that once brought the *Volk* to Hans Koeppen. Until recent events caused me to reassess, I even entertained a theory — my only stab at a Tom Friedman–like, one-phrase-tells-all formulation — that I call "¿Quien es mas macho?" According to this theory, a country led by a man with a mustache is more likely to start a war, and more likely to lose it.* Because such a country is certain to value machismo over the nerdy qualities that actually win wars. A macho leader will counter a tank division with a cavalry charge — or promise, on the eve of battle, to drive his enemies into the sea. Such a leader will make some of the same mistakes as Hitler: he will overvalue physical courage; he will call on supernatural forces; he will consider even the smallest skirmish a "test of wills"; worst of all, he will answer the question "How will we win?" with the question "¿Quien es mas macho?"

I cut my beard on a Friday. I did what everyone who has ever cut a full beard does: I took it through every configuration. Like passing over the stages of man, or watching cultures rise and fall until the face of Hitler emerged. I went to the closet. What would the Führer wear on a sunny day? It does not matter, I decided. Because I am Hitler — whatever I wear, Hitler is wearing. A dozen Hitlers passed through my mind: Hitler in a sport coat; Hitler in a lab coat.

* Even though George W. Bush does not have a mustache, I like to imagine he does.

Hitler in a Speedo; Hitler in a Camaro. I shook myself and said, "Get it together, Hitler — you're losing your mind!"

I went out. In the street, some people looked at me, but most looked away. A few people said things after I passed. One man gave me a kind of *Heil,* but it was lackadaisical, and I am fairly certain he was being ironic. (People can be so mean!) Even friends said nothing until I asked, or else acted embarrassed for me. A woman said, "I think you were more handsome *without* the mustache." I had been worried someone might try to hurt me. I imagined toughs from the Jewish Defense League attacking with throwing stars — Jewish throwing stars! But it turns out, when you shave like Hitler, you follow the same rule you follow with bees: they're more scared of you than you are of them. Because either you really are Hitler or you're a nut. So people do with little Hitlers what people always do with lunatics in New York, the harmless or dangerous — they ignore, they avert, they move away. If you want to fly coach without being hassled, grow a Toothbrush mustache.

I wore the mustache for about a week. It preceded me into stores and hung in the air after I exited. It sat on my face as I slept. I was Hitler in my dreams. I went to the Jewish Museum. I went to Zabar's. I went to the Met. I went to the modern wing. I said, "All of this art is decadent." I stood on the corner of 82nd and Fifth. I stared into space. When you stare into space with a Toothbrush mustache, you are glowering. You can't help it. You're looking into crowds. You're looking at the names on the census that end in "-berg" and "-stein" while thinking, How do we get all these *Juden* onto trains? But in the end, my project, in its broader aims, was a failure. Because no matter how long, or how casually, or how sarcastically I wore the mustache, it still belonged to Hitler. You cannot claim it, or own it, or clean it as a drug lord cleans money. Because it's too dirty. Because it's soaked up too much history. It's his, and, as far as I'm concerned, he can keep it. When you wear the Toothbrush mustache, you are wearing the worst story in the world right under your nose.

BERNARD COOPER

The Constant Gardener

FROM *Los Angeles*

BRIAN SITS BESIDE ME at the edge of our bed, gritting his teeth as he rolls up his sleeve. He's worried that his PICC line — seven inches of flexible tubing that protrudes from the flesh at the crook of his arm — might catch in the fabric. I'd make a move to help him, but he insists on carrying out this part of the procedure himself, lifting and guiding the sleeve with his free hand, blue eyes alert to the slightest snag. These are perhaps the only moments in a given day when he has the power to protect himself from pain. The moments don't last long.

The full length of the PICC line unfurls, its loose end dangling over Brian's forearm. He's grown alarmingly thin over the past year and so vascular that his once submerged veins seem to have risen in compliance with the doctors and nurses who extract his blood, a dark red portent on which they base prognostications and an ever-changing regimen of drugs. The shelves in our kitchen are packed with plastic vials, bottles in every shape and size, foil gel packs, transdermal patches, and a pill cutter dusted with chalky powder.

I force my fingers into a pair of purple Safeskin examination gloves, then clench my fists a few times to loosen the fit. The gloves are numbing; when I touch Brian's outstretched arm, the touch conveys few details, as if his body, and not the sensation in my fingertips, has grown fainter.

The volume is turned up on the television set in the next room so we can hear tonight's episode of *Jeopardy!* Despite the fatigue that overcomes him most evenings, Brian has the presence of mind to give several right answers at the same time as the show's contestants. Sometimes he even beats them to the punch. Alex Trebek says, "Legumes absorb this element from the air and are often planted to restore it to the soil."

"What's nitrate?" asks Brian.

"What's nitrate?" a contestant echoes.

"How did you know that?" I ask.

"From working in the garden."

It's hard to think of him as the host to a virus, and yet I know he's inhabited, yielding against his will to a microscopic force that makes him appear less and less like the young man I met more than two decades ago, his body once agile, thoughtless in its health, responsive to pleasure instead of pain. Exercise, errands; he never seemed to tire. Tonight he wears a polar fleece jacket over a sweatshirt and thermal long johns beneath a pair of jeans. A wool ski cap covers his head. Each foot is padded by several pairs of socks. All these layers give him a temporary density; he's robust from clothes. I'd probably find some comfort in his bulky appearance if it weren't summer in Los Angeles, the heater in our bedroom cranked up full blast. Since he barely possesses any insulating fat, Brian shivers, cold to the bone.

I pop the cap off a syringe filled with saline solution. Keeping its blunt tip upright, I rotate the shaft, trying to gauge the size and relative danger of silvery air bubbles. As I press the plunger a fraction of an inch, excess air is squeezed from the syringe and a drop of saline glitters at its tip. This is Brian's cue to sterilize the treads at the end of his PICC line with a fresh alcohol pad. As soon as he's through, before airborne bacteria can contaminate the surface, I screw the syringe and PICC line together, making an airtight seal.

"Ready?" I ask.

"As I'll ever be," he says.

I push the plunger with my thumb and stop at regular intervals, pulsing saline with enough force to wash away any proteins that have accumulated in the tubing. During this stage of the infusion, our foreheads almost touch, mine perspiring. His breath is sour from chemicals, and though I want to close my eyes and find within those exhalations a scent I recognize as his, I can't afford to break my concentration. We've been warned that an unnoticed air bubble could pass through the filter and cause him to die. Until the syringe is empty, we live on the verge of this fatal mistake. Each second is a precipice.

Once the PICC line has been flushed, Brian and I absorb the fact that he's still alive. Time, which never stopped, continues. We gaze through the bedroom's glass doors at the cacti and succulents he planted along two narrow terraces that make up our backyard, a drought-resistant garden that can survive long periods without his care. Dusk is coming on, and the reflection of our lamp-lit bedroom is superimposed over the dimming plants and low stone retaining walls.

A large plastic bag of paranutrition hangs from a metal hook high atop the IV pole next to our bed. I rise to my feet and squeeze it a few times to stir up what the instruction sheet refers to as the "particulate matter" that has settled at the bottom. Paranutrition's long and cryptic list of ingredients includes lysine, phenylalanine, histidine, tyrosine, acetate, chloride, and something called glacial acetic acid, an additive that Brian facetiously insists is the one that makes his teeth chatter. But what intrigues us as much as its contents is its color, a rich ivory that looks as if elephant tusks and cameos and piano keys have been refined into a medicinal liquid that radiates light. Back when these nightly infusions began, I mentioned to Brian that the bag of liquid hanging above us glowed like a lantern, to which he added, "A lantern made of milk." Bolstering this association, the bag bulges like an udder, three short nozzles protruding from the bottom. I pierce one of these with the spike end of an extension tube, connecting it to Brian's PICC line. We're not sure why the other two nozzles exist, though our running joke is that there's one for Brian and one for our dog, Cubby, and one for me. Tucked within this joke is the truth that, after Brian has fallen asleep, his intravenous feeding under way, my nights are long and solitary, and I find myself wishing that I *could* suckle a source of nutrient-rich supermilk, sustenance to quell my fear, to fill me up until I'm lulled into a sensation I rarely feel these days: sleepy.

Next I thread the tubing through the grooves of a Flo-Gard 1260 Volumetric Infusion Pump, a boxy computerized device clamped to the IV pole. The line must be set snugly against a row of wheels called "pumping/sensing fingers," an anthropomorphic term that makes them sound more dexterous and tender than they are.

When the pump is switched on, the wheels will turn and move the fluid along its course. The last time I performed a similar task was when I threaded 8-millimeter film through the reels of my parents' home-movie projector. This was back in the 1960s, when the world's major contagions — polio, whooping cough, smallpox — had been nearly eradicated and a retrovirus like HIV was unimaginable. Now that idyll of medical innocence is hard to imagine.

Brian and I are in our early fifties. We've lived in this house for twenty-four years, longer than we lived in our boyhood homes — mine in Hollywood, his in a small Canadian province. For seventeen of those twenty-four years we've known that he was HIV positive and I was not. For ten of those seventeen years he's been symptomatic. For four of those ten years he's been sick with greater frequency and for longer periods of time. His T cells have dwindled to the triple, then double, then single digits. The news of his body is composed of numbers. Sometimes the numbers bear little relationship to how he actually feels. There are days when he is sick on paper but fine in fact. Or sick in fact and fine on paper. Often a change in the numbers from one blood test to the next is made meaningless by the test's statistical margin of error. Most of the test results are open to interpretation. In other words, they aren't results at all. Our job, says Brian, is to keep our moods from rising and falling along with the numbers. His odds for survival may fluctuate, he says, but our love for each other is dependable. "Yes," I agree. Then I catch myself thinking, *as dependable as a headstone.* In ways such as this, grief defeats me, undermines my best efforts to remain brave.

Because Brian had volunteered for one of the first trials of protease inhibitors and received low doses as a precautionary measure, he developed a resistance to an entire class of new drugs. His wasting has been temporarily arrested but not reversed by an arsenal of medicines and supplements. Gaining weight became even more difficult after he developed diabetes from taking medications so strong they damaged his pancreas. If he fails to eat modest portions of food low in sugar and fat, he risks slipping into a diabetic coma, the onset of which is a bout of sleepiness and fatigue that can pass for the harmless lassitude of a nap. At five feet six and one hundred pounds, he's forty pounds under his normal weight. He teeters just this side of starvation. Infusions of paranutrition are

perhaps the last treatment left to help him put on a few pounds.
Ten would be excellent, but he'd settle for five, just enough to protect him from the cold of summer — his body's harsh, incongru-
ous climate — and buffer the friction of flesh against bone.

Several months ago, Brian's primary physician, Dr. K., began a gentle but insistent campaign for home infusions of paranutrition. A
peripherally inserted central catheter — the PICC line — would
have to be implanted. "Patients have been able to benefit from
paranutrition for years," Dr. K. told us during a consultation. I
should have grasped the finality of his remark, the brick wall of
it, but I thought he meant that his patients benefited from paranutrition until they were able to eat solid food.

Brian understood the doctor's meaning from the start. One
morning, as he was getting dressed for work, he informed me that
he'd given it a great deal of thought and had decided to take Dr.
K.'s advice. He asked if I'd be willing to learn how to administer
the infusions.

"Absolutely," I said. "Anything."

"I'll probably be hooked up to an infusion pump every night for
the rest of my life."

"You mean, 'for the rest of our lives.'"

"No," he said. "I mean the rest of mine."

I'd been sitting in bed, editing the book I was still working on
months past the deadline. I'd spent the morning fiddling with syntax, but parsing his remark was the greater challenge. "You're saying you won't ever be able to go off it?"

"Probably not. I've done some research," he continued, "and at
least I can sleep through infusions. My only other choice is to be
the guinea pig for an experimental injectable that will leave painful knots at the injection sites. And they don't go away. Eventually,
I wouldn't be able to sit at my desk or lie in bed without hurting. I
wouldn't be able to rest. Ever." Perhaps mistaking my silence for acceptance, he announced that he was off to Nordstrom to get his
shoes shined before work.

I realize that Brian's decision to have his shoes shined at that
particular moment may strike some people as a flight from otherwise bleak and inescapable circumstances — and if so, so what? —
but as his meticulous notebook shows, he's not one to fool himself

about the state of his health. If you ask him how he is, he could (but wouldn't) give you an answer down to the platelet. It's not that he takes his illness lightly. He takes it gravely but pursues his routines to whatever extent his strength allows. When a friend of ours with AIDS proclaimed that having the virus was a blessing in disguise, forcing the person infected to live in a state of acute appreciation for every instant of his or her life, Brian looked skyward and clasped his hands in prayer. "If this is a blessing, then unbless me, Father, fast!" There are times I've seen him dumbstruck by despair, but despair burns inside him for only so long before it runs its course and passes like a fever, restoring him to the ordinary.

A few weeks ago, for example, we were looking out the window at the garden. The prongs and thorny paddles of the succulents made them seem, in the fiery late-afternoon light, especially primeval, and I started to dwell on the vastness of time and the transience of all things, and of course I thought about the threat to Brian's life. The stone retaining walls were cracked and buckled where the hillside had settled. I pictured intricate root systems burrowing into the soil where worms and grubs were writhing blindly. To keep myself from sinking even further into the underworld, I turned to make conversation with Brian and saw that he too was staring somberly out the window, stricken with what I assumed was a similar twinge of mortality. His forehead was furrowed, his shoulders sloped. I asked what he was thinking.

He said, "The euphorbia needs water."

His remark proved without a doubt that his slough of despair was a mere puddle compared to mine. It's not just that Brian is the most genuinely cheerful person I've ever known; he's practically the *only* cheerful person I've ever known. None of my wonderfully complicated and unconventional friends would so much as consider doing the wave in a stadium full of people, for example, which is one of Brian's favorite things to do. Most people I know would rather have their hands lopped off than clap along to some saccharine song, whereas Brian claps along to any old song just to have a taste of collective glee. Group behavior fills me with a discomfort I'm afraid to let show for fear that I'll be seen as a spoiler, and so I grin miserably while everyone around me becomes a marionette whose strings are yanked in a dance of mass hysteria. Brian, on the other hand, loves parades, political rallies, square dances, ice-skating rinks, and other gatherings in which large groups of people move in unison, subordinate parts of a single-mindedly jubilant whole.

Although he tends toward the cheerful end of the spectrum, Brian also qualifies as a staunch realist. Until a few months ago he delivered meals to people with AIDS, and I sometimes went with him, meeting a number of men and women covered with Kaposi's sarcoma lesions or jaundiced from having to take liver-damaging doses of Crixivan, and I couldn't help asking Brian if it frightened him to see their health deteriorate week after week. "They're not me," he said, a little surprised that I had to ask. "I feel bad for them more than frightened for myself." On the same excursion he'd taken along a pair of disposable diapers in case he got the runs, which had become an increasingly frequent side effect of his medications, and when I suggested putting the diapers in a plastic bag to protect them from the fur Cubby had shed all over the car seats, he said, "Why bother? They're just going to get shit on them anyway." I marvel at such remarks because I'm pretty sure that if I had AIDS — to the degree I can imagine having it — the disease would turn me into a fatalist at worst and an absurdist at best. But a realist, never.

Anyway, back to the day he decided to begin infusions. I was sitting on the bed, manuscript in hand — and on lap, legs, bedspread, floor — and when I could finally bring myself to speak, to say something consoling or empathic about what was perhaps the last medical option available to prevent him from losing even more weight, this is what came out of my mouth: "There's a shoe shiner at Nordstrom?"

"In the men's department," he said. He cinched his tie, kissed me on the forehead, and left the house.

A few days after Brian made up his mind to begin infusions, a postcard came to remind us of the upcoming date, address, and time of our appointment at his HMO. That day the PICC line would be implanted, and immediately afterward I'd learn how to infuse him. "Your wellness is our first concern," the postcard read. "So please be on time!"

Over the years Brian had endured medical procedures too numerous to count — too ghoulish to want to count — and he'd cultivated a dignified, if somewhat reticent, surrender when it came to letting strangers palpate his glands, press their stethoscopes against his chest, and pierce his skin with their needles. But shortly after the postcard arrived, the prospect of having a catheter implanted caused an uncharacteristic spike in his anxiety, despite Dr. K.'s assurances that the procedure would be painless and over in a flash.

Brian and I have been a lucky couple in that one of us is usually steadfast (him) when the other is fretful (me), and this division of emotional labor has suited us well. I can say with a fair degree of certainty that I'm good at fretting. Better than good. I'm a world-class fretter. I can fret with both hands tied behind my back. I come from a long line of professional fretters who would have no trouble making the association between, say, a drafty room and full-blown pneumonia. I bring to worry a far greater dedication than Brian ever could, and this, I'd like to think, has allowed him lots of free time in which to get his bearings, dig in his heels, and remain resolute. With my considerable skill in this area, I've been able to take at least some of the burden off Brian's shoulders, and he, in turn, gives me hope for the future by insisting that I worry too much. We've managed, with this kind of delicate imbalance, to husband each other through several crises.

But now Brian's nervousness worsened the closer we came to the day of the appointment. This meant I had to pick up his constitutional slack, so to speak, and I'm happy to say that I met the challenge head-on, becoming a relatively levelheaded fellow who doled out the kind of comments — *Even if getting the implant hurts, which Dr. K. says it doesn't, it won't hurt for long* — that usually fell under Brian's purview. Playing at having confidence (in other words, having false confidence) led me to believe that I might master, or at least achieve a basic grasp of, the necessary steps for giving an infusion. This came as very good news indeed, because if I had to receive an infusion, I'm the last person I'd choose to receive it from. I've never, thank goodness, been called upon to give mouth-to-mouth resuscitation or perform the Heimlich maneuver. I've never stanched a geyser of blood or splinted a broken bone. A paper cut is ordeal enough. Stubbed toes have caused me to curse life on earth. That Brian had asked me to give him infusions struck some squeamish part of me as a breach in his otherwise ratio-

nal thinking. Worse, giving him infusions would make me, in a
definitive and daily way, his caretaker, a word I despised for its sug-
gestions of dependency and incapacitation. For more than two
decades I'd assumed that it was he who took care of me, that
he was the dependable one, the organized one, the one who
got things done despite being HIV positive, while I spent days
hunched over a desk, distracted by language to the point of . . . dis-
traction. If I became the infuser and he the infusee, our time-
tested roles would have to be reversed.

Still, I said I'd do anything for him, and I meant it. To prove to
us both that I was up to the task, I prepared for our appointment
with all the forethought of a Boy Scout. In other words, I har-
nessed my knack for imagining disaster and put it to work. On
the morning in question, my gym bag was packed. In case it was
necessary for either of us to take notes during the instructions, I
brought writing pads and ballpoint pens. I packed bottled water
for Brian in case of dehydration. I'd vacuumed dog hair from the
car seats and made sure the tank was filled with gas, even though
the HMO was a ten-minute drive from our house. I'd slipped the
postcard reminder, printed with the instructor's name, into my
wallet, thinking I could start things off on the right foot by pro-
nouncing it correctly. I was determined not only to learn from her
but to ingratiate myself in case I ever needed to ask her for some
medical favor on Brian's behalf. By planning for every contingency
and executing this visit without a hitch, I hoped to make the difference between watching Brian starve to death and saving his life. It
never occurred to me that, locked within my need to do the right
thing, there existed a more desperate need to believe that there
was a right thing to do, an act or decision that could spare him
from harm.

I dropped Brian off at the entrance to the medical facility's
enormous parking structure. When I saw him next, he was reclin-
ing in one of the infusion center's three plumply upholstered
chairs. His head was tilted back. His eyes were closed. His arms and
legs lay absolutely still. I walked closer. Called his name. No response. On a metal rolling cart beside him, packaged in protective
plastic, lay a fresh catheter, the source of his anxiety for the past
few weeks. Now I saw why. All this time I'd confused (willfully perhaps) a catheter with a shunt. As I'd misunderstood it, a blunt,

needle-like device would be inserted an intrusive inch or two into his vein, and from it would trail a PICC line. In fact, the catheter, when uncoiled, must have been at least five feet long. I would have been calmer seeing a snake. "Holy shit," I whispered. "Exactly," said Brian. He attempted, unsuccessfully, to lift his head. His voice was as raspy as vented steam, and I realized that he'd probably taken a sedative before we'd left the house. This was unusual, for he took great pride in having his wits about him in adverse circumstances. He'd been even more fearful than I'd realized.

"How out of it are you?" I asked.

"Not nearly enough."

The pert nurse assigned to insert Brian's catheter wore a smock blooming with yellow flowers, so I'll call her Daisy. Daisy was the nurse who usually drew Brian's blood for tests, and the three of us had developed one of those affable treat-and-go relationships that are common at HMOs. She spoke broken English, but in her effort to amuse us and keep our minds off the procedure, she couldn't have been more eloquent. She bent over Brian. "All set for catheter?" she asked.

Brian nodded lethargically.

I asked Daisy if she thought he'd taken a sedative.

"Yes!" she said, pointing to herself. "I suggest to him yesterday. Make my job easy."

Daisy and I each took Brian by a pliable arm and provided enough counterweight to pull him out of the chair. "He good and ready," she grunted. With Brian sleepily slung between us, we hobbled into a small room that was empty except for an examination table. Daisy rolled out a fresh sheet of paper and together we helped Brian sprawl atop it. I stood on the opposite side of the table from Daisy. "Hold hand," she demanded. Brian's fingers were icy, and though I enfolded them in my palms, my body heat seemed like a hoarded resource; the coldness of his skin cut through me while the warmth of mine did little for him. He peered up at me, or at least in the general vicinity of my face, and began to shiver. That was enough to send Daisy into action before his trembling grew worse. In one quick, continuous movement, she turned up the thermostat and ripped open the clear plastic package that kept the catheter sterile. "Don't look, don't look," she sang. We both obeyed. In the periphery of my vision I saw her take a couple of somethings out of something else to do something to Brian's arm. This was followed by a hand-over-hand motion as she fed the tubing into his vein. When at last her movements slowed, she pressed her gloved fingers firmly against his chest, trying to gauge when the tip of the catheter was moored just inches above his heart.

My eyes must have widened because Brian blurted, "What's wrong?"

"Friend," said Daisy, "talk to your Bri so he not be thinking."

"Do you want to go out to lunch after this?" I asked him.

"No!" snapped Brian.

The time that elapsed between deciding what else I could say to distract him and coming up with something distracting to say probably wasn't as long as it seemed, but I had never assessed and rejected topics of conversation at such a breakneck pace.

"Done!" announced Daisy. "I fast get bandage, patch you up, and then we take x-ray so make sure catheter in good position. All you need now," she said in my direction, "is learn to do infusion! Instructor come in twenty minutes sharp." She tapped her watch for emphasis. Before she left the room, Daisy paused and stroked Brian's forehead.

"Thank you," he said. "You did a great job."

She laughed. "How you know? You not look at arm."

"That's correct," said Brian. "I have not looked."

Regardless of whether or not he'd looked, his praise applied: Daisy had executed the procedure flawlessly, which bore out Dr. K.'s prediction that it would be painless, which in turn confirmed that Brian was in good hands, which proved that the implant was a wise idea, which suggested that he might gain weight, which led to a full sixty seconds of hope. I don't mean to disparage that hope by measuring its length in seconds. When you're hope-deprived, seconds of hope equal hours, days.

No sooner had Daisy left the room than Brian decided to examine her handiwork. I looked too. The PICC line trailed from a crimson incision. It could have been a wayward vein stripped of flesh and exposed to the air. The crook of his arm had been smeared with Betadine, a disinfectant as brown as dried blood. The sight was incomprehensible, as wrong as a limb turned inside out, and my impulse was to call an ambulance until I remembered we were already at the hospital. Brian wrenched his head in my direction, slightly overshooting the sight line. "Honey," he said. "My stomach. Did you bring diapers?"

The one thing I forgot.

He asked if I would run home and get him a pair. "They're on the bathroom counter. Plus the bottle of Lomotil."

"What about our appointment with the infusion nurse?"

"It's not for twenty minutes."

"I'm sure they have adult diapers and Lomotil here."

"You'd have to get a prescription and wait in line at the pharmacy. That could take hours. If you leave for the house now, you could be back by —"

"I can't miss the instructions."

"You won't. But if you do, I'll tell you what she says later."

"You're too stoned to remember the instructions. Too stoned to realize how stoned you are. I can't — sorry — trust you with the instructions." How did I go from being the person whose task was to help him to being the person whose duty was refusal? "I've been gearing up for this for two weeks, Brian! I can't leave now." A nurse with a clipboard glanced through the open doorway to see if we were okay. I lowered my voice. "Twenty minutes is cutting it too close. Besides, we can't reschedule the instructions now that you have that tube sticking out of you."

"Please," he said. He didn't plead or wheedle or implore. He merely asked — the most persuasive tactic of all — and that was that.

As I raced back into the infusion center, I saw that M., our instructor, was already in the examination room with Brian, setting down her briefcase. She must have just arrived. With her gold-rimmed bifocals and tailored skirt, she looked every bit a woman in the know. "I'm here!" I yelled, still several yards short of the open door. M. and Brian watched me barrel toward them. Despite my relief at returning on time, I was panting like an animal and basted in sweat. I also rattled with every step. Dangling from each wrist were plastic grocery bags crammed to bursting with all of Brian's medications. I'd swept them off the shelves by the armful and sent them tumbling into bag after bag. Once the bags were full, I gathered up the bottles that had fallen onto the floor and stuffed them into my pants and shirt pockets. I figured that Brian would recognize the Lomotil even if he had to riffle through several grocery bags to find it. Clamped under my arm was an economy-size package of Depends. My stride was brisk with a sense of mission. I felt as auspicious as a cargo ship appearing on the horizon of a remote island, or a rescue dog pawing through an avalanche. The second I stepped over the threshold, I greeted M. by her first name, just as I'd planned.

"Do I know you?" she asked. Her black eyebrows were crimped with suspicion. Her scrutiny was as bright as a searchlight.

I introduced myself and reached out to shake her hand. The bags rattled. "You're the partner?" asked M.

"That would be me!" I was too jaunty by half, but the other half couldn't do a thing about it. "It's really humid today," I said, to put my sweat in context.

M. opened her briefcase and peered inside. "Do you need to get settled?" she asked without looking up.

Brian caught the package of diapers as I unclamped my arm. I let the grocery bags slide off my wrists and onto a built-in counter with a sink. I unloaded fistfuls of pill bottles from my pockets and turned to Brian. "Here are the medications you asked me to run home and get for you at the very last minute, which is why I'm late and out of breath," I said in an expository rush, hoping M. had heard every word.

"I didn't say to bring them all!"

"I couldn't find the Lomotil. I brought them all to be on the safe side. I didn't know what else to do."

Brian grabbed a bag at random and reached into it with his uncatheterized arm. He rummaged around inside for a second, then pulled out a bottle. "Here it is!" he said. "Atropine sulfate!"

"Atropine sulfate?"

"Generic for Lomotil."

"How the hell was I supposed to know that?"

"I told you."

"No you didn't!"

"I'm sure I did," Brian said uncertainly.

I began to think he actually might have.

"Well," he conceded, "maybe I didn't."

"No," I said, "you probably did."

"Here's some important information I'd like you both to have," M. interrupted. She handed us a folder titled "Home Infusion." It showed a black-and-white illustration that at first looked to me like a drawing of a kite on a string, but on closer examination turned out to be an IV bag trailing a tube. M. noticed me squinting at the image. She switched off her cell phone. She sighed the sigh of a woman whose work was cut out for her. "I take it," she asked me, "that you'll be in charge?"

I plucked a Kleenex from a nearby box and tamped my forehead. "I realize I must look a little frazzled, what with racing in at the last minute, but please understand that I take this responsibility as seriously as anyone without medical experience can take it. Not that my not having medical experience will be a problem. What I'm saying is, *despite* my lack of medical experience, I'm ready and willing to learn everything there is to know about giving foolproof infusions."

"Foolproof?" she asked.

Brian and I looked at each other.

"The authorities have ways of determining if an air bubble has passed through the filtration system and killed a patient on purpose."

"Listen," I said to M., "I know you don't know me from Adam, and I appreciate your concern, but believe me, there's no way I'm going to kill him on purpose!"

She kept on staring.

"Not by accident either!"

"He won't," mumbled Brian, a Lomotil on his tongue.

"We've been together for over twenty years," I told M., realizing too late that a twenty-year relationship might seem to her like a reason for foul play instead of against it.

"I'm going to trust you," M. told me. "Begrudgingly" doesn't do her tone justice; her trust had to be extracted like a tooth. "You must understand that I'm here not only to instruct but to assess the suitability of the parties involved."

"Listen," I said, "the two of us have been dealing with this disease for —"

"Seventeen years," said Brian. "Can I have a glass of water?"

"— And I think it's safe to say that if we weren't suitable to help each other through this, we would have found out by now."

M. paused, taking this in. "That's what I like to hear!" She seemed pleased to have me insist on my commitment in the face of opposition. Her smile implied that I'd passed a test. A moment ago, when I thought that earning her approval was impossible, I resented having to prove my suitability, but once she deemed me suitable, I needed her approval more than before.

While M. prepared her demonstration, laying out a PICC line and its attachments on a small table, I brought Brian a gulp's worth of water in one of those tiny pleated paper cups. He tossed it back and swallowed the pill. Daisy rolled an IV pole, complete with computerized pump, into the room. An empty IV bag hung atop it. "Here I come for practice," she announced.

She plugged the cord into the wall and the computer let out a shrill, repeated beep. Brian and I winced. Daisy and M. went about their business unbothered. Although the dictionary defines a beep as a short burst of sound, that word is as wanting as a referent can get. *Flo-Gard* is to *beep* as *air horn* is to *tweet*. Like a baby's wail, the sound stimulated an involuntary biological response, its pitch able to wrest the attention of anyone within fifty yards. You couldn't eat or read or relax while that thing was beeping. You certainly couldn't sleep through it, which was precisely the point; no state of repose, no seductive dream, was safe from its many decibels.

"The beep lets you know the machine is on," said M. in a masterstroke of understatement. "During the night it will also alert you to clogs in the PICC line — we call them *occlusions* — and other malfunctions in the apparatus. We want the lumen to stay clear at all times."

Brian wedged a question between beeps.

"Lumen," explained M., "is what we call the inside of the tube. Unusual movements can twist the line, which blocks the lumen and sets off the alarm. You mustn't bounce on the bed unless you absolutely have to."

I said, "I'll hold him down if he bounces."

"My bouncing days are over," said Brian.

"You gentlemen won't think this is so funny if you have to wake up ten times a night to turn off the alarm." M. pressed a button labeled SILENCE. The machine made good on its word, though what followed wasn't silence so much as an agitated vacuum.

"Where these come from?" asked Daisy. She'd just noticed the bags of medication heaped on the counter.

Brian and I both said, "Home."

"So many," she exclaimed. In his previous conversations with Daisy, Brian must have given her some idea of the number of medications he was taking, and she'd no doubt referred to his medical charts many times, but seeing the sum of those drugs with her own eyes was another story. She thrust her hands into the pockets of her smock, sunk in flowers up to her wrists. M. removed her bifocals to get a better look, revealing a permanent furrow that the bridge of her glasses had hidden. The four of us faced the bags and bottles scattered across the countertop. It was hard to believe that someone had ingested, and would continue to ingest, such large quantities of medication. Brian's life was lived by the milligram, the precise titration. Still, we were running out of drugs, and drug combinations, that would prolong his life.

Our staring brought to the room an interval of silence so deep and complete that I could hear the brittle skin of the plastic bags settling with the weight of their contents, a faint rustling as of dry leaves. Fluorescent lights buzzed in the recessed ceiling. Air blew through the vents in an icy, inscrutable whisper. I would have been unnerved by the sudden, almost hallucinatory intensity of these sounds if I hadn't also been astonished by them, snapping to attention the way I would if a symphony orchestra were tuning up in that cramped examination room.

M. said, "Seventeen years."

"What?" I asked.

Her eyes met mine. "That's a long time. Longer than I've lived in America. When I first came to the States, my parents warned me that America was a place forsaken. I was told that few people prayed to Allah. But it looked to me like people were praying all the time, day and night. Of course, it wasn't the kind of prayer I thought."

"What was it?" asked Daisy.

"Cell phones."

Brian said, "You saw people praying over the phone?"

"This was before I had a cell myself," M. continued. "I saw men and women everywhere lifting their hands to their ears just as I had when I was growing up in Iran, and I thought, it's *qiyam*, the posture taken just after one decides to pray. A sign of readiness. Soon I understood my mistake, but I still like to see it as I used to: prayer everywhere. Every one of these people is giving a sign of readiness whether they believe in prayer or not. Call and answer, call and answer. How else can a man or a woman know God? We're making way for prayer even if what we're making is appointments."

M. slid her glasses back into place and cleared her throat. "Shall we begin?" she asked, slightly timid after what she might have considered a regrettable lapse into candor. She waved me over to the sink. Attached to the wall beside it was a soap dispenser. She said she couldn't overemphasize the importance of proper hand-washing. "Everything you're about to learn means nothing if your hands aren't clean." This remark was as weighty as any aphorism I'd ever heard, though now wasn't the time to contemplate its nuances. I cracked my knuckles, took off my watch.

I washed longer than was strictly necessary, to demonstrate my good intentions and win a few extra points. I held out my dripping hands for inspection. "Excellent," M. said. "The challenge is to dry your hands without allowing them to contact any potentially unclean surface." This required touching everything with either my elbows or a fresh, protective paper towel until I could slip my sterilized hands into a pair of the purple Safeskin examination gloves that were stocked throughout the hospital.

M. showed us the catheter's components and demonstrated how to connect them to the Flo-Gard. She explained that 1,725 milligrams of liquid nutrition would be channeled into Brian's bloodstream over the course of a twelve-hour period, from 7 P.M. to 7 A.M., seven days a week, for all the days to come. M. let me practice inputting numbers on the computer's touch pad. She took us through the gamut of digital readouts, each brief but luminous text — PRI RATE, TOT VOL, UPSTREAM OCCLUSION — subject to what poets and scholars would consider a close reading. In case we forgot what the messages meant, she provided us with a xeroxed glossary to keep by our bed.

After nearly a dozen trial runs, I was able to perform a simulated infusion without missing a step or making an error serious enough to set off the alarm. Keeping that machine from beeping was an excellent incentive.

"Are you feeling more confident?" M. asked me.

"Relatively," I said. "But even in the best circumstances, my confidence is clouded with doubt."

"Bernard," said Brian.

"She asked me," I said.

When our hour of instruction was up, I loaded my pockets with stray medicine bottles and grabbed the bulging plastic bags. They hung from my arms like ballast. Brian stood up, a little unsteady on his feet, and glanced around the room. "Do we have everything?" he asked.

We had dozens of drugs, sets of instructions, disposable diapers, and a complimentary box of Safeskin gloves.

"Everything," I said.

Brian tilted back his head, opened his mouth, and shook a drop of water from the paper cup. The sedative was losing its hold; he looked weary but alert. He rolled down his sleeve and buttoned the cuff. Hours from now he would do his best to understand, with neither optimism nor despair, what had changed for him that day. With every cell under siege, his blood muddied by chemicals, a tube burrowing inside his biceps, how was it possible that some unmistakable self remained — obdurate, Brian-like?

M. closed her briefcase. "Brian," she said before we left the room. "I don't mean to pry, but I have to ask. Is there a secret to your longevity?"

"Yes," he told her. "I'd rather not die."

Alex Trebek says, "When driving in the rain, be sure to steer into it."

"What's the skid?" asks Brian. "I know that from driving on black ice in Canada. You steer into the skid and accelerate."

"Accelerate?"

"It's counterintuitive. You have to go against your reflexes. But that's the only way to keep the car from swerving off the road."

I get down on my knees so that I'm at eye level with the Flo-Gard's pump compartment. I press the red safety clamp and latch the pump compartment's door. Both lock into place with an audible click that should be reassuring but isn't.

The temperature is a few degrees cooler near the floor, and the change, though slight, is bracing. Kneeling here, surrounded by boxes of individually wrapped syringes, my hands perspiring in a pair of purple gloves, a rigid dog watching from the corner, I'm able to perceive, with rare clarity, the unlikely shape our lives have taken. Ten years ago, when I was in my early forties, I thought of myself as a person who'd come to expect anything, but I hadn't expected anything like this.

Brian is dying. I will not allow myself to say this aloud. I'm so certain of the incantatory power of words that to utter them aloud, I fear, would bring about his death. To voice them would mean there was no going back, no reprieve to hope for. In the anteroom of unspoken thoughts, the words are closer to silence than to sound.

As I rise to my feet, Brian says, "I'm perishing."

It's as if he's read my mind. I have to stop myself from gasping.

"I'm freezing," he says. "Hurry."

"Perishing" is an expression he's used before. Until now its meaning had been singular. Brian is holding on tightly to what's left of his life as he moves through it — this strikes me as a physically impossible feat, like carrying yourself on your own back — and I try to follow his lead and soldier forward. Not until he's fallen asleep do I give in to an expression I don't want him to see, afraid the desolation on my face might undermine his resolve. If that happened, whom would I draw strength from? Those are the hours when I can turn and look at him without his being aware of it. I can stare with impunity at his thinning skin, balding eyebrows, cheeks sunken in their yoke of bone, and observe the prone whole of him in small, self-imposed doses.

Only once has he ever stirred and caught me staring. He blinked himself awake and took me in. For a moment there was nothing but the hum of the infusion pump. Without a question or preface, he said, "This kind of thing is harder for the person who has to watch."

This kind of thing.

I said, not unkindly, "Do you have to be so decent?" By then I'd entered a new universe where I was stung by his offers of comfort, which only reminded me how much I'd need his presence to survive his death.

"Sorry," he said, and before I could weigh his intonation — was he apologizing for his decency or for his illness? — he'd fallen back asleep.

I press PRI START. The Flo-Gard lets out the ear-piercing beep we heard that day with M. The first ivory bead of paranutrition falls through the drip chamber. Cubby rises to his feet. I grab Brian's jeans off the floor and begin to fold them, but my hands grow suddenly huge against the waistband, the pant legs. "Nordstrom," he says, seeing me bewildered. "I bought new pants in the boys' department."

His remark keeps me awake for hours. In the time-lapse of my imagination, I picture him wasting away until he's little more than a strand of himself, as white and lifeless as a length of thread. This image visits me repeatedly while I lie beside him and try to read, scanning the same sentence, the same paragraph, over and over; regardless of how compelling the prose, its representation of the world beyond this room is never quite as urgent as the world within it, a world where the air is close and overheated, aglow with milky light, dense with emanations from our lungs and bowels and the acrid odor of his body striving, even in sleep, to stay alive. The recurring image of Brian's diminishment is also, I'm ashamed to admit, a wish for his absence to be realized rather than impending, a wish for everything that has been protracted and incremental about his illness to be hastened, accomplished, over at last, the advent of his death transformed into something as ordinary as a loose thread, as easy for me to break free of. Then, as happens several times a night, I turn to him and listen, reassured by his breathing, firmly tethered to the last days of his life.

The Way We Age Now

FROM *The New Yorker*

THE HARDEST SUBSTANCE in the human body is the white enamel of the teeth. With age, it wears away nonetheless, allowing the softer, darker layers underneath to show through. Meanwhile, the blood supply to the pulp and the roots of the teeth atrophies, and the flow of saliva diminishes; the gums tend to become inflamed and pull away from the teeth, exposing the base, making them unstable and elongating their appearance, especially the lower ones. Experts say they can gauge a person's age to within five years from the examination of a single tooth — if the person has any teeth left to examine.

Scrupulous dental care can help avert tooth loss, but growing old gets in the way. Arthritis, tremors, and small strokes, for example, make it difficult to brush and floss, and, because nerves become less sensitive with age, people may not realize that they have cavity and gum problems until it's too late. In the course of a normal lifetime, the muscles of the jaw lose about forty percent of their mass and the bones of the mandible lose about twenty percent, becoming porous and weak. The ability to chew declines, and people shift to softer foods, which are generally higher in fermentable carbohydrates and more likely to cause cavities. By the age of sixty, Americans have lost, on average, a third of their teeth. After eighty-five, almost forty percent have no teeth at all.

Even as our bones and teeth soften, the rest of our body hardens. Blood vessels, joints, the muscle and valves of the heart, and even the lungs pick up substantial deposits of calcium and turn stiff. Under a microscope, the vessels and soft tissues display the same form of calcium that you find in bone. When you reach inside an elderly patient during surgery, the aorta and other major vessels often feel crunchy under your fingers. A recent study has found that loss of bone density may be an even better predictor of death from atherosclerotic disease than cholesterol levels. As we age, it's as if the calcium flows out of our skeletons and into our tissues.

To maintain the same volume of blood flow through narrowed and stiffened blood vessels, the heart has to generate increased pressure. As a result, more than half of us develop hypertension by the age of sixty-five. The heart becomes thicker-walled from having to pump against the pressure, and less able to respond to the demands of exertion. The peak output of the heart decreases steadily from the age of thirty. People become gradually less able to run as far or as fast as they used to, or to climb a flight of stairs without becoming short of breath.

Why we age is the subject of vigorous debate. The classical view is that aging happens because of random wear and tear. A newer view holds that aging is more orderly and genetically driven. Proponents of this view point out that animals of similar species and exposure to wear and tear have markedly different life spans. The Canada goose has a longevity of 23.5 years; the emperor goose only 6.3 years. Perhaps animals are like plants, with lives that are, to a large extent, internally governed. Certain species of bamboo, for instance, form a dense stand that grows and flourishes for a hundred years, flowers all at once, and then dies.

The idea that living things shut down and not just wear down has received substantial support in the past decade. Researchers working with the now famous worm *C. elegans* (two of the last five Nobel Prizes in medicine went to scientists doing work on the little nematode) were able to produce worms that live more than twice as long and age more slowly by altering a single gene. Scientists have since come up with single-gene alterations that increase the life spans of *Drosophila* fruit flies, mice, and yeast.

These findings notwithstanding, scientists do not believe that our life spans are actually programmed into us. After all, for most of our hundred-thousand-year existence — all but the past couple of hundred years — the average life span of human beings has been thirty years or less. (Research suggests that subjects of the Roman Empire had an average life expectancy of twenty-eight years.) Today, the average life span in developed countries is almost eighty years. If human life spans depend on our genetics, then medicine has got the upper hand. We are, in a way, freaks living well beyond our appointed time. So when we study aging, what we are trying to understand is not so much a natural process as an unnatural one. Inheritance has surprisingly little influence on longevity. James Vaupel, of the Max Planck Institute for Demographic Research, in Rostock, Germany, notes that only six percent of how long you'll live, compared with the average, is explained by your parents' longevity; by contrast, up to ninety percent of how tall you are, compared with the average, is explained by your parents' height. Even genetically identical twins vary widely in life span: the typical gap is more than fifteen years.

If our genes explain less than we imagined, the wear-and-tear model may explain more than we knew. Leonid Gavrilov, a researcher at the University of Chicago, argues that human beings fail the way all complex systems fail: randomly and gradually. As engineers have long recognized, many simple devices do not age. They function reliably until a critical component fails, and the whole thing dies instantly. A windup toy works smoothly until a gear rusts or a spring breaks, and then it doesn't work at all. But complex systems — power plants, say — have to survive and function despite having thousands of critical components. Engineers therefore design these machines with multiple layers of redundancy: with backup systems, and backup systems for the backup systems. The backups may not be as efficient as the first-line components, but they allow the machine to keep going even as damage accumulates. Gavrilov argues that, within the parameters established by our genes, that's exactly how human beings appear to work. We have an extra kidney, an extra lung, an extra gonad, extra teeth. The DNA in our cells is frequently damaged under routine conditions, but our cells have a number of DNA repair systems. If a key gene is permanently damaged, there are usually extra copies of the gene nearby. And, if the entire cell dies, other cells can fill in.

Nonetheless, as the defects in a complex system increase, the time comes when just one more defect is enough to impair the whole, resulting in the condition known as frailty. It happens to power plants, cars, and large organizations. And it happens to us: eventually, one too many joints are damaged, one too many arteries calcify. There are no more backups. We wear down until we can't wear down anymore.

It happens in a bewildering array of ways. Hair grows gray, for instance, simply because we run out of the pigment cells that give hair its color. The natural life cycle of the scalp's pigment cells is just a few years. We rely on stem cells under the surface to migrate in and replace them. Gradually, however, the stem-cell reservoir is used up. By the age of fifty, as a result, half of the average person's hairs have gone gray.

Inside skin cells, the mechanisms that clear out waste products slowly break down and the muck coalesces into a clot of gooey yellow-brown pigment known as lipofuscin. These are the age spots we see in skin. When lipofuscin accumulates in sweat glands, the sweat glands cannot function, which helps explain why we become so susceptible to heat stroke and heat exhaustion in old age.

The eyes go for different reasons. The lens is made of crystallin proteins that are tremendously durable, but they change chemically in ways that diminish their elasticity over time — hence the farsightedness that most people develop beginning in their fourth decade. The process also gradually yellows the lens. Even without cataracts (the whitish clouding of the lens caused by excessive ultraviolet exposure, high cholesterol, diabetes, cigarette smoking, and other unhelpful conditions), the amount of light reaching the retina of a healthy sixty-year-old is one-third that of a twenty-year-old.

I spoke to Felix Silverstone, who for twenty-four years was the senior geriatrician at the Parker Jewish Institute in New York and has published more than a hundred studies on aging. There is, he said, "no single, common cellular mechanism to the aging process." Our bodies accumulate lipofuscin and oxygen free-radical damage and random DNA mutations and numerous other microcellular problems. The process is gradual and unrelenting. "We just fall apart," he said.

This is not an appealing prospect, and people naturally prefer to avoid the subject of their decrepitude. There have been dozens of best-selling books on aging, but they tend to have titles like *Younger*

Next Year, The Fountain of Age, Ageless, The Sexy Years. Still, there are costs to averting our eyes from the realities. For one thing, we put off changes that we need to make as a society. For another, we deprive ourselves of opportunities to change the individual experience of aging for the better.

For nearly all of human existence, people died young. Life expectancy improved as we overcame early death — in particular, deaths from childbirth, infection, and traumatic injury. By the 1970s, just four out of every hundred people born in industrialized countries died before the age of thirty. It was an extraordinary achievement, but one that seemed to leave little room for further gain; even *eliminating* deaths before thirty would not raise overall life expectancy significantly. Efforts shifted, therefore, to reducing deaths during middle and old age, and, in the decades since, the average life span has continued upward. Improvements in the treatment and prevention of heart disease, respiratory illness, stroke, cancer, and the like mean that the average sixty-five-year-old can expect to live another nineteen years — almost four years longer than was the case in 1970. (By contrast, from the nineteenth century to 1970, sixty-five-year-olds gained just three years of life expectancy.)

The result has been called the "rectangularization" of survival. Throughout most of human history, a society's population formed a sort of pyramid: young children represented the largest portion — the base — and each successively older cohort represented a smaller and smaller group. In 1950, children under the age of five were eleven percent of the U.S. population, adults aged forty-five to forty-nine were six percent, and those over eighty were one percent. Today, we have as many fifty-year-olds as five-year-olds. In thirty years, there will be as many people over eighty as there are under five.

Americans haven't come to grips with the new demography. We cling to the notion of retirement at sixty-five — a reasonable notion when those over sixty-five were a tiny percentage of the population, but completely untenable as they approach twenty percent. People are putting aside less in savings for old age now than they have in any decade since the Great Depression. More than half of the very old now live without a spouse, and we have fewer children than ever before — yet we give virtually no thought to how we will live out our later years alone.

Equally worrying, and far less recognized, medicine has been slow to confront the very changes that it has been responsible for — or to apply the knowledge we already have about how to make old age better. Despite a rapidly growing elderly population, the number of certified geriatricians fell by a third between 1998 and 2004. Applications to training programs in adult primary-care medicine are plummeting, while fields like plastic surgery and radiology receive applications in record numbers. Partly, this has to do with money — incomes in geriatrics and adult primary care are among the lowest in medicine. And partly, whether we admit it or not, most doctors don't like taking care of the elderly.

"Mainstream doctors are turned off by geriatrics, and that's because they do not have the faculties to cope with the Old Crock," Felix Silverstone, the geriatrician, explained to me. "The Old Crock is deaf. The Old Crock has poor vision. The Old Crock's memory might be somewhat impaired. With the Old Crock, you have to slow down, because he asks you to repeat what you are saying or asking. And the Old Crock doesn't just have a chief complaint — the Old Crock has fifteen chief complaints. How in the world are you going to cope with all of them? You're overwhelmed. Besides, he's had a number of these things for fifty years or so. You're not going to cure something he's had for fifty years. He has high blood pressure. He has diabetes. He has arthritis. There's nothing glamorous about taking care of any of those things."

There is, however, a skill to it, a developed body of professional expertise. And until I visited my hospital's geriatrics clinic and saw the work that geriatricians do, I did not fully grasp the nature of that expertise, or how important it could be for all of us.

The geriatrics clinic — or, as my hospital calls it, the Center for Older Adult Health — is only one floor below my surgery clinic. I pass by it almost every day, and I can't remember ever giving it a moment's thought. One morning, however, I wandered downstairs and, with the permission of the patients, sat in on a few visits with Juergen Bludau, the chief geriatrician.

"What brings you here today?" the doctor asked Jean Gavrilles, his first patient of the morning. She was eighty-five years old, with short, frizzy white hair, oval glasses, a lavender knit shirt, and a sweet, ready smile. Small but sturdy in appearance, she had come in walking steadily, her purse and coat clutched under one arm, her daughter trailing behind her, no support required beyond her mauve orthopedic shoes. She said that her internist had recommended that she come.

About anything in particular? the doctor asked.

The answer, it seemed, was yes and no. The first thing she mentioned was a lower-back pain that she'd had for months, which shot down her leg and sometimes made it difficult to get out of bed or up from a chair. She also had bad arthritis, and she showed us her fingers, which were swollen at the knuckles and bent out to the sides with what's called a swan-neck deformity. She'd had both knees replaced a decade earlier. She had high blood pressure "from stress," she said, and handed him her list of medications. She had glaucoma and needed to have eye exams every four months. She never used to have "bathroom problems," but lately, she admitted, she'd started wearing a pad. She'd also had surgery for colon cancer and, by the way, now had a lung nodule that the radiology report said could be a metastasis — a biopsy was recommended.

Bludau asked her to tell him about her life. She said that she lived alone, except for her Yorkshire terrier, in a single-family house in the West Roxbury section of Boston. Her husband died of lung cancer twenty-three years ago. She did not drive. She had a son living in the area who did her shopping once a week and checked on her each day — "just to see if I'm still alive," she joked. Another son and two daughters lived farther away, but they helped as well. Otherwise, she took care of herself quite capably. She did her own cooking and cleaning. She managed her medicines and her bills. "I have a system," she said. She had a high school education, and during the war she'd worked as a riveter at the Charlestown Navy Yard. She also worked for a time at the Jordan Marsh department store in downtown Boston. But that was a long time ago. She stuck to home now, with her yard and her terrier and her family when they visited.

The doctor asked her about her day in great detail. She usually woke around five or six o'clock, she said — she didn't seem to need much sleep anymore. She would get out of bed as the back pain allowed, take a shower, and get dressed. Downstairs, she'd take her medicines, feed the dog, and eat breakfast. Bludau asked what she had for breakfast. Cereal and a banana. She hated bananas, she said, but she'd heard they were good for her potassium, so she was afraid to stop. After breakfast, she'd take her dog for a little walk in the yard. She did chores — laundry, cleaning, and the like. In the late morning, she took a break to watch *The Price Is Right*. At lunchtime, she had a sandwich and orange juice. If the weather was nice, she'd sit out in the yard afterward. She'd loved working in her garden, but she couldn't do that anymore. The afternoons were slow. She might do some more chores. She might nap or talk on the phone. Eventually, she would make dinner — a salad and maybe a baked potato or a scrambled egg. At night, she watched the Red Sox or the Patriots or college basketball — she loved sports. She usually went to bed at about midnight.

Bludau asked her to sit on the examining table. As she struggled to climb up, her balance teetering on the step, the doctor held her arm. He checked her blood pressure, which was normal. He examined her eyes and ears and had her open her mouth. He listened to her heart and lungs briskly, through his stethoscope. He began to slow down only when he looked at her hands. The nails were neatly trimmed.

"Who cuts your nails?" he asked.

"I do," Gavrilles replied.

I tried to think what could be accomplished in this visit. She was in good condition for her age, but she faced everything from advancing arthritis and incontinence to what might be metastatic colon cancer. It seemed to me that, with just a forty-minute visit, Bludau needed to triage by zeroing in on either the most potentially life-threatening problem (the possible metastasis) or the problem that bothered her the most (the back pain). But this was evidently not what he thought. He asked almost nothing about either issue. Instead, he spent much of the exam looking at her feet.

"Is that really necessary?" she asked, when he instructed her to take off her shoes and socks.

"Yes," he said. After she'd left, he told me, "You must always examine the feet." He described a bow-tied gentleman who seemed dapper and fit, until his feet revealed the truth: he couldn't bend down to reach them, and they turned out not to have been cleaned in weeks, suggesting neglect and real danger.

Gavrilles had difficulty taking her shoes off, and, after watching her struggle a bit, Bludau leaned in to help. When he got her socks off, he took her feet in his hands, one at a time. He inspected them inch by inch — the soles, the toes, the web spaces. Then he helped her get her socks and shoes back on and gave her and her daughter his assessment.

She was doing impressively well, he said. She was mentally sharp and physically strong. The danger for her was losing what she had. The single most serious threat she faced was not the lung nodule or the back pain. It was falling. Each year, about 350,000 Americans fall and break a hip. Of those, forty percent end up in a nursing home, and twenty percent are never able to walk again. The three primary risk factors for falling are poor balance, taking more than four prescription medications, and muscle weakness. Elderly people without these risk factors have a twelve percent chance of falling in a year. Those with all three risk factors have almost a hundred percent chance. Jean Gavrilles had at least two. Her balance was poor. Though she didn't need a walker, he had noticed her splay-footed gait as she came in. Her feet were swollen. The toenails were unclipped. There were sores between the toes. And the balls of her feet had thick, rounded calluses.

She was also on five medications. Each was undoubtedly useful, but together, the usual side effects would include dizziness. In addition, one of the blood pressure medications was a diuretic, and she seemed to drink few liquids, risking dehydration and a worsening of the dizziness. Her tongue was bone dry when Bludau examined it.

She did not have significant muscle weakness, and that was good. When she got out of her chair, he said, he noted that she had not used her arms to push herself up. She simply stood up — a sign of well-preserved muscle strength. From the details of the day she described, however, she did not seem to be eating nearly enough calories to maintain that strength. Bludau asked her whether her weight had changed recently. She admitted that she had lost about seven pounds in the previous six months.

The job of any doctor, Bludau later told me, is to support quality of life, by which he meant two things: as much freedom from the ravages of disease as possible, and the retention of enough function for active engagement in the world. Most doctors treat disease, and figure that the rest will take care of itself. And if it doesn't — if a patient is becoming infirm and heading toward a nursing home — well, that isn't really a *medical* problem, is it?

To a geriatrician, though, it *is* a medical problem. People can't stop the aging of their bodies and minds, but there are ways to make it more manageable, and to avert at least some of the worst effects. So Bludau referred Gavrilles to a podiatrist, whom he wanted her to visit once every four weeks, for better care of her feet. He didn't see medications that he could eliminate, but he switched her diuretic to a blood pressure medicine that wouldn't cause dehydration. He recommended that she eat a snack during the day, get all the low-calorie and low-cholesterol food out of the house, and see whether family or friends could join her for more meals. "Eating alone is not very stimulating," he said. And he asked her to see him again in three months, so that he could make sure the plan was working.

Nine months later, I checked in with Gavrilles and her daughter. She turned eighty-six this past November. She is eating better, and has even gained a pound or two. She still lives comfortably and independently in her own home. And she has not had a single fall.

In the story of Jean Gavrilles and her geriatrician, there's a lesson about frailty. Decline remains our fate; death will come. But, until that last backup system inside each of us fails, decline can occur in two ways. One is early and precipitately, with an old age of enfeeblement and dependence, sustained primarily by nursing homes and hospitals. The other way is more gradual, preserving, for as long as possible, your ability to control your own life.

Good medical care can influence which direction a person's old age will take. Most of us in medicine, however, don't know how to think about decline. We're good at addressing specific, individual problems: colon cancer, high blood pressure, arthritic knees. Give us a disease, and we can do something about it. But give us an elderly woman with colon cancer, high blood pressure, arthritic knees, and various other ailments besides — an elderly woman at risk of losing the life she enjoys — and we are not sure what to do.

Several years ago, researchers in St. Paul, Minnesota, identified 568 men and women over the age of seventy who were living independently but were at high risk of becoming disabled because of chronic health problems, recent illness, or cognitive changes. With their permission, the researchers randomly assigned half of them to see a team of geriatric specialists. The others were asked to see their usual physician, who was notified of their high-risk status.

Within eighteen months, ten percent of the patients in both groups had died. But the patients who had seen a geriatrics team were a third less likely to become disabled and half as likely to develop depression. They were forty percent less likely to require home health services.

Little of what the geriatricians had done was high-tech medicine: they didn't do lung biopsies or back surgery or PET scans. Instead, they simplified medications. They saw that arthritis was controlled. They made sure toenails were trimmed and meals were square. They looked for worrisome signs of isolation and had a social worker check that the patient's home was safe.

How do we reward this kind of work? Chad Boult, who was the lead investigator of the St. Paul study and a geriatrician at the University of Minnesota, can tell you. A few months after he published his study, demonstrating how much better people's lives were with specialized geriatric care, the university closed the division of geriatrics.

"The university said that it simply could not sustain the financial losses," Boult said from Baltimore, where he is now a professor at the Johns Hopkins Bloomberg School of Public Health. On average, in Boult's study, the geriatric services cost the hospital $1,350 more per person than the savings they produced, and Medicare, the insurer for the elderly, does not cover that cost. It's a strange double standard. No one insists that a $25,000 pacemaker or a coronary-artery stent save money for insurers. It just has to *maybe* do people some good. Meanwhile, the twenty-plus members of the proven geriatrics team at the University of Minnesota had to find new jobs. Scores of medical centers across the country have shrunk or closed their geriatrics units. Several of Boult's colleagues no longer advertise their geriatric training for fear that they'll get too many elderly patients. "Economically, it has become too difficult," Boult said.

But the finances are only a symptom of a deeper reality: people have not insisted on a change in priorities. We all like new medical gizmos and demand that policymakers make sure they are paid for. They feed our hope that the troubles of the body can be fixed for good. But geriatricians? Who clamors for geriatricians? What geriatricians do — bolster our resilience in old age, our capacity to weather what comes — is both difficult and unappealingly limited.

It requires attention to the body and its alterations. It requires vigilance over nutrition, medications, and living situations. And it requires each of us to contemplate the course of our decline, in order to make the small changes that can reshape it. When the prevailing fantasy is that we can be ageless, the geriatrician's uncomfortable demand is that we accept we are not.

For Felix Silverstone, understanding human aging has been the work of a lifetime. He was a national leader in geriatrics for five decades. But he is now himself eighty-seven years old. He can feel his own mind and body wearing down, and much of what he spent his career studying is no longer abstract to him.

Felix has been fortunate. He didn't have to stop working, even after he suffered a heart attack in his sixties which cost him half his heart function; nor was he stopped by a near cardiac arrest at the age of seventy-nine. "One evening, sitting at home, I suddenly became aware of palpitations," he told me. "I was just reading, and a few minutes later I became short of breath. A little bit after that, I began to feel heavy in the chest. I took my pulse, and it was over two hundred." He is the sort of person who, in the midst of chest pain, would take the opportunity to examine his own pulse. "My wife and I had a little discussion about whether or not to call an ambulance. We decided to call."

When Felix got to the hospital, the doctors had to shock him to bring his heart back. He'd had ventricular fibrillation, and an automatic defibrillator had to be installed in his chest. Within a few weeks, though, he felt well again, and his doctor cleared him to return to work full time. He stayed in medical practice after the attack, multiple hernia repairs, gallbladder surgery, arthritis that ended his avid piano playing, compression fractures of his aging spine that stole three full inches of his once five-foot-seven-inch height, and hearing loss. "I switched to an electronic stethoscope," he said. "They're a nuisance, but they're very good."

Finally, at eighty-two, he had to retire. The problem wasn't his health; it was that of his wife, Bella. They'd been married for more than sixty years. Felix had met Bella when he was an intern and she was a dietitian at Kings County Hospital in Brooklyn. They brought up two sons in Flatbush. When the boys left home, Bella got her teaching certification and began working with children who had

learning disabilities. In her seventies, however, retinal disease diminished her vision, and she had to stop working. A decade later,
she became almost completely blind. Felix no longer felt safe leaving her at home alone, and in 2001 he gave up his practice. They
moved to Orchard Cove, a retirement community in Canton, Massachusetts, outside Boston, where they could be closer to their
sons.

"I didn't think I would survive the change," Felix said. He'd observed in his patients how difficult the transitions of age could be.
Examining his last patient, packing up his home, he felt that he
was about to die. "I was taking apart my life as well as the house,"
he recalled. "It was terrible."

We were sitting in a library off Orchard Cove's main lobby.
There was light streaming through a picture window, tasteful art
on the walls, white-upholstered Federal-style armchairs. It was like
a nice hotel, only with no one under seventy-five walking around.
Felix and Bella have a two-bedroom apartment with forest views
and plenty of space. In the living room, he has his grand piano
and, at his desk, piles of medical journals that he still subscribes to
— "for my soul," he said. Theirs is an independent-living unit. It
comes with housekeeping, linen changes, and dinner each evening. When they need to, they can upgrade to assisted living,
which provides three prepared meals and up to an hour with a
personal-care assistant each day.

This was not the average retirement community, but even in an
average one, rent runs $32,000 a year. Entry fees are typically
$60,000 to $120,000 on top of that. Meanwhile, the median in-
come of people eighty and older is only about $15,000. More than
half of the elderly who live in long-term-care facilities go through
their entire savings and have to go on Medicaid — welfare — in order to afford it. And, ultimately, the average American spends a
year or more of his old age disabled and living in a nursing home
(at twice the cost), which is a destination Felix desperately hopes to
avoid.

He tries to note the changes he's experiencing objectively, like a
good geriatrician. He notices that his skin has dried out. His sense
of smell has diminished. His night vision has become poor. He
tires easily. He has begun to lose teeth. He takes measures where
he can. He uses lotion to avoid skin cracks; he protects himself

from the heat; he gets on an exercise bike three times a week; he sees a dentist twice a year.

He's most concerned about the changes in his brain. "I can't think as clearly as I used to," he said. "I used to be able to read the *Times* in half an hour. Now it takes me an hour and a half." Even then, he's not sure that he has understood as much as he did before, and his memory gives him trouble. "If I go back and look at what I've read, I recognize that I went through it, but sometimes I don't really remember it," he said. "It's a matter of short-term registration. It's hard to get the signal in and have it stay put."

He makes use of methods that he once taught his patients. "I try to deliberately focus on what I'm doing, rather than do it automatically," he told me. "I haven't lost the automaticity of action, but I can't rely on it the way I used to. For example, I can't think about something else and get dressed and be sure I've gotten all the way dressed." He recognizes that the strategy doesn't always work. He sometimes told me the same story twice in a conversation. The lines of thought in his mind would fall into well-worn grooves and, however hard he tried to put them onto a new path, sometimes they resisted. Felix's knowledge as a geriatrician has forced him to recognize his own decline, but that hasn't made it easier to accept.

"I get blue occasionally," he said. "I think I have recurring episodes of depression. They are not enough to disable me, but they are . . ." He paused to find the right word. "They are uncomfortable."

What buoys him, despite his limitations, is having a purpose. It's the same purpose, he says, that sustained him in medicine: to be of service, in some way, to those around him. He had been in Orchard Cove for only a few months before he was helping to steer a committee to improve the health care services there. He tried to form a journal-reading club for retired physicians. He even guided a young geriatrician through her first independent-research study — a survey of the residents' attitudes toward Do Not Resuscitate orders.

More important is the responsibility that he feels for his children and grandchildren — and, most of all, for Bella. Her blindness and recent memory troubles have made her deeply dependent. Without him, I suspect, she would probably be in a nursing home. He helps her dress. He administers her medicines. He makes her breakfast and lunch. He takes her on walks and to doctors' appointments. "She is my purpose now," he said. Bella doesn't always like his way of doing things. "We argue constantly — we're at each other about a lot of things," Felix said. "But we're also very forgiving."

He does not feel this responsibility to be a burden. With the narrowing of his own life, his ability to look after Bella has become his main source of self-worth. "I am exclusively her caregiver," he said. "I am glad to be." And this role has heightened his sense that he must be attentive to the changes in his own capabilities; he is no good to her if he isn't honest with himself about what he can and can't do.

One evening, Felix invited me to dinner. The formal dining hall was restaurant-like, with reserved seating, table service, and jackets required. I was wearing my white hospital coat and had to borrow a navy blazer from the maître d'. Felix, in a brown suit and a stone-colored oxford shirt, gave his arm to Bella, who wore a blue-flowered knee-length dress that he'd picked out for her, and guided her to the table. She was amiable and chatty and had youthful-seeming eyes. But once she'd been seated, she couldn't find the plate in front of her, let alone the menu. Felix ordered for her: wild-rice soup, an omelet, mashed potatoes, and mashed cauliflower. "No salt," he instructed the waiter; she had high blood pressure. He ordered salmon and mashed potatoes for himself. I had the soup and a London broil.

When the food arrived, Felix told Bella where she could find the different items on her plate by the hands of a clock. He put a fork in her hand. Then he turned to his own meal.

Both made a point of chewing slowly. She was the first to choke. It was the omelet. Her eyes watered. She began to cough. Felix guided her water glass to her mouth. She took a drink and managed to get the omelet down.

"As you get older, the lordosis of your spine tips your head forward," he said to me. "So when you look straight ahead it's like looking up at the ceiling for anyone else. Try to swallow while looking up: you'll choke once in a while. The problem is common in the elderly. Listen." I realized that I could hear someone in the dining room choking on his food every minute or so. Felix turned to Bella. "You have to eat looking down, sweetie," he said.

A couple of bites later, though, he himself was choking. It was the salmon. He began coughing. He turned red. Finally, he was able to cough up the bite. It took a minute for him to catch his breath. "Didn't follow my own advice," he said.

Felix Silverstone is, without question, up against the debilities of his years. Once, it would have been remarkable simply to have lived to see eighty-seven. Now what's remarkable is that he has the control over his life that he does. When he started in geriatric practice, it was almost inconceivable that an eighty-seven-year-old with his history of health problems could live independently, care for his disabled wife, and continue to contribute to research. Even today, most people his age cannot live as he does.

Partly, he has been lucky. His memory, for example, has not deteriorated significantly. But he has also managed his old age well. His goal has been modest: to have as decent a life as medical knowledge and the limits of his body will allow. So he saved and did not retire early, and therefore is not in financial straits. He kept his social contacts and avoided isolation. He monitored his bones and teeth and weight. And he has made sure to find a doctor who had the geriatric skills to help him hold on to an independent life.

I asked Chad Boult, the geriatrics professor now at Johns Hopkins, what can be done to ensure that there are enough geriatricians for our country's surging elderly population. "Nothing," he said. "It's too late." Creating geriatricians takes years, and we already have far too few. This year, just three hundred doctors will complete geriatrics training, not nearly enough to replace the geriatricians going into retirement, let alone meet the needs of the next decade.

Yet Boult believes that we still have time for another strategy: he would direct geriatricians toward training all primary-care doctors in caring for the very old, instead of providing the care themselves. Even this is a tall order — ninety-seven percent of medical students take no course in geriatrics, and the strategy requires that the nation pay geriatricians to teach rather than to provide patient care. But if the will is there, Boult estimates that it would be possible to establish courses in every medical school and internal-medicine training program within a decade. "We've got to do something," he said. "Life for older people can be better than it is today."

Boult and his colleagues have yet another strategy, just in case —

a strategy that they have called Guided Care and that doesn't depend on doctors at all. They're recruiting local nurses for a highly compressed, three-week course in how to recognize specific problems in the elderly, such as depression, malnutrition, isolation, and danger of falling; how to formulate a plan to remedy those problems; and how to work with patients, families, and doctors to follow through on the plan. In a test of the strategy, the researchers are putting the nurses to work in primary-care practices around Baltimore and Washington, D.C., and studying the results. It is a meager solution for a huge problem, but it is cheap, which insurers demand, and if it provides even a fraction of the benefit geriatricians have, it could nudge medical care in the right direction.

"I can still drive, you know," Felix Silverstone said to me. "I'm a very good driver."

After our dinner together, he had to go on an errand to refill Bella's prescriptions in Stoughton, a few miles away, and I asked if I could go along. He had a gold 1998 Toyota Camry with automatic transmission and thirty-nine thousand miles on the odometer. It was pristine, inside and out. He backed out of a narrow parking space and zipped out of the garage. His hands did not shake. Taking the streets of Canton at dusk on a new-moon night, he brought the car to an even stop at the red lights, signaled when he was supposed to, took turns without a hitch.

I was, I admit, braced for disaster. The risk of a fatal car crash with a driver who's eighty-five or older is more than three times higher than it is with a driver between sixteen and twenty. The very old are the highest-risk drivers on the road. This past fall in Los Angeles, George Weller was convicted of manslaughter after he confused the accelerator with the brake pedal and plowed his Buick into a crowd of shoppers at the Santa Monica Farmers' Market. Ten people were killed and more than sixty were injured. He was eighty-six.

But Felix showed no difficulties. At one point during our drive, poorly marked road construction at an intersection channeled our line of cars almost directly into oncoming traffic. Felix corrected course swiftly, pulling over into the proper lane. There is no saying how much longer he will be able to count on his driving ability. The day may well come when he will have to give up his keys.

At the moment, though, he wasn't concerned; he was glad simply to be on the road. The evening traffic was thin as he turned onto Route 138. He brought the Camry to a tick over the forty-five-mile-per-hour speed limit. He had his window rolled down and his elbow on the sash. The air was clear and cool, and we listened to the sound of the wheels on the pavement.

"The night is lovely, isn't it?" he said.

ALBERT GOLDBARTH

Everybody's Nickname

FROM *The Georgia Review*

"MAROONED ON A WORLD OF MONSTERS!"
"SHOWDOWN ON THE SUN'S LAST PLANET!"
"WAS SHE MISTRESS OF MIRACLES OR PUPPET OF
    SUPER-SCIENCE?"
"BEWARE THE MASKS OF MARS!"
"BACKWARD WORLD — OR SECRET OUTPOST OF ANOTHER
    GALAXY?"

These explosive bursts of words that act as ramped-up verbal pheromones, as flirts and barkers wooing us into ever-further sticky embrace, are the cover descriptions under (usually; sometimes over) titles of such allure, you'd think they could easily be self-sufficient. In order: *The Forgotten Planet, World of the Masterminds, The Green Queen, Space Station #1, Warlord of Kor.*

I suppose it's a maxim of marketing that nothing will be left to chance. Someone believed the novel *Voodoo Planet* — check *that* out: *Voodoo Planet!* — still required the extra beckoning power of "DUEL OF THE COSMIC MAGICIANS!" And so, almost all 262 of the gaudy lilies published as "Ace science-fiction doubles" were gilded with lovely, punchy, overly zaftig descriptions. "PRESENT AND FUTURE CLASH IN A WORLD OF THE PAST!" You betcha. Resistance was futile.

And then, of course, there was the cover art. Although a later master of the form — say, Jack Gaughan — let you know that surrealists like de Chirico and Magritte were in his experience, the world of the classic Ace covers never effervesced out of solidity into abstraction. There were no Mondrian or Rothko wannabes here. A spaceship glittered pinpoints of nebula-dazzle off its hull with the credible tonnage that Rockwell Kent would have brought to a breaching whale. That bubble helmet a spaceman wore was *real;* you could hold it, like a goldfish bowl. And the slinky, silver-saronged space sirens — whether depicted as haughtily command-ing or imperiled — had a pleasurably heated heft, the way that Vargas pinup beauties did. Each weirdly spired twenty-third-century city, and every yellow electro-zap out of a ray gun's futuristically coiled muzzle, encouraged your confidence and belied its own airy fancy. This was enormously effective: to have an impossible subject — hordes of eight-armed Arcturians rampaging under pur-ple heavens — done with all of the stolid fidelity of a sitting of Frans Hals's realistic Dutch burgher-musketeers.

But, naturally, the surest inducement to part with your thirty-five cents (as opposed to the quarter for any other paperback of the day) was the very doubleness of the enterprise: two books in one, each upside-down to the other, each with its independent enticing cover and title page. Two books in one! You *couldn't* say no to *Ring Around the Sun* and *Cosmic Manhunt* in a single clamoring package. (Although, if you wavered, the latter's descriptive tag would surely cinch the deal: "FROM A WONDER WORLD HIDEAWAY SHE DEFIED THE CODE OF SPACE!")

But why am I using the past tense? They're in front of me as I'm writing this, on a drugstore spinner rack I've purchased especially to display — to daily live with — my collection. Here's the interga-lactic beauty of *Cosmic Manhunt* herself, although a touch more like a carnival side-tent hootchie-koo dancer than you'd think the far-advanced techno-world of tomorrow might permit. And here's the *Rocket to Limbo* — so full of zoom! And here's the pon-derous, wrinkled, eye-tentacled, seaweed-headed, lobster-clawed green alien who, in 1960, when I was twelve and thirty-five cents was a treasure (and I was aburst with dreams, with vague shapes of Adventure and Accomplishment and Ava Edelman sitting across the aisle in Astronomy), successfully encouraged my first-ever re-tail paperback purchase (outside of schoolroom orders): *Bow Down to Nul* by Brian Aldiss (the tag line, "WHEN MONSTERS RULE"; the cover, Ed Emshwiller art). Its mate: *The Dark Destroyers.*

The colorful paperback-cover bluster and showy iconography that some of us would call "tawdry" or "lurid" simply reclaim their heritage from predecessor pulp fiction magazines. Enter Aaron A. Wyn, sharp businessman and founder in 1928 of the Ace line of pulp magazines — *Secret Agent X, Ten Detective Aces, Eerie Stories** — "some of the livelier second-rung pulps in the golden age," as Lee Server puts it in *Over My Dead Body,* his history of that industry. In 1940 Wyn entered the burgeoning comic book field with *Sure-Fire Comics,* followed by an array of genre hopefuls: *Super Mystery, Love Experiences, War Heroes, Men Against Crime, Hap Hazard, Indian Braves.* They were successful enough, but by the 1950s Wyn could sense the winds of readership beginning to blow in a new direction, and once again he yielded to those currents; in 1952 he launched a paperback line, Ace Books, retaining that aegis from twenty-four years in the fields of high-acid-content paper.

Wyn's associate Walter Zacharius first suggested the gimmick of doubling up books in a single binding, topsy-turvying them in the now familiar format, and Wyn then hired Donald A. Wollheim to edit this new "Ace Doubles" series. (Some were to be crime and western books, but as time went on the series became increasingly outer-spaced.) A number of tumblers were ready to click into place, with Wollheim the first of them.

Born to be a hobnobbing fan and soon after that a professional, Wollheim was, at twenty-three in 1937, forming science fiction's earliest amateur press association, distributing (to its fifty members) those hectographed magazines of fantasy orientation that driven enthusiasts cranked out ("cranked out" literally) in a circulation of twenty to thirty-five. In 1943 he was connected enough to edit what's normally credited as the first mass-market paperback anthology of science-fiction stories, *The Pocket Book of Science Fiction* (for Pocket Books, a major player), having already cut his editorial teeth on the pulp science-fiction magazines *Stirring Science Stories* and *Cosmic Stories* — which, says sci-fi historian James Gunn, "had an editorial budget of exactly nothing, but nevertheless lasted four and three issues respectively."† Wollheim also wrote *The Universe*

---

* *Eerie Stories* has been described by pop culture maven Bud Plant as "one of many 1930s pulps too hot for most newsstands." Titles from a typical issue: "The Soul-Scorcher's Lair" and "Virgins of the Stone Death."

† In the March 1941 *Cosmic Stories:* A tag line, "KELLOGG'S TIME EXPLORERS WERE TRAPPED IN A JUNGLE OF MAN-HUNTING MACHINES!" A story, "The Martians Are Coming!" An ad for the Remington Portable Noiseless Typewriter *and* desk "for as little as 10¢ a day," an ad for "Sex Secrets of Love and Marriage Daringly

Makers (Harper and Row, 1971), a sturdy history of science fiction; indeed, in the published photographs of him that I have, he *looks like* a historian out of central casting, bespectacled and slightly turtley-owlish. Avidity, expertise, the ability to generate product out of nonexistent cash flow: he was the man for A. A. Wyn!

Now . . . enter Allen Ginsberg.

In 1956 the mad young hipster Carl Solomon (Lee Server: "a high-strung screwup and devotee of Antonin Artaud") would enter the annals of literary history as the dedicatee of Ginsberg's seminal anthem, *Howl*. They'd met in 1949 in the New York State Psychiatric Institute. Ginsberg was there under false (well, semi-false) pretenses. Nabbed by the cops for joyriding in the company of some burglar pals (along with their boodle of stolen dresses), and finding his quickly concocted alibi unaccepted (a newspaper headline laconically noted, "BOY JOINS GANG TO GET 'RESEARCH' FOR STORY"), he'd pled insanity as preferable to jail. Here he was now, in the nuthouse.

Solomon, though, was a version of the real-deal certifiable nut outsider, and was undergoing shock treatments, the results of which were amnesia and convulsions. This accidental friendship of theirs provided the neophyte poet with material from Solomon — long-winded diatribe-stories of his adventures ("who talked continuously seventy hours from park to pad to bar to Bellevue to museum to the Brooklyn Bridge . . .") — that seven years later would fuel the mid-twentieth-century's most explosive American poem.

But *three* years after their seraphic-demonic talkfests in the mental institution, Carl Solomon would be making the attempt to reenter everyday straight life, as symbolized mainly by his taking on a job, an "acquiring editor's position" at the offices of his uncle — the publisher A. A. Wyn. At this same moment Ginsberg had also taken on a job, more unofficially, acting as literary agent for some of his wanderlust-afflicted writer friends. And so one day in 1952 finds Ginsberg on West 47th Street, at Ace Books, trying to peddle two manuscripts.

Revealed!" (And another story, "The Man from the Future," by one Donald A. Wollheim, billed as the "Author of 'Planet of Illusion.'")

Solomon is worried that his endorsement of the edgy stuff might only reconfirm his family's dubious opinion of his sanity. On the other hand, Ginsberg's zeal is infectious, and the writing — street-smart and visceral — is abristle with compelling hooks . . . and, to Ginsberg's delight and Solomon's credit, a couple of low three-figure offers eventually are extended.

One of these books — the one with its manuscript handwritten on a roll of uncut Teletype paper — is never to be published by Ace. Solomon requested substantial rewrites, and the author — impatient, egotistical, chafing under the criticism — entered into a series of rancorous shouting bouts with his editor, one time threatening to break Solomon's glasses, and finally withdrew his wunderkind tome from the paper empire of A. A. Wyn.

And thus was Kerouac's *On the Road*, that ur-text of Beat literature, only a tantrum away from joining the ranks of *Android Avenger*; *Earthman, Go Home!*; *The Stars Are Ours!*; and *Slavers of Space*.

And thus did Ginsberg's other (and somewhat more standardly written) offering join the list of Ace doubles as D-15: *Junkie* by the pseudonymous William Lee, paired up (or "69d," as Ginsberg described it) with Maurice Helbrant's *Narcotic Agent*. Today, that thirty-five-cent book — "William Lee," of course, was William Burroughs — can be valued at over a thousandfold (if near mint) in a vintage-paperback auction. Some might want it as well for the showily shadowy dames-and-needles-and-handcuffs covers by genre artist Al Rossi.

Not that *Junkie* ever sold astoundingly well, and soon thereafter Ginsberg lost his "in" at Ace — his dreams of foisting types like Jean Genet and Neal Cassady on a mass-market readership dissipated in tandem with the stability of Solomon, who shortly began to unravel under the pressures of an editor's day.

And thus we leave him, that difficult man, in only four more years to be memorialized by *Howl* ("ah, Carl . . . now you're really in the total animal soup of time"), but right now scampering crazily "through traffic on Eighth Avenue," says Lee Server, "screaming and throwing his suitcase and shoes at passing vehicles."

And yet we *don't* leave him. We can never leave him, or at least we can't leave what he comes to represent, or *it* won't leave us. We

ACE

DOUBLE NOVEL BOOKS 35c

D-443

WHEN MONSTERS RULE

BOW DOWN TO NUL

BRIAN W. ALDISS

First Book Publication

can't shake the workaday man in the suit and tie, the pick-up-the-kids-and-the-groceries mom, who turn around and — voilà! — the gibbering, capering, levitating, gods-conversing, screw-you, fuck-me, soaring-through-the-risen-cream-of-the-origin-of-the-universe otherself is on display to the world. Nor can we free ourselves from the opposite knowledge: inside the incarcerated and the hopeless, the beyond-the-fringe and the up-for-grabs, is a man who longs to mow his lawn to the neighborhood-association code and a woman who's fossicking the checkbook at the end of her day. What thin spit and ephemeral synaptic flimmer bind these halves together!

And we *are* compounded of halves. The heart is our great bicameral house. Our cells are the glorious ringing echo of the duet between a Y chromosome and an X. We're each a working system of an impossibillion positive and negative specter-charges in a delicate ritual balance, and in this of course we're the infrastructure of even larger systems that began at the Bang and function the same. All of our myths almost uniformly reflect this: male/female; Fire Bringer/Bearer of Waters; mind/matter; angel/ape-thing lurking in the dark — ineradicably. Religious precept understands (and fears) how the philanderer is the unspoken twin of the penitent. Popular fiction understands — all of those pulp extravaganzas: Zorro! The Spider! The Whisperer! — how a superhero somehow consists of the same collection of molecules as his more mundane identity.

Here are two stories out of the midsize Midwest city in which I live.

The first is one of those heart-tug pieces my local paper so loves to dote over. In May 1997, Ray Robinson Jr., age eleven, was written up as "mayor for the day." A formerly troublesome (and, one can tell, "disadvantaged") student at College Hill Elementary School, the now fifth-grader had "turned himself around" and "even started helping . . . work with a troubled first-grader."

When Robinson told his teacher, Nancy Hughey, that current mayor Bob Knight "was his hero" ("I didn't think he was aware [we] *had* a mayor," said Hughey), word escaped, and in a snap of media time it was photo-op heaven: "Knight had the boy come to City Hall [and] sit in the mayor's seat in the council chambers." In the photograph that finally ran, we see a beaming black child (his smile could warm its way through permafrost) with his arms around the waist of a benevolently smiling middle-aged white politico guy, who hugs him back. It's the paradigmatic 1997 feel-good shot.

"Ray is very focused these days about his goals and what he wants," Hughey said. "Sometimes he slips and says, 'If I am mayor . . .' then immediately corrects himself, saying, 'When I am mayor . . .' And then, 'I want to be somebody when I grow up.'"

The second story is also about a grade school student who once assumed a short-term political office: Chelsea Brooks, landslide-elected vice president of the "fifth-grade project to study how government works." "She took her job very seriously," said her classroom teacher. "Leadership and charisma were everyday traits for Chelsea." The praises continue: "very bright, confident," "loyal," "such an amazing girl," "funny, smiling," "so much promise." You can start to see all this in the photo the paper keeps using: another smile that beams — from out of the usual daily murk of war and inflation and global warming — like a lighthouse.

A few days after Chelsea's eighth-grade graduation, on June 15, 2006, her body was found by workers, strangled to death and nine months pregnant, in a shallow grave by a wheat field off a rutted dirt road in Butler County. She had planned "to go to college." She was going to name the baby Alexa Lynn.

Her murder was contracted out, the state claims, by the father — who had been pressuring her to keep his identity secret, afraid he'd otherwise wind up in jail on charges of statutory rape. She was crazy about him, her friends say; she'd do anything for him. "'I love him to death,'" her friend Kali quotes Chelsea as saying. Presumably his pressure was starting to fail, and a more secure measure occurred to him. On the night of June 9 Chelsea left the Skate South skate park, on MacArthur near Hydraulic, "to see," she told her friends, "the father of [my] baby." The next time anyone saw her, she was a corpse.

In one accompanying photograph two classmates of Chelsea's hold each other and weep — a common shot by now, "the Columbine pose" I call it. Their faces are buried in one another's grief. In another photograph — paired with hers, as she would have paired up pictures of them on the inside of her locker — is the father, staring sullenly. He's charged with capital murder, aggravated kidnapping, and two counts of rape "for allegedly having sex with

Chelsea before her 14th birthday." (Chelsea's mother claims, "In 2004 he was [also] caught in a park with [another] 14-year-old girl.") His face is dazed and scared and insolent and hardly recognizable at all as that of Elgin "Ray-Ray" Robinson, nine years after his one day as guest mayor.

An extreme example, for sure, but which of us *isn't* two people nestled together? Or wrestled. "My father was a political radical," Betsy Wollheim writes in a reminiscence, "but he was conservative personally." And she says, "Many people loved him." And she adds, "Many people feared him."

It seems that Donald A. Wollheim had it right. Everyone's backed by a second narrative. Everybody's nickname is Ace.

In some of the doubles, the halves are conjoined with an easy inevitability. D-295, for instance: two Jack Vance novels seamed together, both of them barnstorming, gutsy, other-galactic tours (*Slaves of the Klau* and *Big Planet*) done in an early stage of his highly distinctive style. Or later, D-403: *The Pirates of Zan* and *The Mutant Weapon,* both by Murray Leinster.

Other duos are more discrepant: a story of time travel (ancient Rome) matched with a look at some twenty-fourth-century outpost on Mars. And how, among all of the swashbuckle/gung-ho/wondrous interplanetary voyaging of so many of these titles, to find a fit partner for one of Philip K. Dick's increasingly dyspeptic, dour, and psychopharmacologically inspired views of "tomorrow"?

All of this halving and doubling reaches a lovely critical mass on the cover (I'd guess it's by Robert Schultz, although it's uncredited) of Andre Norton's *The Crossroads of Time* ("A CHASE THROUGH ALTERNATE WORLDS"). Its central image is of a man staring out at us, full-front. The face's left-hand side we clearly read as a portrait of a soldier of the future (he wears a soldier-of-the-future helmet); in back, a futuristic city skyline: plump cigar-silhouetted rocket ship and buildings that muscle upward with flanges and doohickey walkways bespeaking a leap of centuries. The right-side face is a portrait of a twentieth-century man (the book appeared in 1956, the year of *Howl*'s publication); in back, a mid-twentieth-century downtown cityscape, with airplane and an Empire-State-Building building lifting out of the foggy streets. They merge: they make a single face. So tell me, is the invisible ver-

ACE
DOUBLE NOVEL
BOOKS

D-164

TWO COMPLETE NOVELS 35c

THE CROSSROADS OF TIME

Complete and Unabridged

A CHASE THROUGH ALTERNATE WORLDS

ANDRE NORTON

tical line between the two a glitch? — or a bridging? Keep in mind
that the novel itself is half of D-164 and so is backed by (at the
same time, is the back of) *Mankind on the Run* (Gordon R. Dick-
son). Keep in mind that the prolific Andre Norton ("author of
over one hundred novels") is a woman — she also published as
Andrew North. (And for whoever finally produces Mary Alice
Norton's biography: I recommend you use the cover of *The Crossroads of Time* as a template, with a female-male division-and-blend
laid over the original.)

The more I look at this book in the days of my writing this essay,
the more the rest of the world conforms. A man named John
Rybicki has asked if I'll supply a blurb for his first collection of poems; on one page I find:

> "You're living two lives now," I tell him rolling out
>   of Detroit in my truck . . .

> "You slip your arms out of a fur coat made of bricks.
>   And when we get back home, trade it

>   for a fur coat made of cornfields."

There you have it. I open an issue of *Fortean Times,* that monthly
compilation of "unusual phenomena," and I find that Jessica Sandy
Booth attempted "to hire a hitman to kill four men and steal a
block of cocaine she had seen in their house in Memphis." The
"cocaine" "turned out to be Mexican queso fresco cheese"; the
"hitman" was an undercover cop. *They make a single face . . .* — "A
CHASE THROUGH ALTERNATE WORLDS" indeed.

As if a map of our own bilateral neocortex weren't enough to
conjure up that cover of Andre Norton's book as a hovering tute-
lary spirit. The brain is butterflied into its left-right hemispheres:
sometimes, in a certain aspect, they work with a uniform will; at
other times, these wings have seemingly landed here, each from a
different world, and become hinged arbitrarily.

If you snip and peel back the dura, the thin but leathery mem-
brane-shield over the brain, then there they are: the mirror-image
mazes where our thought exists and where our commands to ourselves are created. Carl Sagan refers to them as "two semi-indepen-

dent brains." But we do — and really it's most proper to — consider them parts of a single thing, the one "grey vault of Heaven," as Shakespeare puts it in *Henry IV, Part II.*

Even so, there are maladies so unfortunate that a few of us undergo hemispherectomies (1923 was the first, by a Baltimore neurosurgeon). The patients usually do surprisingly well. Although, as Christine Kenneally says, "it is generally thought that language is situated in the left half of the brain," it turns out all left-lobe hemispherectomees still talk. "Many children who have had [the operation] are in high school, and one, a college student, is on the dean's list."

Still, grievous aversion to any removal of our symmetries is understandably woven throughout the fabric of us. At the same time that my local paper is covering Chelsea Brooks's murder, it's covering the trial of the (now convicted) murderer of county sheriff's deputy Kurt Ford. Testifying in court was twin sister Karla Ford: "The other half of me is gone."

In the earliest days of the hemispherectomy process, at the conclusion of it, when one of the Gemini lobes was gone and the suddenly empty space called out for filling, "they would put all kinds of things in the cranial cavity — one surgeon used sterile Ping-Pong balls." I *like* the image of stuffing the skull with those small light spheres that, after all, were made exactly to travel back and forth across the halves of a whole.

First on the statistical side. Then on the creative side. Speech over here. Motor skills there. Potayto. Potahto. Tomayto. Tomahto.

Somehow we bring it all off. I'm reminded of Ginsberg's bon mot "69d." In a cheezoid porn mag I have is a photographic sequence of a couple performing exactly that. In the final scene, they're satiated and resting: not engaged in sexual pleasure any longer, but still in that same position: relaxed now into a circle — *the* circle — of difference-and-similarity.

She said her name was Gaea now.

And so it made a kind of "poetic sense" that I met her in what they termed an "Earth Sciences" course.

I couldn't pull my gaze away. If she *were* the earth, then she had two orbiting satellites: my eyes.

She was the standard "coed hippie chick" of the era — this was

1968 — but given the lower-middle-class neighborhood of my upbringing, she was the sweep of a fresh, invigorating breeze, with
her ass-length unpermed hair, her genuine and unadorned smile,
her tiny massage-me toes in their sensible sandals. I would have followed her to set up a treehouse residence at the heart of any leech-
infested rainforest of her choosing, she was so . . . "different" is the
only way I could say it, although my sappiest poems of that year attempted an eloquence on her behalf, with "halcyon" and "alabas-
ter" and "beauteous" and — a loosely Ginsbergian influence —
"heart-electricity-sylph."

"Different," but . . . familiar too, the way she sat across from me
in class. Like . . . she was Ava, I realized. Ava Edelman. Wow. From
seventh grade. And look at how she'd willfully metamorphosed
from that shallow, eye-shadowed, cashmered girl. The strength to
which I attributed that transformation only further ratcheted up
my infatuation. Stratosphere-level. Ionosphere-level. There was no
stopping my lust-and-googoo trajectory up from the launchpad.

She had taken her current name, she said, to match her "current being": she was "an advocate of our mother planet." Okay by
me. Whatever.

And she was flattered I'd remembered her — flattered, I think,
that out of all the men who gathered around the dancing slopes
below the showcase scoop of her peasant blouse and the cling of
the African-pattern skirt to her hips, I was the only one who knew
enough to appreciatively chart the arc of her evolution. One day
she got out the old class notes from Astronomy, and the textbook,
and we reminisced. And then we carnally tussled.

She was so . . . "pure." She was so pure and "free" — "like the animals in nature." She was sexy but pure, if pure is a way of saying no
to makeup and choosing a bicycle over "fossil fuels." And under
the lure of the musks of her body, I wanted to be pure too. I think
she enjoyed, in her own way, having an acolyte, a trainee. This was
a time when my friend Mitch became a Marxist mainly to gain the
affections of Frances Shteck and spent three nights in the city jail
martyring himself (in vain, it turned out) to that cause. And Darcy
— she left an A average and invitations from seven East Coast graduate schools in favor of leather leashes and a man whose biker
name was Seven Sins. So it didn't seem odd to me to mold myself
toward Gaea's needs. I doubt I even knew that I was doing it.

She liked that I was "gentle." Fine: I emphasized my gentleness. It was like natural selection. And her daily code *was* admirable. "No" to preservatives. "No" to meat foods. "No" to artificial soup-to-nuts. Ah, but the "yes" she'd murmur at night, when her roommates had blessedly left us alone for an hour . . . For that I'd have gouged the fillings out of my teeth — such man-made obscenities!

You can tell, I'm sure, where this is leading. Before we reached that point, however, we *did* share wonderful times. They didn't need to be outwardly major moments — a European tour, a backstage pass. The smallest event could feel as if it let extra worlds into this one: reading her a passage out of Thoreau while she reclined in the bath, the candlelight bringing his sure-grip words and her slippery shoulder into an alliance. And I came to see myself as I believed *she* saw myself: it wasn't shyness, it was tenderness. I was a kind of sachem of tenderness.

The falling apart was total cliché. It happened out of town — down at the beach, in fact — at a Green-Think Weekend Getaway. She got away, all right. Around seven o'clock on that Saturday night I turned a corner of heaped-up brush and abandoned jetty piles, and there she was with another man, a specialist on recycling waste into energy sources. I'm telling you, *with* another man. Her neon fuchsia bikini bottom was floating out on the blue of the bay as loud as a four-car pileup.

So we had it out in the room that night — anger, guilt, defensiveness, and all of the other carrion birds. I called her a slut. She'd *told* me she was "free," she hadn't *lied* to me, wasn't I *listening?* And then I punched her, lightly, once, or maybe I slapped her, I can't quite see it anymore. Yes, that's what Mr. Gentle did in his pig-blind rage. I must have thought it didn't come *close* to the hurt that she'd dealt me. You want to be "free," huh? "Like an animal," Miss Purity? Go watch a nature movie. (And then my hand struck.) There! *That's* how animals act.

We never completely recovered from that confrontation, although some do. The trouble, as you can see, was not her betrayal of me with Victor Vegan, nor was it my one-time violent swipe. The real trouble was the way we'd seen each other all along — as singular things, that meant one message only. Yes, but we each had another side too, like anyone. That shouldn't have been surprising. Still, we were young and we were inflexible, and whatever those "other sides" of us were, they hadn't fit the dynamic as we'd been living it. The following morning I sulked off by myself and had a triple bacon cheeseburger: breakfast. It was *goooood.*

We never completely recovered, but twice that year we made an attempt. I'm thinking right now of a night with wine and slightly drunken petting over at her apartment. She goes to bed and leaves me restlessly awake still, at her work desk. I can look through the door and watch the moon's long intimacy with that shoulder I used to suds.

And I idly page through her papers. There, the old textbook: Astronomy. A picture of the earth from space, exactly one half in the full touch of the sun and exactly one half in shadow. Not a single thing at all.

I look at that earth, through time and wine and a thousand compounded emotions, and I look until there are many earths, or anyway many planets, zooming amazingly through the skies of those books I used to read for just thirty-five cents. In one, the aliens clobbered us. In another, we emerged triumphant. Whoever the "aliens" were by then — and, of course, whoever "we" were.

EMILY R. GROSHOLZ

On Necklaces

FROM *Prairie Schooner*

This essay is dedicated to Roald Hoffmann, who has brought me back beads from Calcutta, Bangkok, Singapore, Madagascar via Tucson, Arizona, and the Atacama Desert in Chile.

Anthropology

What is the charm of necklaces? Why would anyone put something extra around her neck and then invest it with special significance? A necklace doesn't afford warmth in cold weather, like a scarf, or protection in combat, like chain mail; it only decorates. We might say it borrows meaning from what it surrounds and sets off: the head with its supremely important material contents, and the face, that register of the soul. When photographers discuss the way in which a photograph reduces the reality it represents, they mention not only the passage from three dimensions to two, but also the se-lection of a *point de vue* that favors the top of the body rather than the bottom, and the front rather than the back. The face is the jewel in the crown of the body, and so we give it a setting.

When people are intensely concerned with something that is ob-viously impractical, anthropologists take note, for lovely useless things often express archaic structures in the human soul. Fire-places, for example, have little reason to exist in contemporary American houses already heated by gas and electricity, yet most people want one and it is still the *focus* of the living room. This de-sire testifies, I think, to the hundreds of thousands of years during which we *Homo sapiens* huddled around a cave fire. We watch our-

selves, rather anxiously, vanish backward down those long tempo-
ral corridors, as my daughter gazes at her infinitely multiplied
small self in the mutually opposed mirrors of the beauty salon, and
wonders, is it me? Our fireplaces and necklaces and tombstones
say it is, they are.

So we have the corporeal-cultural custom of wearing something
around our necks, useless except for the emphasis or commentary
it provides. A necklace is very *meta*. A friend of mine in Paris, Lucie
Vines, learning of my newly acquired fascination with bead craft,
brought out two necklaces that she had made from objects purchased over a period of decades in the antiquarian shops of Paris.
The first was a necklace made entirely of Neolithic beads, great
oversize, roundly geometrical, roughly granitic things. Taken together, they were gorgeous and not a little disturbing, for they
were the literal embodiment of the archaic figure of the necklace.
So too the second, composed entirely of Egyptian amulets and
scarabs, each two or three thousand years old. And then she emptied a box of African trade beads that she'd been saving up, and let
me take my pick of them to celebrate my unwonted excursion into
color and form. (She's an artist.) In three or four different experiments, I mixed them up with *faux* and *vrai* Murano millefiore
beads; amber, red, and blue glass lozenges; heavy round dark
crushed-glass-coated oversize beads; green aventurine beads from
a garage sale; silver filigree beads from an antiques barn near Lan-
caster; and coral beads from the Philippines, coated in shellac,
with the grain and striation of little apples.

In American culture, an interest in necklaces seems to be rather
gender specific. Many men to whom I mention the enterprise
feign polite interest and then change the subject, though I know
some who admire, construct, and wear necklaces, including the
distinguished scientist and poet to whom this essay is dedicated.
Most women, by contrast, become mildly to wildly enthusiastic. A
doctor in Blois brought out her entire collection of costume jewelry for me, exhibited the most splendid pieces with an account of
where and when they were purchased, and then explained them
all with the help of a large glossy book on the history of costume
jewelry, with dozens of pictures. A former student who had moved
to California mailed me six plastic boxes full of beads gleaned
from a warehouse managed by an eccentric friend who just likes to
amass: a trove of freshwater pearls I had to detach one by one from

their settings; a feature bead painted with a naked lady; crystal ron-
dels of truly exceptional shine; and tiny silver hematite seed beads.
My daughter's dance teacher, learning that I was on the lookout
for tree-shaped beads, directed me to the local stained-glass artist,
and as an afterthought lent me a book on the internationally recognized glass artist Dale Chihuly, who reminds us that glass is like
water (as crystal is like ice). Our babysitter brought me back a box
from Colorado Springs with various treasures: large topazes, azure
cloisonné beads, bone beads carved like dice, and snake vertebrae.
One college friend requested a purple necklace; another, bright
lemon and lime, because she was sad; another, blue, because she
wasn't. Beads lend themselves to exchange. Beads travel. And
clearly these two facts are related.

History

My fourth book of poetry, *The Abacus of Years,* includes a poem titled "The Historian's Pursuit," written a couple of years ago for
Christine Heyrman, who had just won the Bancroft Prize for her
book *Southern Cross: The Beginnings of the Bible Belt.* When we were
fellow Fellows at the National Humanities Center (with my husband, Robert Edwards, who wasn't yet), I learned a great deal from
her — mostly over lunch — about the methods and romance of
historical research: how she talked her way into archives and sifted
patiently through dusty boxes in the unventilated basements of
churches or the un-air-conditioned storerooms of county court-
houses; how she wove narrative warp threads in and out of the weft
of statistical data, numbers compiled from phone books, tax records, medical records, deeds, wills, newspapers. That year, when
we were not exchanging scholarly notes, we were shopping for
shoes at the outlets. E. B. White said of the gifted spider Charlotte
that it is rare to find someone who is both a good friend and a
good writer; I might add, and a good shopper.

   I didn't realize that she had another hidden talent until, in response to my poem, one day she observed by e-mail, "Emily, I can't
make you immortal in verse, but I certainly can make you sparkle." Shortly thereafter, she arrived for a visit with two packages.
One contained a longish necklace composed of gold Czech glass
squares with blue edges, big amber beads, mottled brown-and-

white seeds, clay stars, and in the middle a milky blue marble bead that looks like the earth seen from the moon. In the other was a shorter necklace of polished rose quartz and softly faceted clear crystal. They both indeed sparkled, and so did I when I wore them, cheered by the thought that Christine made them herself especially for me.

Later, I asked her to restring a strand of jet and pearl beads my mother-in-law once gave me; the title poem of *Abacus* is dedicated to her, and come to think of it, centers around the image of a necklace, construed as wooden counters on the wire of an abacus, strands of Christmas tree lights, and stars flung out along the conceptual filaments of light-years. Along with that broken strand I threw in two other derelict sets, one blue, one green, which had been rolling around for a decade in a bureau drawer. I meant for Christine to use them in her own creations, but when she returned the repaired necklace, she also brought two new ones. The irregular green serpentine beads were interspersed with silver spacers and green glass stars and reorganized around one large heart-shaped and two smaller oval green-and-white-marble feature beads; and the little metallic blue beads were enlivened and extended with multiple small olive, bottle-green, and azure glass cylinders to a strand I could wrap three times around my neck. Wow. My daughter and I took to laying out and admiring my new trove of necklaces, which made the white bedspread resemble a corner of Aladdin's cave. Like crackers and marshmallows, speakers and air conditioners, necklaces had always seemed to me items that one must buy at the store, involving in their manufacture skills or equipment beyond the ambit of ordinary humans. And yet here suddenly was a king's ransom, conjured up by a friend: magic!

Initiation

So one day I called up Christine and said to her, What if I come down to visit with a couple of the kids and you show me how to make necklaces? A few weeks later, we arrived at her house in the Maryland countryside; the children occupied themselves with her astonishingly patient dog, and Christine and I sat down to bead. She had kindly bought me a pair of wire cutters, a pair of needle-nose pliers, some glass seed beads of various color and degree of sparkle, and the new space-age substitute for thread (in three diameters, .12, .15, and .18 centimeters) that makes beading easy: supple, nylon-coated steel wire. Also a few other essential, though diminutive, items: crimp beads, clasps, and spacers (both gold and silver in, well, tone), which prove to be the commas, semicolons, and periods in the expressive sentence of the necklace.

I hope I may be pardoned for giving it all away, but the technical secret of necklaces is what happens at the end of your row of beads. You feed the wire through a cylindrical metal crimp bead, through one end-loop of your clasp, then back through the crimp bead; you make sure that the beads are tightly lined up and secure, and then squash the crimp bead flat with your pliers and cut off the stray end with your cutters. Voilà. The procedure has to be carried out twice, of course, and the second time is always a little harder (because there is less wiggle room) and riskier (because at that point your necklace is about to become a fait accompli). "Is that *it?*" I asked Christine in amazement after having just elevated my first strand of beads to the rank of necklace with a flourish of jeweler's tools. It was so much easier than the exacting procedures required to deploy a sewing machine that I'd usually gotten wrong in seventh grade, for example. "That's it!" she announced, and brought us out another beer from the fridge. I was in business.

Business

The easy part of making necklaces is finishing them, once you have the right equipment. The hard part is making necklaces that aren't ugly (disproportionate, mismatched, or unbalanced) but at the same time aren't boring. I suppose the exception to the rule is a single strand of pearls, which from the perspective of design is about as boring as a necklace can be; but in this case the investment is all in the materials, real pearls, which made dozens of real oysters miserable for a long time. Otherwise, the trick is to take materials of variable quality and provenance, and mix them up according to various formal principles, intuition, and the hard cautionary knocks of experience, so that in combination they look gorgeous. A good necklace, like an organism or a poem, is a counterexample to the metaphysical thesis of reductionism: it is much more than the sum of its parts. What it will look like when you finally tote it all up and fasten it on is always a surprise. You don't know that you have achieved, or failed to achieve, gorgeousness (or even sober elegance) until the last moment when, if you're lucky, you give an involuntary sigh of wonder and recognition.

Another way to put the point is that making a good necklace is not the application of formal rules, nor can a necklace be deduced from its beads. You have to keep moving between rules and memories and hunches to discover what certain beads in concert may be encouraged to become. The wisdom of experience precipitates a cascade of rules, but then you have to choose and apply them. Don't depart too far from symmetry. Perfect symmetry is boring. Increase bead size as you work toward the center. Don't place interesting beads too close to the clasp; they'll be hidden behind the curve of neck and shoulder, and hair. But don't put trivial beads near the clasp either, because sometimes, after all, they show. Be reasonable in your use of spacers; syntax should not be allowed to overwhelm semantics. Heavy central beads turn the curved drape of a strand into a V. Two- and three-strand drapes are much harder to estimate than one. Don't juxtapose really big and really small, or round and rectilinear, beads without mediation. Choose your central beads with care, because they draw attention even when they're not feature beads: make sure they're not chipped or dirty. Wash your beads if they need it, in vinegar or soapsuds or jeweler's solution. Be lavish in mixing colors, but let your eye guide you.

You have to have a good eye. Like the musician's ear or the poet's heart, this is an innate attribute, though possible to cultivate if you have it. Moreover, no amount of experience seems to prevent the occasional disappointment of a failed hypothesis; an awkward necklace, however lovely it seemed in the prospect of imagination, declares itself as firmly as the data of experiment fail to measure up to what the scientist predicted. And you never know when unexpected gorgeousness will thrill you.

Shops and Souks

Once I began to make necklaces, I also began to see the world through a highly specific filter: wherever I went, I was on the lookout for material. My children learned to sense the onset of bead fever, and tried to resist when I shepherded them into a dollar store or a Saks or a dark alley. Beads show up in fancy and lowly places, and no possibility should be scorned. Finding bargains is half the fun, though sometimes the discovery is nuanced by sadness, for beads travel, and they are often cheap because in the lands they come from no one earns a living wage. One of the few women who haven't responded to my new project with enthusiasm is a Taiwanese friend who runs a restaurant I go to almost every week. When she was a child, she spent many summers stringing beads to make money to support herself and her family, so the idea of doing it voluntarily and for pleasure to her fell just short of the unthinkable, in the no man's land where the natural numbers get close to infinity. The provenance of beads in general can't be tracked like that of Adidas sneakers. Was your bead carved by an artisan in Bali who relishes and is rewarded for her craft, or by a Burmese peasant who is trying not to starve? On the other hand, sometimes the discovery is nuanced by malice: if a neighbor is silly enough to let go of a strand of good cloisonné pearls for two dollars at her garage sale, my contraband adds a certain spice to each necklace in which I plant it.

The most expensive way to buy beads is to cut up necklaces you've bought at a jeweler's. I've done this once or twice, when I really needed a certain kind of bead, but discourage the practice. Wholesalers who supply jewelers are a more rational source, but then you have to find them. There are quite a few in the Marais in Paris, behind the Place des Vosges and the Picasso Museum; I bought some lovely white-amber beads there, which look like a smooth compound of vanilla taffy and butterscotch. In Rome, behind the Piazza Navona, you can buy strands of coral, from the Mediterranean Sea just off the harbor of Naples, for ten or twenty dollars. My soberest wholesale purchase was the fifty euros I laid down for a long string of faceted Tibetan crystal in a shop just above Pigalle, which has meanwhile proved to be worth every centime. In New York, the pertinent neighborhood centers around Thirty-sixth and Forty-sixth streets and Broadway. Not long ago, I spent an hour there discussing findings and philosophy with three generations of the charming family of Myron Toback; his daughter persuaded me to buy my first two- and three-strand clasps, which opened up a whole new set of quasi-geometrical construction problems.

Antique stores have offered some treasures. At a *brocante* in Cusset, a medieval suburb of Vichy, I bought a dozen strands of tiny silver seed beads made in Murano in the 1930s, which endow any necklace I put them in with a shimmer like light reflected from the lagoon off the rosy façades of Piazza San Marco. The most spectacular clasp I ever bought, a kind of rhinestone clock face, came from an antique store off the Via Nomentana in Rome, though I had to detach it from some high-class plastic pearls. The Goodwill in my town is a well of bargains: I looked at a strand of intricately carved bone rosettes there for months before snatching it up for fifteen dollars when it was finally marked down, and once pounced on a glorious set of yellow jade beads for even less. It is also a reliable source of staples: black glass beads of all sizes, glass pearls, gold spacers, and lobster-claw clasps. Garage sales regularly yield discoveries, but only if you get up at the crack of dawn: a bracelet of rock-crystal beads for a dollar, a necklace of polished hematite chips for two. There are also stores that purvey beads to people who make necklaces, like the chain Beadazzled or La Pharmacie, whose Paris branch hides in the shadow of Les Halles. I mostly avoid them, because it seems like cheating, but I did buy five sets of large flat oval "palazzo" beads with swirls of gold in purple, black, yellow, green, and amber, and smooth mahogany-brown seeds that resemble shaped-up horse chestnuts at La Pharmacie, and had to wait in line forty-five minutes for the privilege.

Betrayal

Bargains also turn up when you aren't really looking for them. I once bought polished topaz and garnet chips in an Indian grocery store at the same price demanded by a wholesaler off Forty-seventh Street. I've stumbled upon *faux* but dazzling Murano millefiore beads in an art supply store at home and at a newspaper stand next to the Pantheon, moss agate lozenges in the shop of a natural history museum on the Sioule River featuring the skeleton of a thirty-thousand-year-old rhinoceros, and carved jade in a souvenir store facing the august Romanesque church at Orcival. One attribute of beads is their stubborn democracy: good ones turn up in both high-heeled and flip-flop establishments.

But bargains, as ever in the economy of life, must be paid for by betrayals, which are also democratic: I have been gulled at all levels. I was once disappointed to discover that a *vide-grenier* held in a small French village did not actually consist of French villagers emptying out their attics, but rather of professional dealers who go from town to town selling collectibles. One such dealer talked me into an imitation Coco Chanel necklace that seemed to be made of sea glass, those wine-bottle shards worn opaque by waves and sand that beachcombers treasure. *Mais oui, madame.* She assured me it was, but I had forgotten my glasses and was too embarrassed to bite it, a sure-fire way to distinguish stone from glass and glass from plastic. Teeth turn out to be remarkably sensitive organs. In any case, great was my disappointment when, upon returning home, I uncoupled them from their enormous gold-tone spacers, which hid half the bead, and discovered they were only plastic after all. I gave them to my daughter, but she also scorned them, because under the shadows left by the spacers they were dirty.

An elderly lady and her young gay assistant talked to me for half an hour about my projects in an upscale Roman boutique, and assured me that there were no wholesalers in Rome. I explained to them (in English, French, and approximate Italian) that I never used plastic beads but was happy to employ all kinds of glass, and they ultimately sold me a long string of glass beads the color of Piero della Francesca's skies that I never want to part with, and another long string (for the same price) of delicious coral-colored beads that proved, when I bit them back in the hotel room, to be plastic. The charming Korean gentleman who sold me white amber in the Marais also sold me a graduated set of yellow amber beads with fascinating interior crackles. When I tried to use them a few weeks later, they turned out to have no holes.

Mathematics

Those who string beads in patterns count, like weavers, like Goethe composing verse by tapping out the meter, delicately, with his fingers on his Roman mistress's back. *Four green seed beads given to me in Paris twenty years ago, one of Christine's sparkly turquoise seed beads, two Murano silvers, one turquoise, four more greens, and then the big one; begin again.* So it goes, and so I whisper to myself. Because I have a long-standing interest in geometry and its mathematical off-spring, I often also reflect on the curve a necklace makes as I work on it. Stretched out and unclasped, it's a line ($ax + by + c = 0$). A choker encircles the neck, so it is by and large a circle ($x^2 + y^2 + c = 0$). We might think that a necklace, extending longer, droops into an ellipse or a parabola or one of the fugitive branches of a hyperbola ($ax^2 + by^2 + cx + dy + e = 0$). However, the form is in the end probably not an algebraic curve, expressible like those above by a polynomial equation with a finite number of terms and positive integral exponents, but rather more like a famous transcendental curve, the catenary. Leibniz called it *la chainette,* because it is the form assumed by an ideal chain with links of vanishingly small fineness (and who among us has not wished for such a chain, in gold, fashioned by the masters of Jaipur?) when suspended from two points. Generally speaking, it stands for a minimal energy state, and since such "minimal surfaces" are especially important in physics and chemistry, *la chainette* and the surface it generates when rotated turn up all over, as the catenoid of a soap bubble stretched between two loops or of the lipid bilayer in cell membranes; another such minimal surface is the helicoid of DNA. I thought of trying to make a necklace with a glass helix winding around a certain section of the beads, but haven't yet found the right occasion.

Apropos surfaces, what makes the drape of a necklace so hard to estimate in abstraction, up in the air (the way you hold a necklace up to see how it's developing), is the complicated surface formed by a woman's neck, shoulders, and breasts. They are a set of saddle curves. A flat surface has zero curvature; a sphere, where the curviness all curves in one way, so to speak, has constant positive curvature; but a saddle has negative curvature, since some of its curviness goes up and some goes down. A neck and shoulder form such a curve and so does the valley between two breasts, and the clavicle adds its own angular interruption. Now, how will the circle or ellipse or catenary of the necklace (in one, two, or three strands) fall over this surface? The question is further vexed by the varying weight and size of the beads. A long bead in the middle tends to go horizontal; a heavy feature bead pulls the whole thing into a V that then intersects in various ways with the curves of a buxom girl.

Moreover, people have necks that vary from willowy to columnar, so what droops on one person will work fine as a choker on her friend.

The Glass Blower

Recently my family spent a month in Châtel-Montagne, a hilltop village in the Bourbonnais, south of Bourgogne and north of the Auvergne. We chose it by chance from the hundred offerings in a Gîtes de France catalog, but once arrived we realized it was a great discovery. It combined the advantages of French rural life — no e-mail, coin-only public telephone, fragrant bakery, established population of wild cats, friendly postmaster, tidy fields, and ravishing views — with a lively aesthetic scene. During the past decade, the mayor realized that the imposing Romanesque church brought into the village a stream of tourists steady enough to turn a cultural waterwheel. So he invited artisans to settle in the village: glass blower, basket weaver, carpenter, leather worker, glass engraver, sculptor, photographer, potter. He turned the public building next to the *mairie* into an art gallery with rotating exhibitions, and booked frequent concerts into the church and the tent erected in the *place* beside the church, where there is also a good restaurant.

As soon as I arrived at Châtel-Montagne, I went around to various ateliers to see if anyone would make me beads. Many expressed interest, but the only person who really followed through was the glass blower, a young man named Laurent Joignaud, whose shop is always filled with relatives, friends, ruly dogs, glassworks that show how willfully he tests the boundaries between craft and art, and children drawn by the twice daily, sorcerer's apprentice exhibitions of his powers as a glass blower. So I often found myself sitting on the threadbare sofa in the rear of the atelier with a couple of children balanced on my lap, trying not to stare into the inferno behind the open doors of the furnace, marveling as M. Joignaud turned molten clumps of glass into vases, platters, kittens, apples, wings, snowflakes, and northern lights.

At first he made me beads that were globes of clear glass with a floating island of gold, like earth when Pangaea was the only continent; the squarish fragments of gold leaf came from a booklet with the fine sheets pressed between its pages. Next there were pink flat flowerets and then leaves, which were green and blue until I told him about the autumn hardwood forests of New England and thereupon red, gold, and amber. After further speculation, he tried more abstract spiral forms, sometimes with spirals of color twisted inside the spirals, including one double helix whose black *tourbillon* proved, when held up to the light, to have oxidized to purple. That one inspired my first two-strand necklace, made with the silver 1930s Murano seed beads, amethyst, and jet. I left a few of our coauthored necklaces for him to sell in his shop, along with matching chokers. The last thing he brought me, as the landlords were checking us out on the final day, was a blue lizard with gold speckles on its back, its tail curled in a loop like the Seine just before it disperses into the Atlantic Ocean at Honfleur.

Landscapes

Now when I have to drive far away, usually to New York City, instead of listening to the radio I invent imaginary necklaces. You can conjure up a necklace around a feature bead, as I often did with M. Joignaud's glass pendants. But it is also instructive to plan necklaces with no center, whose patterns wax and wane or just remain constant all the way around. Perhaps it's like planning a melody in a certain key versus a melody progressing without emphasis in the twelve-tone system, or planning a sonnet in accentual verse versus a ghazal written *à la française* in syllabics. Either way, you can achieve good effects. There is the question of length, and the question of multiple strands, and the questions of uniform or graduated size, curvilinear or rectilinear bead shape, smooth or rough texture. And color, of course, is the deepest source of formal conundrum. I invented rainbow necklaces, springtime and autumn necklaces, nightclub and hearthside necklaces, snow and fire.

My best invention was initially sparked by a Chinese blue-and-white porcelain bead, a cat with a quizzical look on its whiskery face. I thought it was hungry, so I put it on the trail of four fish beads, who swam away from it through lapis and crystal water while I landlocked the kitty in green jade beads dotted with blue glass flowers. At first I thought of the necklace as a narrative, but then realized it was also a landscape. Many painted depictions of land-scape on two-dimensional canvas or silk scroll make use of linear conventions: they are often organized around or summed up in a winding road, the curve of a riverbank, the crest of a hill, or a cir-rus cloud. So why couldn't my necklaces also linearize a place on earth?

With that insight, many places occurred to me. I thought of a necklace corresponding to Châtel-Montagne. Starting from the clasp, I would use a few green-gray jade beads, the color of sunlight waning from a cloudy sky. Bronze-green jasper, delicately lobed and veined, leaf beads from China to represent by synecdoche the dark maples beside my favorite wall, and sand-colored, squarish beads for the wall. A clear hand-blown glass hummingbird with flecks of gold, from M. Joignaud, suspended at the center. Then a spray or sequence of fine coral branch beads, real ones from the Piazza Navona, which do rather resemble, iconically, the flowers called coral bells that lined the base of the wall and drew the elfin hummingbirds out of hiding. Then a few more sandstone beads, asymmetrically disposed with respect to those on the other side, and leaves all the rest of the way up. If I could find the right kind of fat black bee beads, perhaps carved from pyrite (fool's gold), or some indication of the faded metallic red of the gate in the wall, I'd put them in too.

I thought of another for Olympia, with cypress trees climbing the little hills, redbud blooming before its leaves come out, dwarf iris and wild geranium, the Alpheus River plunging among vine-yards. Another for Aegina with olive trees, gold terraces, and the Mediterranean lost in the blue of distance. Another for the woods behind my house in Pennsylvania, with rabbit and deer, blue jays and robins, my children playing hide-and-seek behind black wal-nut and wild cherry trees. Each place, each necklace, also had its poem, and the stylization of the landscape impressed upon it by the poem suggested to me the elements of the necklace.

Genealogy

When I was a child, my mother and I kept a "glitter box" filled with a hodgepodge of sequins, rickrack, buttons, seed beads, old bits of jewelry, ribbons, and felt cut up into shapes. We got it out mostly to make Christmas tree ornaments, by decorating Styrofoam balls or bells or reindeer with the stuff held in place by half-length straight pins. Perhaps because my mother's real jewelry was lost for a time after her death (although later recovered), I always kept careful track of the glitter box. From time to time I'd get it out of the closet for my little boys, just for fun, but only when my daughter Mary-Frances and I started making necklaces in tandem did I realize it might include beads we could use. Then I spent a couple of days, off and on, sorting out beads from its bright jumble: coral beads shaped like miniature branches; real but tiny conch shells either *au nature* or colored in 1950s aquamarine and mauve, with neat holes; matte-black round metal beads; clear glass rosettes; turquoise glass seed beads; rainbow-colored wooden beads of various shapes; and graduated beads the decorous, shiny white of dinner plates in a French bistro.

I put them back, mostly sorted, in the postwar shoebox they'd always inhabited, and then in a glorious moment of recognition set it on the needlepoint footstool that belonged to my great-great-aunt Emily, next to the Italian shoebox in which I keep my own beads (sorted by color in freezer bags with zipper tops, which in turn contain finer sortings by texture and weight in postcard- to stamp-size plastic bags) and the Adidas box in which Mary-Frances keeps her beads, mostly plastic and not much sorted and extremely brilliant. Tears came to my eyes. There we were, four generations of women represented by the work of our hands, with interlocking names: Emily Paddock, Frances Skerrett, Emily Grosholz, Mary-Frances Grosholz Edwards.

During the years of my early fifties, the grief of my mother's death has often reoccurred to me, because she died at fifty-two. The triggering event was September 11, but somehow every threat of dispersion, every important thing I'd ever lost, every bitter disappointment, came back to haunt me. For a while, the center could not hold. Taking up the construction of necklaces was, I think, at first almost obsessive and then therapeutic and then, at last, another occasion for the pleasures of invention. It is a commonplace that disaster often causes a retreat into intense aestheticism, domesticity, and the miniature (and therefore manageable), and I don't deny my own need for retreat. But to compose a necklace is also to endow lost or dispersed elements with meaning and pattern, to make them beautiful again, to warm them with the touch of human flesh. They ride, after all, where our blood comes close to the surface, where we feel a pulse, where we dab perfume to emanate from cleavage, nape, and temple. And their allure reflects the face they underline.

Linearization

As it happened, just when I was dreaming up the landscape necklaces — a project that proceeds slowly because it's hard to find beads that resemble trees or rivers or the red tile roofs of the Mediterranean in cross section — I was writing about the way science linearizes real things in order to understand them, to reveal their conditions of intelligibility. For example, a molecule (indeed, any physical or algebraic system) may be studied in terms of its symmetries, using groups that are in turn reduced to matrices and then to numbers. In general, and over a longer period of time, I have been musing about the linearization of things in the symbolic strings of language, natural language or the formal languages of logic and abstract algebra, and even of space itself in the analytic geometry Descartes invented but didn't fathom, and even of love in the sonnets of Shakespeare and Sidney. Linearization is a distortion, an oversimplification, a reduction of complexity: but *pari passu* it also illuminates and engenders, highlighting elements and patterns against a shadowy background of forgetfulness.

As Borges knew so well, if we couldn't forget, we would never discover, prefer, or bless. So it may be that the poems and theorems I especially treasure are like necklaces on the great breast of darkness, underwriting a lovely and terrible face up to whose furnace-like eyes I don't dare turn my own, and with reason. If it seems pretentious to end an essay on necklaces with an excursion into metaphysics, keep in mind that the four figures who (arguably) invented modernity around 1600 were the philosopher Descartes, the scientist Bacon, the poet Shakespeare, and the essayist Montaigne, who took the pebbles to which skepticism reduces knowledge and the fragments explorers carried back to Europe from the realms of gold, and fashioned them into a new line of civilization.

ANTHONY LANE

Candid Camera

FROM *The New Yorker*

FIFTY MILES NORTH OF Frankfurt lies the small German town of Solms. Turn off the main thoroughfare and you find yourself driving down tranquil suburban streets, with detached houses set back from the road, and, on a warm morning in late August, not a soul in sight. Nobody does bourgeois solidity like the Germans: you can imagine coming here for coffee and cakes with your aunt, but that would be the limit of excitement. By the time you reach Oskar-Barnack-Strasse, the town has almost petered out; just before the railway line, however, there is a clutch of industrial buildings, with a red dot on the sign outside. As far as fanfare is concerned, that's about it. But here is the place to go if you want to find the most beautiful mechanical objects in the world.

Many people would disagree. Bugatti fans, for instance, would direct your attention to the Type 57 Atlantic, the only car I know that appears to have been designed by masseuses. Personally, I would consider it a privilege to die at the wheel of a Lamborghini Miura — not difficult when you're nudging 170 miles per hour and waving at passersby. But automobiles need gas, whereas the truest mechanisms run on nothing but themselves. What is required is a machine constructed with such skill that it renders every user — from the pro to the banana-fingered fumbler — more skillful as a result. We need it to refine and lubricate, rather than block or coarsen, our means of engagement with the world: we want to look not just *at* it, however admiringly, but through it. In that case, we need a Leica.

There have been Leica cameras since 1925, when the Leica I was introduced at a trade fair in Leipzig. From then on, as the camera has evolved over eight decades, generations of users have turned to it in their hour of need, or their millisecond of inspiration. Aleksandr Rodchenko, André Kertész, Walker Evans, Henri Cartier-Bresson, Robert Capa, Robert Frank, William Klein, Garry Winogrand, Lee Friedlander, and Sebastião Salgado: these are some of the major league names that are associated with the Leica brand — or, in the case of Cartier-Bresson, stuck to it with everlasting glue.

Even if you don't follow photography, your mind's eye will still be full of Leica photographs. The famous head shot of Che Guevara, reproduced on millions of rebellious T-shirts and student walls: that was taken on a Leica with a portrait lens — a short telephoto of 90 millimeters — by Alberto Díaz Gutiérrez, better known as Korda, in 1960. How about the pearl-gray smile-cum-kiss reflected in the wing mirror of a car, taken by Elliott Erwitt in 1955? Leica again, as is the even more celebrated smooch caught in Times Square on V-J Day, 1945 — a sailor craned over a nurse, bending her backward, her hand raised against his chest in polite half-protestation. The man behind the camera was Alfred Eisenstaedt, of *Life* magazine, who recalled: "I was running ahead of him with my Leica, looking back over my shoulder. But none of the pictures that were possible pleased me. Then suddenly, in a flash, I saw something white being grabbed. I turned around and clicked."

He took four pictures, and that was that. "It was done within a few seconds," he said. All you need to know about the Leica is present in those seconds. The photographer was on the run, so whatever he was carrying had to be light and trim enough not to be a drag. He swiveled and fired in one motion, like the Sundance Kid. And everything happened as quickly for him as it did for the startled nurse, with all the components — the angles, the surrounding throng, the shining white of her dress and the kisser's cap — falling into position. Times Square was the arena of uncontrolled joy; the job of the artist was to bring it under control, and the task of his camera was to bring life — or, at least, an improved version of it, graced with order and impact — to the readers of *Life*.

Still, why should one lump of metal and glass be better at fulfilling that duty than any other? Would Eisenstaedt really have been worse off, or failed to hit the target, with another sort of camera? These days, Leica makes digital compacts and a beefy SLR, or single-lens reflex, called the R9, but for more than fifty years the pride of the company has been the M series of 35-millimeter range-finder cameras — durable, companionable, costly, and basically unchanging, like a spouse. There are three current models, one of which, the MP, will set you back a throat-drying four thousand dollars or so; having stood outside dustless factory rooms in Solms, and watched women in white coats and protective hairnets carefully applying black paint, with a slender brush, to the rim of every lens, I can tell you exactly where your money goes. Mind you, for four grand you don't even get a lens — just the MP body. It sits there like a gum without a tooth until you add a lens, the cheapest being available for just under a thousand dollars. (Five and a half thousand will buy you a 50-millimeter $f/1$, the widest lens on the market; for anybody wanting to shoot pictures by candlelight, there's your answer.) If you simply want to take a nice photograph of your children, though, what's wrong with a Canon PowerShot? Yours online for just over two hundred bucks, the PowerShot SD1000 will also zoom, focus for you, set the exposure for you, and advance the frame automatically for you, none of which the MP, like some sniffing aristocrat, will deign to do. To make the contest even starker, the SD1000 is a digital camera, fizzing with megapixels, whereas the Leica still stores images on that frail, combustible material known as film. Short of telling the kids to hold still while you copy them onto parchment, how much further out of touch could you be?

To non-photographers, Leica, more than any other manufacturer, is a legend with a hint of scam: suckers paying through the nose for a name, in a doomed attempt to crank up the credibility of a picture they were going to take anyway, just as weekend golfers splash out on a Callaway Big Bertha in a bid to convince themselves that, with a little more whippiness in their shaft, they will swell into Tiger Woods. To unrepentant aesthetes, on the other hand, there is something demeaning in the idea of Leica. Talent will out, they say, whatever the tools that lie to hand, and in a sense they are right: Woods would destroy us with a single rusty five-iron found at the back of a garage, and Cartier-Bresson could have picked up a Box Brownie and done more with a roll of film — summoning his usual miracles of poise and surprise — than the rest of us would manage with a lifetime of Leicas. Yet the man himself was quite clear on the matter: "I have never abandoned the Leica, anything different that I have tried has always brought me back to it. I am not saying this is the case for others. But as far as I am concerned it is the camera. It literally constitutes the optical extension of my eye."

Asked how he thought of the Leica, Cartier-Bresson said that it felt like "a big warm kiss, like a shot from a revolver, and like the psychoanalyst's couch." At this point, five thousand dollars begins to look like a bargain.

Many reasons have been adduced for the rise of the Leica. There is the hectic progress of the illustrated press, avid for photographs to fill its columns; there is the increased mobility, spending power, and leisure time of the middle classes, who wished to preserve a record of these novel blessings, if not for posterity, then at least for show. Yet the great inventions, more often than not, are triggered less by vast historical movements than by the pressures of individual chance — or, in Leica's case, by asthma. Every Leica employee who drives down Oskar-Barnack-Strasse is reminded of corporate glory, for it was Barnack, a former engineer at Carl Zeiss, the famous lens makers in Jena, who designed the Leica I. He was an amateur photographer, and the camera had first occurred to him, as if in a vision, in 1905, twenty years before it actually went on sale: "Back then I took pictures using a camera that took 13 by 18 plates, with six double-plate holders and a large leather case similar to a salesman's sample case. This was quite a load to haul around when I set off each Sunday through the Thüringer Wald. While I struggled up the hillsides (bearing in mind that I suffer from asthma) an idea came to me. Couldn't this be done differently?"

Five years later, Barnack was invited to work for Ernst Leitz, a rival optical company, in Wetzlar. (The company stayed there until 1988, when it was sold, and the camera division, renamed Leica, shifted to Solms, fifteen minutes away.) By 1913–14, he had developed what became known as the ur-Leica: a tough, squat, rectangular metal box, not much bigger than a spectacles case, with rounded corners and a retractable brass lens. You could tuck it into a jacket pocket, wander around the Thüringer woods all week-end, and never gasp for breath. The extraordinary fact is that, if you were to place it next to today's Leica MP, the similarities would far outweigh the differences; stand a young man beside his own great-grandfather and you get the same effect.

Barnack took a picture on August 2, 1914, using his new device. Reproduced in Alessandro Pasi's comprehensive study *Leica: Witness to a Century* (2004), it shows a helmeted soldier turning away from a column on which he has just plastered the imperial order for mobilization. This was the first hint of the role that would fall to Leicas above all other cameras: to be there in history's face. Not until the end of hostilities did Barnack resume work on the Leica, as it came to be called. (His own choice of name was Lilliput, but wiser counsels prevailed.) Whenever you buy a 35-millimeter camera, you pay homage to Barnack, for it was his hand-held invention that popularized the 24-by-36-millimeter negative — a perfect ratio of 2:3 — adapted from cine film. According to company lore, he held a strip of the new film between his hands and stretched his arms wide, the resulting length being just enough to contain thirty-six frames — the standard number of images, ever since, on a roll of 35-millimeter film. Well, maybe. Does this mean that if Barnack had been more of an ape, we might have got forty?

When the Leica I made its eventual debut in 1925, it caused consternation. In the words of one Leica historian, quoted by Pasi, "To many of the old photographers it looked like a toy designed for a lady's handbag." Over the next seven years, however, nearly sixty thousand Leica I's were sold. That's a lot of handbags. The shutter speeds on the new camera ran up to 1/500 second, and the aperture opened wide to f/3.5. In 1932, the Leica II arrived, equipped with a range finder for more accurate focusing. I used one the other day — a mid-thirties model, although production lasted until 1948. Everything still ran sweetly, including the knurled knob with which you wind on from frame to frame, and the simplicity of the design made the Leica an infinitely more friendly proposition, for the novice, than one of the digital monsters from Nikon and Canon. Those need an instruction manual only slightly smaller than the Old Testament, whereas the Leica II sat in my palms like a puppy, begging to be taken out on the streets.

That is how it struck not only the public but also those for whom photography was a living, or an ecstatic pursuit. A German named Paul Wolff acquired a Leica in 1926 and became a high priest to the brand, winning many converts with his 1934 book *My Experiences with the Leica.* His compatriot Ilsa Bing, born to a Jewish family in Frankfurt, was dubbed "the Queen of the Leica" after an exhibit in 1931. She had bought the camera in 1929, and what is remarkable, as one scrolls through a roster of her peers, is how quickly, and infectiously, the Leica habit caught on. Whenever I pick up a book of photographs, I check the chronology at the back. From a monograph by the Hungarian André Kertész, the most wistful and tactful of photographers: "1928 — Purchases first Leica." From the catalog of the 1998 Aleksandr Rodchenko show at MOMA: "1928, November 25 — Stepanova's diary records Rodchenko's purchase of a Leica for 350 rubles." And on it goes.

The Russians were among the first and fiercest devotees, and anyone who craves the Leica as a pure emblem of capitalist desire — what Marx would call commodity fetishism — may also like to reflect on its status, to men like Rodchenko, as a weapon in the revolutionary struggle. Never a man to be tied down (he was also a painter, sculptor, and master of collage), he nonetheless believed that "only the camera is capable of reflecting contemporary life," and he went on the attack, craning up at buildings and down from roofs, tipping his Leica at flights of steps and street parades, upending the world as if all its old complacencies could be shaken out of the bottom like dust. There is a gorgeous shot from 1934 entitled *Girl with a Leica,* in which his subject perches politely on a bench that arrows diagonally, and most impolitely, from lower left to upper right. She wears a soft white beret and dress, and her gaze is blank and misty, but thrown over the scene, like a net, is the shadow of a window grille — modernist geometry at war with reactionary decorum. The object she clasps in her lap, its strap drawn tightly over her shoulder, is of the same make as the one that created the picture.

When it came to off-centeredness, Rodchenko's fellow Russian Ilya Ehrenburg went one better. "A camera is clumsy and crude. It meddles insolently in other people's affairs," he wrote in 1932. "Ours is a guileful age. Following man's example, things have also learned to dissemble. For many months I roamed Paris with a little camera. People would sometimes wonder: why was I taking pic-

tures of a fence or a road? They didn't know that I was taking pictures of them." Ehrenburg had solved the problem of meddling by
buying an accessory: "The Leica has a lateral viewfinder. It's constructed like a periscope. I was photographing at 90 degrees." The
Paris that emerged — poor, grimy, and unposed — was a moral re-
buke to the myth of bohemian chic.

You can still buy a right-angled viewfinder for a new Leica if
you're too shy or sneaky to confront your subjects head-on, although the basic thrust of Leica technique has been to insist that
no extra subterfuge is required: the camera can hide itself. If I had
to fix the source of that reticence, I would point to Marseilles in
1932. It was then that Cartier-Bresson, an aimless young French-
man from a wealthy family, bought his first Leica. He proceeded to
grow into the best-known photographer of the twentieth century,
in spite (or, as he would argue, because) of his ability to walk down
a street not merely unrecognized but unnoticed. He began as a
painter, and continued to draw throughout his life, but his hand
was most comfortable with a camera.

When I spoke to his widow, Martine Franck — the president of
the Henri Cartier-Bresson Foundation in Paris and herself a distinguished photographer — she said that her husband in action with
his Leica "was like a dancer." This feline unobtrusiveness led him
all over the world and made him seem at home wherever he
paused; one trip to Asia lasted three years, ending in 1950, and
produced 850 rolls of film. His breakthrough collection, published
two years later, was called *The Decisive Moment,* and he sought endless analogies for the sensation that was engendered by the press of
a shutter. The most common of these was hunting: "The photographer must lie in wait, watching out for his prey, and have a presen-
timent of what is about to happen."

There, if anywhere, is the Leica motto: watch and wait. If you were
a predator, the moment — not just for Cartier-Bresson, but for
all photographers — became that much more decisive in 1954.
"Clairvoyance" means "clear sight," and when Leica launched the
M3 that year, the clarity was a *coup de foudre;* even now, when you
look through a used M3, the world before you is brighter and
crisper than seems feasible. You half expect to feel the crunch of
autumn leaves beneath your feet. A Leica viewfinder resembles no

ELLIOT ERWITT/MAGNUM PHOTOS

other, because of the frame lines: thin white strips, parallel to each side of the frame, which show you the borders of the photograph that you are set to take — not merely the lie of the land within the shot, but also what is happening, or about to happen, just outside. This is a matter of millimeters, but to Leica fans it is sacred, because it allows them to plan and imagine a photograph as an act of storytelling — an instant grabbed at will from a continuum. If you want a slice of life, why not see the loaf?

The M3 had everything, although by the standards of today it had practically nothing. You focused manually, of course, and there was nothing to help you calculate the exposure; either you carried a separate light meter or you clipped one awkwardly to the top of the camera or, if you were cool, you guessed. Cartier-Bresson was cool. Martine Franck is still cool: "I think I know my light by now," she told me. She continues to use her M3: "I've never held a camera so beautiful. It fits the hand so well." Even for people who know nothing of Cartier-Bresson, and for whom 1954 is as long ago as Pompeii, something about the M3 clicks into place: last year, when eBay and *Stuff* magazine, in the U.K., took it upon themselves to nominate "the top gadget of all time," the Game Boy came fifth, the Sony Walkman third, and the iPod second. First place went to an old camera that doesn't even need a battery. If the Queen subscribes to *Stuff,* she will have nodded in approval, having owned an M3 since 1958. Her Majesty is so wedded to her Leica that she was once shown on a postage stamp holding it at the ready.

It's no insult to call the M3 a gadget. Such beauty as it possesses flows from its scorn for the superfluous; as any Bauhaus designer could tell you, form follows function. The M series is the backbone of Leica; we are now at the M8 (which at first glance is barely distinguishable from the M3), and, with a couple of exceptions, every intervening camera has been a classic. Richard Kalvar, who rose to become president of the Magnum photographic agency during the nineties, remembers hearing the words of a Leica fan: "I know I'm using the best, and I don't have to think about it anymore." Kalvar bought an M4 and never looked back: "It's almost a part of me," he says. Ralph Gibson, whose photographs offer an unblinking survey of the textures that surround us, from skin to stone, bought his first Leica, an M2 (which, confusingly, postdated the M3), in 1961. It cost him three hundred dollars, which, considering that he was earning a hundred a week, was quite an outlay, but his loyalty is undimmed. "More great photographs have been made with a Leica and a fifty-millimeter lens than with any other combination in the history of photography," Gibson said to me. He advised Leica beginners to use nothing except that standard lens for two or three years, so as to ease themselves into the swing of the thing: "What you learn you can then apply to all the other lengths."

One could argue that, since the 1950s and '60s, the sense of Europe as the spiritual hearth of Leica, with the Paris of Kertész and Cartier-Bresson glowing at its core, has been complemented, if not superseded, by America's attraction to the brand. The Russian love of the angular had exploited the camera's portability (you try bending over a window ledge with a plate camera); the French had perfected the art of reportage, netting experience on the wing; but the Leicas that conquered America — the M3, the M4, and later the M6, with built-in metering and the round red Leica logo on the front — were wielded with fresh appetite, biting at the world and slicing it off in unexpected chunks. Lee Friedlander, photographing a child in New York in 1963, thought nothing of bringing the camera down to the boy's eye level, and thus semi-decapitating the grownups who stood beside him. (All kids dream of that sometime.) Men and women were reflected in storefront windows or obscured by street signs; many of the photographs shimmered on the brink of a mistake. "With a camera like that," Friedlander has said of the Leica, "you don't believe that you're in the masterpiece business. It's enough to be able to peck at the world." One shot of his, from 1969, traps an entire landscape of feeling — a boundless American sky salted with high clouds, plus Friedlander's wife, Maria, with her lightly smiling face — inside the cab of a single truck, layering what we see through the side window with what is reflected in it. I know of long novels that tell you less.

Before Friedlander came Robert Frank, born in Switzerland; only someone from a mountainous country, perhaps, could come here and view the United States as a flat and tragic plain. *The Americans* (1958), the record of his travels with a Leica, was mostly haze, shade, and grain, stacked with human features resigned to their fate. No artist had ever studied a men's room in such detail before, with everything from the mop to the hand dryer immortalized in the wide embrace of the lens; Jack Kerouac, who wrote the introduction to the book, lauded the result, taken in Memphis, Tennessee, as "the loneliest picture ever made, the urinals that women never see, the shoeshine going on in sad eternity." Then there was Garry Winogrand, the least exhaustible of all photographers. Frank's eighty-three images may have been chosen from five hundred rolls of film, but when Winogrand died, in 1984, at the age of fifty-six, he left behind more than two and a half thousand rolls of film that hadn't even been developed. He leavened the wistfulness of Frank with a documentary bluntness and a grinning wit, incessantly tilting his Leica to throw a scene off balance and seek a new dynamic. His picture of a disabled man in Los Angeles, in 1969, could have been fueled by pathos alone, or by political rage at an indifferent society, but Winogrand cannot stop tracking that society in its comic range; that is why we get not just the wheelchair and the begging bowl but also a trio of short-skirted girls, bunched together like a backup group, strolling through the V's of shadow and sunlight, and a portly matron planted at the right of the frame — a stolid import from another age.

I recently found a picture of Winogrand's M4. The metal is not just rubbed but visibly worn down beside the wind-on lever; you have to shoot a heck of a lot of photographs on a Leica before that happens. Still, his M4 is in mint condition compared with the M2 owned by Bruce Davidson, the American photographer whose work constitutes, among other things, an invaluable record of the civil rights movement. And even his M2, pitted and peeled like the bark of a tree, is pristine compared with the Leica I saw in the display case at the Leica factory in Solms. That model had been in the *Hindenburg* when it went up in flames in New Jersey in 1937. The heat was so intense that the front of the lenses melted. So now you know: Leica engineers test their product to the limits, and they will customize it for you if you are planning a trip to the Arctic, but when you really want to trash your precious camera you need an exploding airship.

If you pick up an M-series Leica, two things are immediately apparent. First, the density: the object sits neatly but not lightly in the hand, and a full day's shooting, with the camera continually hefted to the eye, leaves you with a faint but discernible case of wrist ache. Second, there is no lump. Most of the smarter, costlier cameras in the world are SLRs with a lumpy prism on top. Light enters through the lens, strikes an angled mirror, and bounces upward to the prism, where it strikes one surface after another, like a ball in a squash court, before exiting through the viewfinder. You see what your lens sees, and you focus accordingly. This happy state of affairs does not endure. As you take a picture, the mirror flips up out of the light path. The image, now unobstructed, reaches straight to the rear of the camera and, as the shutter opens, burns into the emulsion of the film — or, these days, registers on a digital sensor. With every flip, however, comes a flip side: the mirror shuts off access to the prism, meaning that, at the instant of release, your vision is blocked, and you are left gazing at the dark.

To most of us, this is not a problem. The instant passes, the mirror flips back down, and lo, there is light. For some photographers, though, the impediment is agony: of all the times to deny us the right to look at our subject, SLRs have to pick *this* one? "Visualus interruptus," Ralph Gibson calls it, and here is where the Leica M series plays its ace. The Leica is lumpless, with a flat top built from a single piece of brass. It has no prism, because it focuses with a range finder — situated above the lens. And it has no mirror inside, and therefore no clunk as the mirror swings. When you take a picture with an SLR, there is a distinctive sound, somewhere between a clatter and a thump; I worship my beat-up Nikon FE, but there is no denying that every snap reminds me of a cow kicking over a milk pail. With a Leica, all you hear is the shutter, which is the quietest on the market. The result — and this may be the most seductive reason for the Leica cult — is that a photograph sounds like a kiss.

From the start, this tinge of diplomatic subtlety has shaded our view of the Leica, not always helpfully. The M-series range finder feels made for the finesse and formality of black-and-white — yet consider the oeuvre of William Eggleston, whose unabashed use of color has delivered, through Leica lenses, a lesson in everyday American surrealism, which, like David Lynch movies, blooms almost painfully bright. Again, the Leica, with its range of wide-aperture lenses, is *the* camera for natural light, and thus inimical to flash, yet Lee Friedlander conjured a series of plainly flash-lit nudes in the 1970s that finds tenderness and dignity in the brazen. Lastly, a Leica is, before anything else, a 35-millimeter camera. Barnack shaped the Leica I around a strip of film, and the essential mission of the brand since then has been to guarantee that a single chemical event — the action of light on a photosensitive surface — passes off as smoothly as possible. Picture the scene, then, in Cologne in the fall of 2006. At Photokina, the biennial fair of the world's photographic trade, Leica made an announcement: it was time, we were told, for the M8. The M series was going digital. It was like Dylan going electric.

In a way, this had to happen. The tide of our lives is surging in a digital direction. My complete childhood is distilled into a couple of photograph albums, with the highlights, whether of achievement or embarrassment, captured in no more than a dozen talismanic stills, now faded and curling at the edges. Yet our own children go on one school trip and return with a hundred images stashed on a memory card: will that enhance or dilute their later remembrance of themselves? Will our experience be any the richer for being so retrievable, or could an individual history risk being wiped, or corrupted, as briskly as a memory card? Garry

Winogrand might have felt relieved to secure those thousands of images on a hard drive rather than on frangible film, although it could be that the taking of a photograph meant more to him than the printed result. The jury is out, but one thing is for sure: film is dwindling into a minority taste, upheld largely by professionals and stubborn, nostalgic perfectionists. Nikon now offers twenty-two digital models, for instance, while the "wide array of SLR film cameras," as promised on its website, numbers precisely two.

Even a company like Leica, servant to the devout, has felt the brunt. For the fiscal year 2004–05, the company posted losses of almost twenty million euros (nearly twenty-six million dollars), and in 2005 the banks partially terminated its credit lines; in short, Leica was heading for extinction. Since then, there has been something of a turnaround. Major restructuring is still under way, with a new CEO — a genial Californian called Steven K. Lee — brought in to oversee the changes. According to a report of June 20, 2007, the past year has seen the company inching back into profitability, and much of that improvement is due to the M8. The camera's birth was fraught with complications, and reports streamed in from owners that in certain conditions, thanks to a glitch in the sensor, black was showing up on digital images as deep purple — troubling news if you happened to be shooting a portrait of Dracula, or a Guinness commercial. There were also rumblings about the quality of the focus, which is the last thing you expect from a Leica. One well-known photographer described the camera to me as "unusable," and said he sometimes felt like throwing it against a wall. But the company responded: cameras were recalled to the factory, Lee signed four thousand letters of apology, and the crisis passed. Nevertheless, the camera still needs a filter fixed to every lens to correct its vision, and Leica will want to do better next time. When I asked Lee about the possibility of an M9 — an upgraded M8, with all the kinks ironed out — he smiled and said nothing.

Lee knows what is at stake, being a Leica lover of long standing. Asked about the difference between using his product and an ordinary camera, he replied: "One is driving a Morgan four-by-four down a country lane, the other one is getting in a Mercedes station wagon and going a hundred miles an hour." The problem is that, for photographers as for drivers, the most pressing criterion these days is speed, and anything more sluggish than the latest Mercedes

— anything, likewise, not tricked out with luxurious extras — belongs to the realm of heritage. There is an astonishing industry in used Leicas, with clubs and forums debating such vital areas of contention as the strap lugs introduced in 1933. There are collectors who buy a Leica and never take it out of the box; others who discreetly amass the special models forged for the Luftwaffe. Ralph Gibson once went to a meeting of the Leica Historical Society of America and, he claims, listened to a retired Marine Corps general give a scholarly paper on certain discrepancies in the serial numbers of Leica lens caps. "Leicaweenies," Gibson calls such addicts, and they are part of the charming, unbreakable spell that the name continues to cast, as well as a tribute to the working longevity of the cameras. By an unfortunate irony, the abiding virtues of the secondhand slow down the sales of the new: why buy an M8 when you can buy an M3 for a quarter of the price and wind up with comparable results? The economic equation is perverse: "I believe that for every euro we make in sales, the market does four euros of business," Lee said.

I have always wanted a Leica, ever since I saw an Edward Weston photograph of Henry Fonda, his noble profile etched against the sky, a cigarette between two fingers, and a Leica resting against the corduroy of his jacket. I have used a variety of cultish cameras, all of them secondhand at least, and all based on a negative larger than 35 millimeters: a Bronica, a Mamiya 7, and the celebrated twin-lens Rolleiflex, which needs to be cupped at waist height. ("If the good Lord had wanted us to take photographs with a 6 by 6, he would have put eyes in our belly," a scornful Cartier-Bresson said.) But I have never used a Leica. Now I own one: a small, dapper digital compact called the D-Lux 3. It has a fine lens, and its grace note is a retro leather case that makes me feel less like Henry Fonda and more like a hiker named Helmut, striding around the Black Forest in long socks and a dark green hat with a feather in it; but a D-Lux 3 is not an M8. For one thing, it doesn't have a proper viewfinder. For another, it costs close to six hundred dollars — the upper limit of my budget but laughably cheap to anyone versed in the M series. So, to discover what I was missing, I rented an M8 and a 50-millimeter lens for four hours, from a Leica dealer, and went to work.

If you can conquer the slight queasiness that comes from walking about with seven thousand dollars' worth of machinery hanging around your neck, an afternoon with the M8 is a dangerously pleasant groove to get into. I can understand that, were you a sports photographer, perched far away from the action, or a paparazzo, fighting to squeeze off twenty consecutive frames of Britney Spears falling down outside a nightclub, this would not be your tool of choice, but for more patient mortals it feels very usable indeed. This is not just a question of ergonomics or of the diamond-like sharpness of the lens. Rather, it has to do with the old, bewildering Leica trick: the illusion, fostered by a mere machine, that the world out there is asking to be looked at — to be caught and consumed while it is fresh, like a trout. Ever since my teens, as one substandard print after another glimmered into view in the developing tray under the brothel-red gloom of the darkroom, my own attempts at photography have meant a lurch of expectation and disappointment. Now, with an M8 in my possession, the shame gave way to a thrill. At one point, I stood outside a bookstore and, in a bid to test the exposure, focused on a pair of browsers standing within, under an "Antiquarian" sign at the end of a long shelf. Suddenly, a pale blur entered the frame lines. I panicked, and pressed the shutter: kiss.

On the digital playback, I inspected the evidence. The blur had been an old lady, and she had emerged as a phantom — the complete antiquarian, with glowing white hair and a hint of spectacles. It wasn't a good photograph, more of a still from *Ghostbusters*, but it was funnier and punchier than anything I had taken before, and I could only have grabbed it with a Leica. (And only with an M. By the time the D-Lux 3 had fired up and focused, the lady would have floated halfway down the street.) So the rumors were true: buy this camera, and accidents will happen. I remembered what Cartier-Bresson once said about turning from painting to photography: "the adventurer in me felt obliged to testify with a quicker instrument than a brush to the scars of the world." That is what links him to the Leicaweenies, and Oskar Barnack to the advent of the M8, and Russian revolutionaries to flash-lit American nudes: the simple, undying wish to look at the scars.

JONATHAN LETHEM

The Ecstasy of Influence

A Plagiarism

FROM *Harper's Magazine*

> All mankind is of one author, and is one volume; when one man dies,
> one chapter is not torn out of the book, but translated into a better
> language; and every chapter must be so translated.
> — *John Donne*

Love and Theft

Consider this tale: a cultivated man of middle age looks back on
the story of an *amour fou,* one beginning when, traveling abroad,
he takes a room as a lodger. The moment he sees the daughter of
the house, he is lost. She is a preteen, whose charms instantly en-
slave him. Heedless of her age, he becomes intimate with her. In
the end she dies, and the narrator — marked by her forever —
remains alone. The name of the girl supplies the title of the story:
Lolita.

The author of the story I've described, Heinz von Lichberg,
published his tale of Lolita in 1916, forty years before Vladimir
Nabokov's novel. Lichberg later became a prominent journalist in
the Nazi era, and his youthful works faded from view. Did Nabokov,
who remained in Berlin until 1937, adopt Lichberg's tale consciously? Or did the earlier tale exist for Nabokov as a hidden,
unacknowledged memory? The history of literature is not without
examples of this phenomenon, called cryptomnesia. Another hy-

pothesis is that Nabokov, knowing Lichberg's tale perfectly well, had set himself to that art of quotation that Thomas Mann, himself a master of it, called "higher cribbing." Literature has always been a crucible in which familiar themes are continually recast. Little of what we admire in Nabokov's *Lolita* is to be found in its predecessor; the former is in no way deducible from the latter. Still: did Nabokov consciously borrow and quote?

"When you live outside the law, you have to eliminate dishonesty." The line comes from Don Siegel's 1958 film noir, *The Lineup,* written by Stirling Silliphant. The film still haunts revival houses, likely thanks to Eli Wallach's blazing portrayal of a sociopathic hit man and to Siegel's long, sturdy auteurist career. Yet what were those words worth — to Siegel, or Silliphant, or their audience — in 1958? And again: what was the line worth when Bob Dylan heard it (presumably in some Greenwich Village repertory cinema), cleaned it up a little, and inserted it into "Absolutely Sweet Marie"? What are they worth now, to the culture at large?

Appropriation has always played a key role in Dylan's music. The songwriter has grabbed not only from a panoply of vintage Hollywood films but from Shakespeare and F. Scott Fitzgerald and Junichi Saga's *Confessions of a Yakuza.* He also nabbed the title of Eric Lott's study of minstrelsy for his 2001 album *Love and Theft.* One imagines Dylan liked the general resonance of the title, in which emotional misdemeanors stalk the sweetness of love, as they do so often in Dylan's songs. Lott's title is, of course, itself a riff on Leslie Fiedler's *Love and Death in the American Novel,* which famously identifies the literary motif of the interdependence of a white man and a dark man, like Huck and Jim or Ishmael and Queequeg — a series of nested references to Dylan's own appropriating, minstrel-boy self. Dylan's art offers a paradox: while it famously urges us not to look back, it also encodes a knowledge of past sources that might otherwise have little home in contemporary culture, like the Civil War poetry of the Confederate bard Henry Timrod, resuscitated in lyrics on Dylan's newest record, *Modern Times.* Dylan's originality and his appropriations are as one.

The same might be said of *all* art. I realized this forcefully when one day I went looking for the John Donne passage quoted above. I know the lines, I confess, not from a college course but from the movie version of *84, Charing Cross Road* with Anthony Hopkins and

Anne Bancroft. I checked out *84, Charing Cross Road* from the library in the hope of finding the Donne passage, but it wasn't in the book. It's alluded to in the play that was adapted from the book, but it isn't reprinted. So I rented the movie again, and there was the passage, read in voice-over by Anthony Hopkins but without attribution. Unfortunately, the line was also abridged so that, when I finally turned to the web, I found myself searching for the line "all mankind is of one volume" instead of "all mankind is of one author, and is one volume."

My Internet search was initially no more successful than my library search. I had thought that summoning books from the vasty deep was a matter of a few keystrokes, but when I visited the website of the Yale library, I found that most of its books don't yet exist as computer text. As a last-ditch effort I searched the seemingly more obscure phrase "every chapter must be so translated." The passage I wanted finally came to me, as it turns out, not as part of a scholarly library collection but simply because someone who loves Donne had posted it on his homepage. The lines I sought were from Meditation 17 in *Devotions upon Emergent Occasions,* which happens to be the most famous thing Donne ever wrote, containing as it does the line "never send to know for whom the bell tolls; it tolls for thee." My search had led me from a movie to a book to a play to a website and back to a book. Then again, those words may be as famous as they are only because Hemingway lifted them for his book title.

Literature has been in a plundered, fragmentary state for a long time. When I was thirteen I purchased an anthology of Beat writing. Immediately, and to my very great excitement, I discovered one William S. Burroughs, author of something called *Naked Lunch,* excerpted there in all its coruscating brilliance. Burroughs was then as radical a literary man as the world had to offer. Nothing, in all my experience of literature since, has ever had as strong an effect on my sense of the sheer possibilities of writing. Later, attempting to understand this impact, I discovered that Burroughs had incorporated snippets of other writers' texts into his work, an action I knew my teachers would have called plagiarism. Some of these borrowings had been lifted from American science fiction of the forties and fifties, adding a secondary shock of recognition for me. By then I knew that this "cut-up method," as Burroughs called it, was central to whatever he thought he was doing, and that he quite literally believed it to be akin to magic. When he wrote about his process, the hairs on my neck stood up, so palpable was the excitement. Burroughs was interrogating the universe with scissors and a paste pot, and the least imitative of authors was no plagiarist at all.

Contamination Anxiety

In 1941, on his front porch, Muddy Waters recorded a song for the folklorist Alan Lomax. After singing the song, which he told Lomax was entitled "Country Blues," Waters described how he came to write it. "I made it on about the eighth of October '38," Waters said. "I was fixin' a puncture on a car. I had been mistreated by a girl. I just felt blue, and the song fell into my mind and it come to me just like that and I started singing." Then Lomax, who knew of the Robert Johnson recording called "Walkin' Blues," asked Waters if there were any other songs that used the same tune. "There's been some blues played like that," Waters replied. "This song comes from the cotton field and a boy once put a record out — Robert Johnson. He put it out as named 'Walkin' Blues.' I heard the tune before I heard it on the record. I learned it from Son House." In nearly one breath, Waters offers five accounts: his own active authorship: he "made it" on a specific date. Then the "passive" explanation: "it come to me just like that." After Lomax raises the question of influence, Waters, without shame, misgivings, or trepidation, says that he heard a version by Johnson, but that his mentor, Son House, taught it to him. In the middle of that complex genealogy, Waters declares that "this song comes from the cotton field."

Blues and jazz musicians have long been enabled by a kind of "open source" culture, in which preexisting melodic fragments and larger musical frameworks are freely reworked. Technology has only multiplied the possibilities; musicians have gained the power to *duplicate* sounds literally rather than simply approximate them through allusion. In seventies Jamaica, King Tubby and Lee "Scratch" Perry deconstructed recorded music, using astonishingly primitive predigital hardware, creating what they called "versions."

The recombinant nature of their means of production quickly spread to DJs in New York and London. Today an endless, gloriously impure, and fundamentally social process generates countless hours of music.

Visual, sound, and text collage — which for many centuries were relatively fugitive traditions (a cento here, a folk pastiche there) — became explosively central to a series of movements in the twentieth century: futurism, cubism, Dada, musique concrète, situationism, pop art, and appropriationism. In fact, collage, the common denominator in that list, might be called *the* art form of the twentieth century, never mind the twenty-first. But forget for the moment chronologies, schools, or even centuries. As examples accumulate — Igor Stravinsky's music and Daniel Johnston's, Francis Bacon's paintings and Henry Darger's, the novels of the Oulipo group and of Hannah Crafts (the author who pillaged Dickens's *Bleak House* to write *The Bondwoman's Narrative*), as well as cherished texts that become troubling to their admirers after the discovery of their "plagiarized" elements, like Richard Condon's novels or Martin Luther King Jr.'s sermons — it becomes apparent that appropriation, mimicry, quotation, allusion, and sublimated collaboration consist of a kind of sine qua non of the creative act, cutting across all forms and genres in the realm of cultural production.

In a courtroom scene from *The Simpsons* that has since entered into the television canon, an argument over the ownership of the animated characters Itchy and Scratchy rapidly escalates into an existential debate on the very nature of cartoons. "Animation is built on plagiarism!" declares the show's hot-tempered cartoon-producer-within-a-cartoon, Roger Meyers Jr. "You take away our right to steal ideas, where are they going to come from?" If nostalgic cartoonists had never borrowed from *Fritz the Cat,* there would be no *Ren & Stimpy Show;* without the Rankin/Bass and Charlie Brown Christmas specials, there would be no *South Park;* and without *The Flintstones* — more or less *The Honeymooners* in cartoon loincloths — *The Simpsons* would cease to exist. If those don't strike you as essential losses, then consider the remarkable series of "plagiarisms" that links Ovid's "Pyramus and Thisbe" with Shakespeare's *Romeo and Juliet* and Leonard Bernstein's *West Side Story,* or Shakespeare's description of Cleopatra, copied nearly verbatim from

Plutarch's life of Mark Antony and also later nicked by T. S. Eliot for *The Waste Land*. If these are examples of plagiarism, then we want more plagiarism.

Most artists are brought to their vocation when their own nascent gifts are awakened by the work of a master. That is to say, most artists are converted to art by art itself. Finding one's voice isn't just an emptying and purifying oneself of the words of others but an adopting and embracing of filiations, communities, and discourses. Inspiration could be called inhaling the memory of an act never experienced. Invention, it must be humbly admitted, does not consist in creating out of void but out of chaos. Any artist knows these truths, no matter how deeply he or she submerges that knowing.

What happens when an allusion goes unrecognized? A closer look at *The Waste Land* may help make this point. The body of Eliot's poem is a vertiginous mélange of quotation, allusion, and "original" writing. When Eliot alludes to Edmund Spenser's "Prothalamion" with the line "Sweet Thames, run softly, till I end my song," what of readers to whom the poem, never one of Spenser's most popular, is unfamiliar? (Indeed, the Spenser is now known largely because of Eliot's use of it.) Two responses are possible: grant the line to Eliot or later discover the source and understand the line as plagiarism. Eliot evidenced no small anxiety about these matters; the notes he so carefully added to *The Waste Land* can be read as a symptom of modernism's contamination anxiety. Taken from this angle, what exactly is postmodernism, except modernism without the anxiety?

Surrounded by Signs

The surrealists believed that objects in the world possess a certain but unspecifiable intensity that had been dulled by everyday use and utility. They meant to reanimate this dormant intensity, to bring their minds once again into close contact with the matter that made up their world. André Breton's maxim "Beautiful as the chance encounter of a sewing machine and an umbrella on an operating table" is an expression of the belief that simply placing objects in an unexpected context reinvigorates their mysterious qualities.

This "crisis" the surrealists identified was being simultaneously diagnosed by others. Martin Heidegger held that the essence of modernity was found in a certain technological orientation he called "enframing." This tendency encourages us to see the objects in our world only in terms of how they can serve us or be used by us. The task he identified was to find ways to resituate ourselves vis-à-vis these "objects," so that we may see them as "things" pulled into relief against the ground of their functionality. Heidegger believed that art had the great potential to reveal the "thingness" of objects.

The surrealists understood that photography and cinema could carry out this reanimating process automatically; the process of framing objects in a lens was often enough to create the charge they sought. Describing the effect, Walter Benjamin drew a comparison between the photographic apparatus and Freud's psychoanalytic methods. Just as Freud's theories "isolated and made analyzable things which had heretofore floated along unnoticed in the broad stream of perception," the photographic apparatus focuses on "hidden details of familiar objects," revealing "entirely new structural formations of the subject."

It's worth noting, then, that early in the history of photography a series of judicial decisions could well have changed the course of that art: courts were asked whether the photographer, amateur or professional, required permission before he could capture and print an image. Was the photographer *stealing* from the person or building whose photograph he shot, pirating something of private and certifiable value? Those early decisions went in favor of the pirates. Just as Walt Disney could take inspiration from Buster Keaton's *Steamboat Bill, Jr.*, the Brothers Grimm, or the existence of real mice, the photographer should be free to capture an image without compensating the source. The world that meets our eye through the lens of a camera was judged to be, with minor exceptions, a sort of public commons, where a cat may look at a king.

Novelists may glance at the stuff of the world too, but we sometimes get called to task for it. For those whose ganglia were formed pre-TV, the mimetic deployment of pop-culture icons seems at best an annoying tic and at worst a dangerous vapidity that compromises fiction's seriousness by dating it out of the Platonic Always, where it ought to reside. In a graduate workshop I briefly passed through, a certain gray eminence tried to convince us that a liter-

ary story should always eschew "any feature which serves to date it"
because "serious fiction must be Timeless." When we protested
that, in his own well-known work, characters moved about electri-
cally lit rooms, drove cars, and spoke not Anglo-Saxon but postwar
English — and further, that fiction he'd himself ratified as great,
such as Dickens's, was liberally strewn with innately topical, commercial, and time-bound references — he impatiently amended
his proscription to those explicit references that would date a story
in the "frivolous Now." When pressed, he said of course he meant
the "trendy mass-popular-media" reference. Here, transgenera-
tional discourse broke down.

I was born in 1964; I grew up watching *Captain Kangaroo*, moon
landings, zillions of TV ads, the Banana Splits, *M*A*S*H*, and *The
Mary Tyler Moore Show*. I was born with words in my mouth —
"Band-Aid," "Q-tip," "Xerox" — object-names as fixed and eternal
in my logosphere as "taxicab" and "toothbrush." The world is a
home littered with pop-culture products and their emblems. I also
came of age swamped by parodies that stood for originals yet mysterious to me — I knew Monkees before Beatles, Belmondo before
Bogart, and "remember" the movie *Summer of '42* from a *Mad* magazine satire, though I've still never seen the film itself. I'm not
alone in having been born backward into an incoherent realm of
texts, products, and images, the commercial and cultural environment with which we've both supplemented and blotted out our
natural world. I can no more claim it as "mine" than the sidewalks
and forests of the world, yet I do dwell in it, and for me to stand a
chance as either artist or citizen, I'd probably better be permitted
to name it.

Consider Walker Percy's *The Moviegoer:*

Other people, so I have read, treasure memorable moments in their
lives: the time one climbed the Parthenon at sunrise, the summer night
one met a lonely girl in Central Park and achieved with her a sweet and
natural relationship, as they say in books. I too once met a girl in Central Park, but it is not much to remember. What I remember is the time
John Wayne killed three men with a carbine as he was falling to the
dusty street in *Stagecoach,* and the time the kitten found Orson Welles in
the doorway in *The Third Man.*

Today, when we can eat Tex-Mex with chopsticks while listening to reggae and watching a YouTube rebroadcast of the Berlin

Wall's fall — i.e., when damn near *everything* presents itself as familiar — it's not a surprise that some of today's most ambitious art is going about trying to *make the familiar strange*. In so doing, in reimagining what human life might truly be like over there across the chasms of illusion, mediation, demographics, marketing, imago, and appearance, artists are paradoxically trying to restore what's taken for "real" to three whole dimensions, to reconstruct a univocally round world out of disparate streams of flat sights.

Whatever charge of tastelessness or trademark violation may be attached to the artistic appropriation of the media environment in which we swim, the alternative — to flinch, or tiptoe away into some ivory tower of irrelevance — is far worse. We're surrounded by signs; our imperative is to ignore none of them.

Usemonopoly

The idea that culture can be property — *intellectual* property — is used to justify everything from attempts to force the Girl Scouts to pay royalties for singing songs around campfires to the infringement suit brought by the estate of Margaret Mitchell against the publishers of Alice Randall's *The Wind Done Gone*. Corporations like Celera Genomics have filed for patents for human genes, while the Recording Industry Association of America has sued music downloaders for copyright infringement, reaching out-of-court settlements for thousands of dollars with defendants as young as twelve. ASCAP bleeds fees from shop owners who play background music in their stores; students and scholars are shamed from placing texts face-down on photocopy machines. At the same time, copyright is revered by most established writers and artists as a birthright and bulwark, the source of nurture for their infinitely fragile practices in a rapacious world. Plagiarism and piracy, after all, are the monsters we working artists are taught to dread, as they roam the woods surrounding our tiny preserves of regard and remuneration.

A time is marked not so much by ideas that are argued about as by ideas that are taken for granted. The character of an era hangs upon what needs no defense. In this regard, few of us question the contemporary construction of copyright. It is taken as a law, both in the sense of a universally recognizable moral absolute, like the law against murder, and as naturally inherent in our world, like the law of gravity. In fact, it is neither. Rather, copyright is an ongoing social negotiation, tenuously forged, endlessly revised, and imperfect in its every incarnation.

Thomas Jefferson, for one, considered copyright a necessary evil: he favored providing just enough incentive to create, nothing more, and thereafter allowing ideas to flow freely, as nature intended. His conception of copyright was enshrined in the Constitution, which gives Congress the authority to "promote the Progress of Science and useful Arts, by securing for limited Times to Authors and Inventors the exclusive Right to their respective Writings and Discoveries." This was a balancing act between creators and society as a whole; second comers might do a much better job than the originator with the original idea.

But Jefferson's vision has not fared well, has in fact been steadily eroded by those who view the culture as a market in which everything of value should be owned by someone or other. The distinctive feature of modern American copyright law is its almost limitless bloating — its expansion in both scope and duration. With no registration requirement, every creative act in a tangible medium is now subject to copyright protection: your e-mail to your child or your child's finger painting, both are automatically protected. The first Congress to grant copyright gave authors an initial term of fourteen years, which could be renewed for another fourteen if the author still lived. The current term is the life of the author plus seventy years. It's only a slight exaggeration to say that each time Mickey Mouse is about to fall into the public domain, the mouse's copyright term is extended.

Even as the law becomes more restrictive, technology is exposing those restrictions as bizarre and arbitrary. When old laws fixed on reproduction as the compensable (or actionable) unit, it wasn't because there was anything fundamentally invasive of an author's rights in the making of a copy. Rather it was because copies were once easy to find and count, so they made a useful benchmark for deciding when an owner's rights had been invaded. In the contemporary world, though, the act of "copying" is in no meaningful sense equivalent to an infringement — we make a copy every time we accept an e-mailed text, or send or forward one — and is impossible anymore to regulate or even describe.

At the movies, my entertainment is sometimes lately preceded by a dire trailer, produced by the lobbying group called the Motion Picture Association of America, in which the purchasing of a bootleg copy of a Hollywood film is compared to the theft of a car or a handbag — and, as the bullying supertitles remind us, "You wouldn't steal a handbag!" This conflation forms an incitement to quit thinking. If I were to tell you that pirating DVDs or downloading music is in no way different from loaning a friend a book, my own arguments would be as ethically bankrupt as the MPAA's. The truth lies somewhere in the vast gray area between these two overstated positions. For a car or a handbag, once stolen, no longer is available to its owner, while the appropriation of an article of "intellectual property" leaves the original untouched. As Jefferson wrote, "He who receives an idea from me, receives instruction himself without lessening mine; as he who lights his taper at mine, receives light without darkening me."

Yet industries of cultural capital, who profit not from creating but from distributing, see the sale of culture as a zero-sum game. The piano-roll publishers fear the record companies, who fear the cassette-tape manufacturers, who fear the online vendors, who fear whoever else is next in line to profit most quickly from the intangible and infinitely reproducible fruits of an artist's labor. It has been the same in every industry and with every technological innovation. Jack Valenti, speaking for the MPAA: "I say to you that the VCR is to the American film producer and the American public as the Boston Strangler is to the woman home alone."

Thinking clearly sometimes requires unbraiding our language. The word "copyright" may eventually seem as dubious in its embedded purposes as "family values," "globalization," and, sure, "intellectual property." Copyright is a "right" in no absolute sense; it is a government-granted monopoly on the use of creative results. So let's try calling it that — not a right but a *monopoly on use,* a "usemonopoly" — and then consider how the rapacious expansion of monopoly rights has always been counter to the public interest, no matter if it is Andrew Carnegie controlling the price of steel or Walt Disney managing the fate of his mouse. Whether the monopolizing beneficiary is a living artist or some artist's heirs or some corporation's shareholders, the loser is the community, including living artists who might make splendid use of a healthy public domain.

The Beauty of Second Use

A few years ago someone brought me a strange gift, purchased at MOMA's downtown design store: a copy of my own first novel, *Gun, with Occasional Music,* expertly cut into the contours of a pistol. The object was the work of Robert The, an artist whose specialty is the reincarnation of everyday materials. I regard my first book as an old friend, one who never fails to remind me of the spirit with which I entered into this game of art and commerce — that to be allowed to insert the materials of my imagination onto the shelves of bookstores and into the minds of readers (if only a handful) was a wild privilege. I was paid six thousand dollars for three years of writing, but at the time I'd have happily published the results for nothing. Now my old friend had come home in a new form, one I was unlikely to have imagined for it myself. The gun-book wasn't readable, exactly, but I couldn't take offense at that. The fertile spirit of stray connection this appropriated object conveyed back to me — the strange beauty of its second use — was a reward for being a published writer I could never have fathomed in advance. And the world makes room for both my novel and Robert The's gun-book. There's no need to choose between the two.

In the first life of creative property, if the creator is lucky, the content is sold. After the commercial life has ended, our tradition supports a second life as well. A newspaper is delivered to a door-step, and the next day wraps fish or builds an archive. Most books fall out of print after one year, yet even within that period they can be sold in used bookstores and stored in libraries, quoted in reviews, parodied in magazines, described in conversations, and plundered for costumes for kids to wear on Halloween. The demarcation between various possible uses is beautifully graded and hard to define, the more so as artifacts distill into and repercuss through the realm of culture into which they've been entered, the more so as they engage the receptive minds for whom they were presumably intended.

Active reading is an impertinent raid on the literary preserve. Readers are like nomads, poaching their way across fields they do not own — artists are no more able to control the imaginations of their audiences than the culture industry is able to control second uses of its artifacts. In the children's classic *The Velveteen Rabbit,* the old Skin Horse offers the Rabbit a lecture on the practice of textual poaching. The value of a new toy lies not in its material qualities (not "having things that buzz inside you and a stick-out handle"), the Skin Horse explains, but rather in how the toy is used. "Real isn't how you are made . . . It's a thing that happens to you. When a child loves you for a long, long time, not just to play with, but REALLY loves you, then you become Real." The Rabbit is fearful, recognizing that consumer goods don't become "real" without being actively reworked: "Does it hurt?" Reassuring him, the Skin Horse says: "It doesn't happen all at once . . . You become. It takes a long time . . . Generally, by the time you are Real, most of your hair has been loved off, and your eyes drop out and you get loose in the joints and very shabby." Seen from the perspective of the toymaker, the Velveteen Rabbit's loose joints and missing eyes represent vandalism, signs of misuse and rough treatment; for others, these are marks of its loving use.

Artists and their surrogates who fall into the trap of seeking recompense for every possible second use end up attacking their own best audience members for the crime of exalting and enshrining their work. The Recording Industry Association of America prosecuting its own record-buying public makes as little sense as the novelists who bristle at autographing used copies of their books for collectors. And artists, or their heirs, who fall into the trap of attacking the collagists and satirists and digital samplers of their work are attacking the next generation of creators for the crime of being influenced, for the crime of responding with the same mixture of intoxication, resentment, lust, and glee that characterizes all artistic successors. By doing so they make the world smaller, betraying what seems to me the primary motivation for participating in the world of culture in the first place: to make the world larger.

Source Hypocrisy, or, Disnial

The Walt Disney Company has drawn an astonishing catalog from the work of others: *Snow White and the Seven Dwarfs, Fantasia, Pinocchio, Dumbo, Bambi, Song of the South, Cinderella, Alice in Wonder-*

land, Robin Hood, Peter Pan, Lady and the Tramp, Mulan, Sleeping Beauty, The Sword in the Stone, The Jungle Book, and, alas, *Treasure Planet,* a legacy of cultural sampling that Shakespeare, or De La Soul, could get behind. Yet Disney's protectorate of lobbyists has policed the resulting cache of cultural materials as vigilantly as if it were Fort Knox — threatening legal action, for instance, against the artist Dennis Oppenheim for the use of Disney characters in a sculpture, and prohibiting the scholar Holly Crawford from using any Disney-related images — including artwork by Lichtenstein, Warhol, Oldenburg, and others — in her monograph *Attached to the Mouse: Disney and Contemporary Art.*

This peculiar and specific act — the enclosure of common-wealth culture for the benefit of a sole or corporate owner — is close kin to what could be called *imperial plagiarism,* the free use of Third World or "primitive" artworks and styles by more privi-leged (and better-paid) artists. Think of Picasso's *Les Demoiselles d'Avignon,* or some of the albums of Paul Simon or David Byrne: even without violating copyright, those creators have sometimes come in for a certain skepticism when the extent of their out-sourcing became evident. And, as when Led Zeppelin found them-selves sued for back royalties by the bluesman Willie Dixon, the act can occasionally be an expensive one. *To live outside the law, you must be honest:* perhaps it was this, in part, that spurred David Byrne and Brian Eno to recently launch a "remix" website where anyone can download easily disassembled versions of two songs from *My Life in the Bush of Ghosts,* an album reliant on vernacular speech sampled from a host of sources. Perhaps it also explains why Bob Dylan has never refused a request for a sample.

Kenneth Koch once said, "I'm a writer who likes to be influ-enced." It was a charming confession, and a rare one. For so many artists, the act of creativity is intended as a Napoleonic imposition of one's uniqueness upon the universe — *après moi le déluge* of copycats! And for every James Joyce or Woody Guthrie or Martin Luther King Jr. or Walt Disney who gathered a constellation of voices in his work, there may seem to be some corporation or liter-ary estate eager to stopper the bottle: cultural debts flow in, but they don't flow out. We might call this tendency "source hypoc-risy." Or we could name it after the most pernicious source hypo-crites of all time: Disnial.

You Can't Steal a Gift

My reader may, understandably, be on the verge of crying, "Communist!" A large, diverse society cannot survive without property; a large, diverse, and modern society cannot flourish without some form of intellectual property. But it takes little reflection to grasp that there is ample value that the term "property" doesn't capture. And works of art exist simultaneously in two economies, a market economy and a *gift economy.*

The cardinal difference between gift and commodity exchange is that a gift establishes a feeling-bond between two people, whereas the sale of a commodity leaves no necessary connection. I go into a hardware store, pay the man for a hacksaw blade, and walk out. I may never see him again. The disconnectedness is, in fact, a virtue of the commodity mode. We don't want to be bothered, and if the clerk always wants to chat about the family, I'll shop elsewhere. I just want a hacksaw blade. But a gift makes a connection. There are many examples, the candy or cigarette offered to a stranger who shares a seat on the plane, the few words that indicate goodwill between passengers on the late-night bus. These tokens establish the simplest bonds of social life, but the model they offer may be extended to the most complicated of unions — marriage, parenthood, mentorship. If a value is placed on these (often essentially unequal) exchanges, they degenerate into something else.

Yet one of the more difficult things to comprehend is that the gift economies — like those that sustain open-source software — coexist so naturally with the market. It is precisely this doubleness in art practices that we must identify, ratify, and enshrine in our lives as participants in culture, either as "producers" or "consumers." Art that matters to us — which moves the heart, or revives the soul, or delights the senses, or offers courage for living, however we choose to describe the experience — is received as a gift is received. Even if we've paid a fee at the door of the museum or concert hall, when we are touched by a work of art something comes to us that has nothing to do with the price. The daily commerce of our lives proceeds at its own constant level, but a gift conveys an uncommodifiable surplus of inspiration.

The way we treat a thing can change its nature, though. Religions often prohibit the sale of sacred objects, the implication being that their sanctity is lost if they are bought and sold. We consider it unacceptable to sell sex, babies, body organs, legal rights, and votes. The idea that something should never be commodified is generally known as *inalienability* or *unalienability* — a concept most famously expressed by Thomas Jefferson in the phrase "endowed by their Creator with certain unalienable Rights." A work of art seems to be a hardier breed; it can be sold in the market and still emerge a work of art. But if it is true that in the essential commerce of art a gift is carried by the work from the artist to his audience, if I am right to say that where there is no gift there is no art, then it may be possible to destroy a work of art by converting it into a pure commodity. I don't maintain that art can't be bought and sold, but that the gift portion of the work places a constraint upon our merchandising. This is the reason why even a really beautiful, ingenious, powerful ad (of which there are a lot) can never be any kind of real art: an ad has no status as gift; that is, it's never really *for* the person it's directed at.

The power of a gift economy remains difficult for the empiricists of our market culture to understand. In our times, the rhetoric of the market presumes that everything should be and can be appropriately bought, sold, and owned — a tide of alienation lapping daily at the dwindling redoubt of the unalienable. In free-market theory, an intervention to halt propertization is considered "paternalistic," because it inhibits the free action of the citizen, now reposited as a "potential entrepreneur." Of course, in the real world, we know that child-rearing, family life, education, socialization, sexuality, political life, and many other basic human activities require insulation from market forces. In fact, paying for many of these things can ruin them. We may be willing to peek at *Who Wants to Marry a Multi-Millionaire?* or an eBay auction of the ova of fashion models, but only to reassure ourselves that some things are still beneath our standards of dignity.

What's remarkable about gift economies is that they can flourish in the most unlikely places — in rundown neighborhoods, on the Internet, in scientific communities, and among members of Alcoholics Anonymous. A classic example is commercial blood systems, which generally produce blood supplies of lower safety, purity, and potency than volunteer systems. A gift economy may be superior when it comes to maintaining a group's commitment to certain extra-market values.

The Commons

Another way of understanding the presence of gift economies — which dwell like ghosts in the commercial machine — is in the sense of a *public commons.* A commons, of course, is anything like the streets over which we drive, the skies through which we pilot airplanes, or the public parks or beaches on which we dally. A commons belongs to everyone and no one, and its use is controlled only by common consent. A commons describes resources like the body of ancient music drawn on by composers and folk musicians alike, rather than the commodities, like "Happy Birthday to You," for which ASCAP, 114 years after it was written, continues to collect a fee. Einstein's theory of relativity is a commons. Writings in the public domain are a commons. Gossip about celebrities is a commons. The silence in a movie theater is a transitory commons, impossibly fragile, treasured by those who crave it, and constructed as a mutual gift by those who compose it.

The world of art and culture is a vast commons, one that is salted through with zones of utter commerce yet remains gloriously immune to any overall commodification. The closest resemblance is to the commons of a *language:* altered by every contributor, expanded by even the most passive user. That a language is a commons doesn't mean that the community owns it; rather, it belongs *between* people, possessed by no one, not even by society as a whole.

Nearly any commons, though, can be encroached upon, partitioned, enclosed. The American commons include tangible assets such as public forests and minerals, intangible wealth such as copyrights and patents, critical infrastructures such as the Internet and government research, and cultural resources such as the broadcast airwaves and public spaces. They include resources we've paid for as taxpayers and inherited from previous generations. They're not just an inventory of marketable assets; they're social institutions and cultural traditions that define us as Americans and enliven us as human beings. Some invasions of the commons are sanctioned because we can no longer muster a spirited commitment to the public sector. The abuse goes unnoticed because the theft of the commons is seen in glimpses, not in panorama. We may occasionally see a former wetland paved; we may hear about the breakthrough cancer drug that tax dollars helped develop, the rights to which pharmaceutical companies acquired for a song. The larger movement goes too much unremarked. The notion of a *commons of cultural materials* goes more or less unnamed.

Honoring the commons is not a matter of moral exhortation. It is a practical necessity. We in Western society are going through a period of intensifying belief in private ownership, to the detriment of the public good. We have to remain constantly vigilant to prevent raids by those who would selfishly exploit our common heritage for their private gain. Such raids on our natural resources are not examples of enterprise and initiative. They are attempts to take from all the people just for the benefit of a few.

Undiscovered Public Knowledge

Artists and intellectuals despondent over the prospects for originality can take heart from a phenomenon identified about twenty years ago by Don Swanson, a library scientist at the University of Chicago. He called it "undiscovered public knowledge." Swanson showed that standing problems in medical research may be significantly addressed, perhaps even solved, simply by systematically surveying the scientific literature. Left to its own devices, research tends to become more specialized and abstracted from the real-world problems that motivated it and to which it remains relevant. This suggests that such a problem may be tackled effectively not by commissioning more research but by assuming that most or all of the solution can already be found in various scientific journals, waiting to be assembled by someone willing to read across specialties. Swanson himself did this in the case of Raynaud's syndrome, a disease that causes the fingers of young women to become numb. His finding is especially striking — perhaps even scandalous — because it happened in the ever-expanding biomedical sciences.

Undiscovered public knowledge emboldens us to question the extreme claims to originality made in press releases and publishers' notices: is an intellectual or creative offering truly novel, or have we just forgotten a worthy precursor? Does solving certain scientific problems really require massive additional funding, or could a computerized search engine, creatively deployed, do the same job more quickly and cheaply? Lastly, does our appetite for creative vitality require the violence and exasperation of another avant-garde, with its wearisome killing-the-father imperatives, or might we be better off ratifying *the ecstasy of influence* — and deepening our willingness to understand the commonality and time-lessness of the methods and motifs available to artists?

Give All

A few years ago, the Film Society of Lincoln Center announced a retrospective of the works of Dariush Mehrjui, then a fresh enthusiasm of mine. Mehrjui is one of Iran's finest filmmakers, and the only one whose subject was personal relationships among the upper-middle-class intelligentsia. Needless to say, opportunities to view his films were — and remain — rare indeed. I headed uptown for one, an adaptation of J. D. Salinger's *Franny and Zooey,* titled *Pari,* only to discover at the door of the Walter Reade Theater that the screening had been canceled: its announcement had brought threat of a lawsuit down on the Film Society. True, these were Salinger's rights under the law. Yet why would he care that some obscure Iranian filmmaker had paid him homage with a meditation on his heroine? Would it have damaged his book or robbed him of some crucial remuneration had the screening been permitted? The fertile spirit of stray connection — one stretching across what is presently seen as the direst of international breaches — had in this case been snuffed out. The cold, undead hand of one of my childhood literary heroes had reached out from its New Hampshire redoubt to arrest my present-day curiosity.

A few assertions, then:

Any text that has infiltrated the common mind to the extent of *Gone With the Wind* or *Lolita* or *Ulysses* inexorably joins the language of culture. A map-turned-to-landscape, it has moved to a place beyond enclosure or control. The authors and their heirs should consider the subsequent parodies, refractions, quotations, and revisions an honor, or at least the price of a rare success.

A corporation that has imposed an inescapable notion — Mickey Mouse, Band-Aid — on the cultural language should pay a similar price.

The primary objective of copyright is not to reward the labor of authors but "to promote the Progress of Science and useful Arts." To this end, copyright assures authors the right to their original expression but encourages others to build freely upon the ideas and information conveyed by a work. This result is neither unfair nor unfortunate.

Contemporary copyright, trademark, and patent law is presently corrupted. The case for perpetual copyright is a denial of the essential gift-aspect of the creative act. Arguments in its favor are as un-American as those for the repeal of the estate tax.

Art is sourced. Apprentices graze in the field of culture.

Digital sampling is an art method like any other, neutral in itself.

Despite hand-wringing at each technological turn — radio, the Internet — the future will be much like the past. Artists will sell some things but also give some things away. Change may be troubling for those who crave less ambiguity, but the life of an artist has never been filled with certainty.

The dream of a perfect systematic remuneration is nonsense. I pay rent with the price my words bring when published in glossy magazines and at the same moment offer them for almost nothing to impoverished literary quarterlies, or speak them for free into the air in a radio interview. So what are they worth? What would they be worth if some future Dylan worked them into a song? Should I care to make such a thing impossible?

Any text is woven entirely with citations, references, echoes, cultural languages, which cut across it through and through in a vast stereophony. The citations that go to make up a text are anonymous, untraceable, and yet *already read;* they are quotations without inverted commas. The kernel, the soul — let us go further and say the substance, the bulk, the actual and valuable material of all human utterances — is plagiarism. For substantially all ideas are secondhand, consciously and unconsciously drawn from a million outside sources, and daily used by the garnerer with a pride and satisfaction born of the superstition that he originated them; whereas there is not a rag of originality about them anywhere except the little discoloration they get from his mental and moral caliber and his temperament, and which is revealed in characteristics

of phrasing. Old and new make the warp and woof of every moment. There is no thread that is not a twist of these two strands. By
necessity, by proclivity, and by delight, we all quote. Neurological
study has lately shown that memory, imagination, and consciousness itself is stitched, quilted, pastiched. If we cut-and-paste our
selves, might we not forgive it of our artworks?

Artists and writers — and our advocates, our guilds and agents
— too often subscribe to implicit claims of originality that do injury to these truths. And we too often, as hucksters and bean counters in the tiny enterprises of our selves, act to spite the gift portion
of our privileged roles. People live differently who treat a portion
of their wealth as a gift. If we devalue and obscure the gift-economy
function of our art practices, we turn our works into nothing more
than advertisements for themselves. We may console ourselves that
our lust for subsidiary rights in virtual perpetuity is some heroic
counter to rapacious corporate interests. But the truth is that with
artists pulling on one side and corporations pulling on the other,
the loser is the collective public imagination from which we were
nourished in the first place, and whose existence as the ultimate
repository of our offerings makes the work worth doing in the first
place.

As a novelist, I'm a cork on the ocean of story, a leaf on a windy
day. Pretty soon I'll be blown away. For the moment I'm grateful to
be making a living, and so must ask that for a limited time (in the
Thomas Jefferson sense) you please respect my small, treasured
usemonopolies. Don't pirate my editions; do plunder my visions.
The name of the game is Give All. You, reader, are welcome to my
stories. They were never mine in the first place, but I gave them to
you. If you have the inclination to pick them up, take them with my
blessing.

Key: I Is Another

This key to the preceding essay names the source of every line I stole,
warped, and cobbled together as I "wrote" (except, alas, those sources
I forgot along the way). First uses of a given author or speaker are
highlighted in bold. Nearly every sentence I culled I also revised, at
least slightly — for necessities of space, in order to produce a more
consistent tone, or simply because I felt like it.

TITLE

The phrase "the ecstasy of influence," which embeds a rebuking play on Harold Bloom's "anxiety of influence," is lifted from spoken remarks by Professor **Richard Dienst** of Rutgers.

LOVE AND THEFT

". . . a cultivated man of middle age . . ." to ". . . hidden, unacknowledged memory?" These lines, with some adjustments for tone, belong to the **anonymous editor** or **assistant** who wrote the dust-flap copy of **Michael Maar**'s *The Two Lolitas*. Of course, in my own experience, dust-flap copy is often a collaboration between author and editor. Perhaps this was also true for Maar.

"The history of literature . . ." to ". . . borrow and quote?" comes from Maar's book itself.

"Appropriation has always . . ." to ". . . Ishmael and Queequeg . . ." This paragraph makes a hash of remarks from an interview with **Eric Lott** conducted by **David McNair** and **Jayson Whitehead**, and incorporates both interviewers' and interviewee's observations. (The text-interview form can be seen as a commonly accepted form of multivocal writing. Most interviewers prime their subjects with remarks of their own — leading the witness, so to speak — and gently refine their subjects' statements in the final printed transcript.)

"I realized this . . ." to ". . . for a long time." The anecdote is cribbed, with an elision to avoid appropriating a dead grandmother, from **Jonathan Rosen**'s *The Talmud and the Internet*. I've never seen *84, Charing Cross Road,* nor searched the web for a Donne quote. For me it was through Rosen to Donne, Hemingway, website, et al.

"When I was thirteen . . ." to ". . . no plagiarist at all." This is from **William Gibson**'s "God's Little Toys," in *Wired* magazine. My own first encounter with William Burroughs, also at age thirteen, was less epiphanic. Having grown up with a painter father who, during family visits to galleries or museums, approvingly noted collage and appropriation techniques in the visual arts (Picasso, Claes Oldenburg, Stuart Davis), I was gratified, but not surprised, to learn that literature could encompass the same methods.

CONTAMINATION ANXIETY

"In 1941, on his front porch . . ." to ". . . 'this song comes from the cotton field.'" **Siva Vaidhyanathan**, *Copyrights and Copywrongs*.

". . . enabled by a kind . . . freely reworked." **Kembrew McLeod**, *Free-*

dom of Expression. In *Owning Culture,* McLeod notes that, as he was writing, he

> happened to be listening to a lot of old country music, and in my casual listening I noticed that *six* country songs shared *exactly* the same vocal melody, including Hank Thompson's "Wild Side of Life," the Carter Family's "I'm Thinking Tonight of My Blue Eyes," Roy Acuff's "Great Speckled Bird," Kitty Wells's "It Wasn't God Who Made Honky Tonk Angels," Reno & Smiley's "I'm Using My Bible for a Roadmap," and Townes Van Zandt's "Heavenly Houseboat Blues." . . . In his extensively researched book, *Country: The Twisted Roots of Rock 'n' Roll,* Nick Tosches documents that the melody these songs share is both "ancient and British." There were no recorded lawsuits stemming from these appropriations . . .

". . . musicians have gained . . . through allusion." **Joanna Demers**, *Steal This Music.*

"In seventies Jamaica . . ." to ". . . hours of music." Gibson.

"Visual, sound, and text collage . . ." to ". . . realm of cultural production." This plunders, rewrites, and amplifies paragraphs from McLeod's *Owning Culture,* except for the line about collage being the art form of the twentieth and twenty-first centuries, which I heard filmmaker **Craig Baldwin** say, in defense of sampling, in the trailer for a forthcoming documentary, *Copyright Criminals.*

"In a courtroom scene . . ." to ". . . would cease to exist." **Dave Itzkoff**, *New York Times.*

". . . the remarkable series of 'plagiarisms' . . ." to ". . . we want more plagiarism." **Richard Posner**, combined from The Becker-Posner Blog and the *Atlantic Monthly.*

"Most artists are brought . . ." to ". . . by art itself." These words, and many more to follow, come from **Lewis Hyde**'s *The Gift.* Above any other book I've here plagiarized, I commend *The Gift* to your attention.

"Finding one's voice . . . filiations, communities, and discourses." Semanticist **George L. Dillon**, quoted in **Rebecca Moore Howard**'s "The New Abolitionism Comes to Plagiarism."

"Inspiration could be . . . act never experienced." **Ned Rorem**, found on several "great quotations" sites on the Internet.

"Invention, it must be humbly admitted . . . out of chaos." **Mary Shelley**, from her introduction to *Frankenstein.*

"What happens . . ." to ". . . contamination anxiety." **Kevin J. H.**

Dettmar, from "The Illusion of Modernist Allusion and the Politics of Postmodern Plagiarism."

SURROUNDED BY SIGNS

"The surrealists believed . . ." to the Walter Benjamin quote. **Christian Keathley**'s *Cinephilia and History, or, The Wind in the Trees*, a book that treats fannish fetishism as the secret at the heart of film scholarship. Keathley notes, for instance, Joseph Cornell's surrealist-influenced 1936 film *Rose Hobart*, which simply records "the way in which Cornell himself watched the 1931 Hollywood potboiler *East of Borneo*, fascinated and distracted as he was by its B-grade star" — the star, of course, being Rose Hobart herself. This, I suppose, makes Cornell a sort of father to computer-enabled fan-creator reworkings of Hollywood product, like the version of George Lucas's *The Phantom Menace* from which the noxious Jar Jar Binks character was purged; both incorporate a viewer's subjective preferences into a revision of a filmmaker's work.

". . . early in the history of photography" to ". . . without compensating the source." From *Free Culture*, by **Lawrence Lessig**, the greatest of public advocates for copyright reform and the best source if you want to get radicalized in a hurry.

"For those whose ganglia . . ." to ". . . discourse broke down." From **David Foster Wallace**'s essay "E Unibus Pluram," reprinted in *A Supposedly Fun Thing I'll Never Do Again*. I have no idea who Wallace's "gray eminence" is or was. I inserted the example of Dickens into the paragraph; he strikes me as overlooked in the lineage of authors of "brand-name" fiction.

"I was born . . . *Mary Tyler Moore Show.*" These are the reminiscences of **Mark Hosler** from Negativland, a collaging musical collective that was sued by U2's record label for its appropriation of "I Still Haven't Found What I'm Looking For." Although I had to adjust the birth date, Hosler's cultural menu fits me like a glove.

"The world is a home . . . pop-culture products . . ." McLeod.

"Today, when we can eat . . ." to ". . . flat sights." Wallace.

"We're surrounded by signs, ignore none of them." This phrase, which I unfortunately rendered somewhat leaden with the word "imperative," comes from **Steve Erickson**'s novel *Our Ecstatic Days*.

USEMONOPOLY

". . . everything from attempts . . ." to "defendants as young as twelve." **Robert Boynton**, the *New York Times Magazine*, "The Tyranny of Copyright?"

"A time is marked . . ." to ". . . what needs no defense." Lessig, this time from *The Future of Ideas.*

"Thomas Jefferson, for one . . ." to "'. . . respective Writings and Discoveries.'" Boynton.

". . . second comers might do a much better job than the originator . . ." I found this phrase in Lessig, who is quoting Vaidhyanathan, who himself is characterizing a judgment written by **Learned Hand**.

"But Jefferson's vision . . . owned by someone or other." Boynton.

"The distinctive feature . . ." to ". . . term is extended." Lessig, again from *The Future of Ideas.*

"When old laws . . ." to ". . . had been invaded." **Jessica Litman**, *Digital Copyright.*

"'I say to you . . . woman home alone.'" I found the Valenti quote in McLeod. Now fill in the blank: Jack Valenti is to the public domain as _____ is to _____.

THE BEAUTY OF SECOND USE

"In the first . . ." to ". . . builds an archive." Lessig.

"Most books . . . one year . . ." Lessig.

"Active reading is . . ." to ". . . do not own . . ." This is a mash-up of **Henry Jenkins**, from his *Textual Poachers: Television Fans and Participatory Culture,* and **Michel de Certeau**, whom Jenkins quotes.

"In the children's classic . . ." to ". . . its loving use." Jenkins. (Incidentally, have the holders of the copyright to *The Velveteen Rabbit* had a close look at *Toy Story*? There could be a lawsuit there.)

SOURCE HYPOCRISY, OR, DISNIAL

"The Walt Disney Company . . . alas, *Treasure Planet* . . ." Lessig.

"Imperial Plagiarism" is the title of an essay by **Marilyn Randall.**

". . . spurred David Byrne . . . *My Life in the Bush of Ghosts* . . ." **Chris Dahlen**, *Pitchfork* — though in truth by the time I'd finished, his words were so utterly dissolved within my own that had I been an ordinary cutting-and-pasting journalist it never would have occurred to me to give Dahlen a citation. The effort of preserving another's distinctive phrases as I worked on this essay was sometimes beyond my capacities; this form of plagiarism was oddly hard work.

"Kenneth Koch . . ." to ". . . *déluge* of copycats!" **Emily Nussbaum**, the *New York Times Book Review.*

YOU CAN'T STEAL A GIFT

"You can't steal a gift." **Dizzy Gillespie**, defending another player who'd been accused of poaching Charlie Parker's style: "You can't steal a gift. Bird gave the world his music, and if you can hear it you can have it."

"A large, diverse society . . . intellectual property." Lessig.

"And works of art . . ." to ". . . marriage, parenthood, mentorship." Hyde.

"Yet one . . . so naturally with the market." **David Bollier**, *Silent Theft*.

"Art that matters . . ." to ". . . bought and sold." Hyde.

"We consider it unacceptable . . ." to "'. . . certain unalienable Rights . . .'" Bollier, paraphrasing **Margaret Jane Radin**'s *Contested Commodities*.

"A work of art . . ." to ". . . constraint upon our merchandising." Hyde.

"This is the reason . . . person it's directed at." Wallace.

"The power of a gift . . ." to ". . . certain extra-market values." Bollier, and also the sociologist **Warren O. Hagstrom**, whom Bollier is paraphrasing.

THE COMMONS

"Einstein's theory . . ." to ". . . public domain are a commons." Lessig.

"That a language is a commons . . . society as a whole." **Michael Newton**, in the *London Review of Books*, reviewing a book called *Echolalias: On the Forgetting of Language* by **Daniel Heller-Roazen**. The paraphrases of book reviewers are another covert form of collaborative culture; as an avid reader of reviews, I know much about books I've never read. To quote Yann Martel on how he came to be accused of imperial plagiarism in his Booker-winning novel *Life of Pi*:

> Ten or so years ago, I read a review by John Updike in the *New York Times Review of Books* [sic]. It was of a novel by a Brazilian writer, Moacyr Scliar. I forget the title, and John Updike did worse: he clearly thought the book as a whole was forgettable. His review — one of those that makes you suspicious by being mostly descriptive . . . oozed indifference. But one thing about it struck me: the premise . . . Oh, the wondrous things I could do with this premise.

Unfortunately, no one was ever able to locate the Updike review in question.

"The American commons . . ." to ". . . for a song." Bollier.

"Honoring the commons . . ." to ". . . practical necessity." Bollier.

"We in Western . . . public good." **John Sulston**, Nobel Prize winner and co-mapper of the human genome.

"We have to remain . . ." to ". . . benefit of a few." **Harry Truman** at the opening of Everglades National Park. Although it may seem the height of presumption to rip off a president — I found claiming Truman's stolid advocacy as my own embarrassing in the extreme — I didn't rewrite him at all. As the poet Marianne Moore said, "If a thing had been said in the *best* way, how can you say it better?" Moore confessed her penchant for incorporating lines from others' works, explaining, "I have not yet been able to outgrow this hybrid method of composition."

UNDISCOVERED PUBLIC KNOWLEDGE

". . . intellectuals despondent . . ." to ". . . quickly and cheaply?" **Steve Fuller**, *The Intellectual.* There's something of Borges in Fuller's insight here; the notion of a storehouse of knowledge waiting passively to be assembled by future users is suggestive of both "The Library of Babel" and "Kafka and His Precursors."

GIVE ALL

". . . one of Iran's finest . . ." to ". . . meditation on his heroine?" **Amy Taubin**, *Village Voice,* although it was me who was disappointed at the door of the Walter Reade Theater.

"The primary objective . . ." to ". . . unfair nor unfortunate." **Sandra Day O'Connor**, 1991.

". . . the future will be much like the past" to ". . . give some things away." Open-source film archivist **Rick Prelinger**, quoted in McLeod.

"Change may be troubling . . . with certainty." McLeod.

". . . woven entirely . . ." to ". . . without inverted commas." **Roland Barthes**.

"The kernel, the soul . . ." to ". . . characteristics of phrasing." **Mark Twain**, from a consoling letter to Helen Keller, who had suffered distressing accusations of plagiarism (!). In fact, her work included unconsciously memorized phrases; under Keller's particular circumstances, her writing could be understood as a kind of allegory of the "constructed" nature of artistic perception. I found the Twain quote in the aforementioned *Copyrights and Copywrongs,* by Siva Vaidhyanathan.

"Old and new . . ." to ". . . we all quote." **Ralph Waldo Emerson**. These guys all sound alike!

"People live differently . . . wealth as a gift." Hyde.

". . . I'm a cork . . ." to ". . . blown away." This is adapted from the Beach Boys song "Til I Die," written by **Brian Wilson**. My own first adventure with song-lyric permissions came when I tried to have a character in my second novel quote the lyrics "There's a world where I can go and / Tell my secrets to / In my room / In my room." After learning the likely expense, at my editor's suggestion I replaced those with "You take the high road / I'll take the low road / I'll be in Scotland before you," a lyric in the public domain. This capitulation always bugged me, and in the subsequent British publication of the same book I restored the Brian Wilson lyric, without permission. *Ocean of Story* is the title of a collection of **Christina Stead**'s short fiction.

Saul Bellow, writing to a friend who'd taken offense at Bellow's fictional use of certain personal facts, said: "The name of the game is Give All. You are welcome to all my facts. You know them, I give them to you. If you have the strength to pick them up, take them with my blessing." I couldn't bring myself to retain Bellow's "strength," which seemed presumptuous in my new context, though it is surely the more elegant phrase. On the other hand, I was pleased to invite the suggestion that the gifts in question may actually be light and easily lifted.

Key to the Key

The notion of a collage text is, of course, not original to me. **Walter Benjamin**'s incomplete *Arcades Project* seemingly would have featured extensive interlaced quotations. Other precedents include **Graham Rawle**'s novel *Diary of an Amateur Photographer,* its text harvested from photography magazines, and **Eduardo Paolozzi**'s collage novel *Kex,* cobbled from crime novels and newspaper clippings. Closer to home, my efforts owe a great deal to the recent essays of **David Shields**, in which diverse quotes are made to closely intertwine and reverberate, and to conversations with editor **Sean Howe** and archivist **Pamela Jackson**. Last year **David Edelstein**, in *New York* magazine, satirized the Kaavya Viswanathan plagiarism case by creating an almost completely plagiarized column denouncing her actions. Edelstein intended to demonstrate, through ironic example, how bricolage such as his own was ipso facto facile and unworthy. Although Viswanathan's version of "creative copying" was a pitiable one, I differ with Edelstein's conclusions.

The phrase *Je est un autre*, with its deliberately awkward syntax, belongs to **Arthur Rimbaud**. It has been translated both as "I is another" and "I is someone else," as in this excerpt from Rimbaud's letters:

For I is someone else. If brass wakes up a trumpet, it is not its fault. To me this is obvious: I witness the unfolding of my own thought: I watch it, I listen to it: I make a stroke of the bow: the symphony begins to stir in the depths, or springs on to the stage.

If the old fools had not discovered only the *false* significance of the Ego, we should not now be having to sweep away those millions of skeletons which, since time immemorial, have been piling up the fruits of their one-eyed intellects, and claiming to be, themselves, the authors!

ARIEL LEVY

The Lesbian Bride's Handbook

FROM *New York*

WHAT IS THE RIGHT THING to wear to a wedding? Women have been asking themselves this question for generations and, I suppose, coming up with many of the same answers as I have. Black and gray, the colors I usually wear, are obviously too somber. Red is a bad idea: too garish, too iconic — the whore instead of the virgin — and, as a saleswoman at Saks explained to me, one doesn't want to draw attention away from the bride. But then, I am the bride. Sort of.

For several months, admitting that detail filled me with a flickering dread. I knew what would inevitably follow: "Why aren't you wearing white?" Eventually, I realized that, obviously, I could just tell Katie at Barneys or Jen at Chloé, "Because I prefer color." But at first, I felt compelled to tell the whole mortifying truth: "Because it's a gay wedding." Or, if I couldn't quite get those words out of my mouth: "Because it's not a real wedding."

A real wedding was not something I was raised to want. My parents were bohemians of a sort, and real weddings were like real jobs: square. As my mother has managed to mention on numerous occasions, she would have liked to elope, but to please her parents, there was a modest reception; she told them to do whatever they wanted and that she and my father would show up. When Amy and I announced that we intended to have a wedding — not a real wedding, of course, but something festive, something that expressed the scale of our glee — my mother's response was less than gushing. "How can you feel okay about spending all that money on one day?" she wanted to know.

Naturally, I yelled at her for saying that, but the truth is I didn't. By the time things starting getting specific and estimated costs of various things started combining to form enormous estimated sums, money was only one of many things I did not feel okay about. I did not feel okay about the word "marriage," for instance, partly because it didn't describe a legal option for me, and partly because the closer that something quite like it loomed, the less it seemed like an attractive condition with which to be afflicted. (This was relatively easy to sidestep, at least in a technical sense: our invitations promised "a party about love," and you can't really argue with that.) I also didn't feel okay about spending all my free time on the phone with the flower guy and the tent man, or about making little checklists of who was coming, and who was not coming, and who was staying at the Goodstone Inn. And I definitely did not feel okay about telling the sales staff of half the better clothing retailers in New York City that I needed something fetching to wear to my big fat gay wedding.

Now that I know what is involved in throwing such an event, it is difficult to remember exactly how we decided to do so . . . hard to retrace the steps that led to my standing in front of a three-way mirror in a $3,700 canary-yellow Donna Karan trapeze dress, completely panicked, knowing that soon, very soon, everyone I knew and loved would be joining me for this hell of my own making, this festival of gayness and commitment.

All I can say for sure is that it started on the blackout. When I met Amy on a friend's balcony that night, I never wanted the lights to come back on. With all the stoplights dead, traffic moved on the streets below to its own ghostly, unpredictable rhythm — everything was different. The idea that we wouldn't be together from then on seemed unnatural, almost immediately. And so it was unsurprising that despite the considerable obstacles of other relationships and opposite coasts, eventually we had one life. We were pretty pleased with ourselves. "Look!" we wanted to say to everyone. "Look how fun! Look what's possible! Let's have a cocktail!" We would celebrate with our friends — our families, even. There should be music and dancing. We'd need hyacinths and shrimps! Let the wild rumpus begin.

I am not a total idiot. I always had the sense to say no wedding cake, no officiant, no first dance, no here comes the bride, no

Times announcement, and absolutely no white dress. Who are we kidding? And why? We just wanted a big, awesome party where everyone could meet and go bananas. It's a special opportunity, you know: the only other time everyone you love will assemble in one place is at your funeral. (At most weddings, some people you don't actually love will also be in attendance. But the silver lining of my parents' being irreverent and Amy's parents' being in denial is that we didn't have to invite anyone we didn't want to.) The thing is, though, you have to serve *something,* and you can't very well go naked. You can call it a party about love all you want, but you still have to make all the same decisions that every other bride has to make, and you have to make them very carefully unless you want everyone you know to schlep to some crummy party in the middle of nowhere.

And I do not believe in crummy parties. I believe in glamour. I believe that when you are on your deathbed clinging to the murk of your memories, some will stay with you purely on the power of atmosphere: the way a punch bowl looked surrounded by daisies at your fifth-birthday party, the feel of a certain set of blue sheets the first time you traveled alone. There was no way I was going to let this thing be shoddy — some pathetic hers-and-hers imitation of the real thing or some vaguely patchouli-scented *ceremony.* If I was going to have a party about love, it was going to be the classiest party about love ever. I did not experience this imperative as relaxing.

This was not the first large, square, optional ceremony I'd insisted on having despite my mother's warnings. As a ten-year-old, I decided that I wanted to have a bat mitzvah. I was the only kid in the history of Westchester County who *demanded* Hebrew school. And as I stood in front of the racks of red at Bergdorf Goodman, I recalled the feeling I'd had at some point in my preteen Jewish odyssey when I looked down at the sacred ancient letters on the scroll: *What have I done?*

But in both cases, by the time the magnitude of my folly revealed itself to me, it was way, way too late to undo. As my stepmother put it with terrifying accuracy when we went to see how many cocktail tables would fit on the porch of the house where she and my dad live in the Blue Ridge Mountains, "This horse is out of the gate." It was too late to cancel those lovely and meticulously worded invitations. Too late to tell Amy's eighty-year-old father, a man who served in MacArthur's honor guard after World War II, that the vibratingly tense dinner at which we'd declared our intention to *faux* wed was a waste of a good steak and two hours of his remaining time on planet Earth. It was too late to do anything but find a dress.

Normally, I love clothes. Really love them. I feel about clothes the way I feel about flowers: they sing to me. But I understand tulips and boots; I understand little jackets. I am a stranger to formalwear. The first dress I brought home was a kind of Grecian muumuu in a cheery shade of coral. It looked like something Mrs. Robinson would have worn to a pool party in *The Graduate*. "Chic, right?" I said to Amy. "Perky and festive."

She appeared confused. "You want to wear a nightgown to our wedding?"

"It's not a wedding!" I shrieked. "It's a party about love!"

Amy rolled her eyes. "I didn't realize it was a pajama party about love."

Back it went. A few days later, I modeled a low-cut pale-gold dress with spaghetti straps and a gauzy skirt from Missoni. "Nice!" said Amy. "You look like a fancy hooker. In Capri." This was not the look I wanted.

Then one day I went to a doctor's appointment uptown. It was a sunny spring morning and I wore sneakers and track pants so I could walk home to the East Village when it was over. Amy was at Jussara Lee, the custom shop on Little West 12th Street where she was having her suit made for the big event, the P.A.L. As I made my way down Madison Avenue, I envied her. (And by envied I mean, obviously, resented.) *Of course* Amy would wear a suit; Amy always wears a suit. Everything about this situation seemed simpler for her — she was neither ambivalent nor insane, while I was rapidly flipping my lid. She didn't care about how uncool it was that we were doing this; Amy has always been cool. While I obsessed about how lame it was to seek public acceptance, to crave ritual, and grew queasy at the mention of marriage, Amy was excited.

Then something in a shop window caught my eye. A dress the color of grass, the shape of a mermaid. A dress that would flash before your eyes on your deathbed and in your dreams. I could no longer think about being cool or being mortified or being heteronormative. I could no longer think. The doorman looked at my sneakers skeptically as I shuffled past him into the Carolina Herrera boutique.

"Hello," I said to the salesgirl, a water lily of a woman. "I need a dress to wear to my wedding. I do not want to wear white. I want to wear that one."

"A gown," she told me. "That one is a gown."

I stood still in my sneakers. "Great."

If you are unfamiliar with the price points at Carolina Herrera, here's a good way to get a sense of them: think of the absolute most you can imagine an article of clothing costing. Now triple that. I must have tried on a hundred thousand dollars' worth of fabric that day. But every dress was exquisite, astounding. Each one made me look thinner and more expensive. And then the saleswoman brought me something I would never have even looked twice at: it was made of pale blue oxford cloth with ribbons for straps and a corseted bodice. The skirt was tight at the top and then exploded with volume and hand-painted floral appliqués. When I put it on, I appeared to be in full bloom. "There's your bouquet," she said.

"I'll take it."

If my mother knew how much money I paid for that dress, I do believe she would disown me. But I wasn't thinking about my mother when the seamstress started pinning me in. I was thinking about Amy's.

Like me, Mrs. Norquist was a journalist before she got married. Like me, she is a chatterbox and a gardener. And like me, she is a clotheshorse. But that's it. Mrs. Norquist is a staunch conservative and a churchgoer, as are two of the three sons she raised. (Her oldest, Bruce, is an Evangelical minister, and her youngest, Todd, works for the creationist movement.) When Amy came out in college (two decades ago), Mrs. Norquist didn't speak to her for a year. In fact, as much as she likes to gab, Mrs. Norquist does not talk about anything that really bothers her, except to say the words "Oh, honestly." She likes to talk about who's had a baby and who's been on a trip, and she likes to talk about weddings, a lot. She talks about weddings as much as my mother talks about shiatsu. Where my family is freaky and loose, foulmouthed and freewheeling, Mrs. Norquist is nurturing and restrained, a woman who makes toasted cheese sandwiches and tomato soup. I fell for her immediately.

When we go to visit Amy's parents, generally Amy and her dad watch sports, and Mrs. Norquist and I drink tea and look at fashion magazines together. This is not something I find boring. It is a shared passion and a neutral territory — we avoid discussing politics, sexuality, ethnicity, and religion (except once, when I let loose an "oy vey" and she said, "What?" And I said, "That's what my people say when we mean 'Oh, honestly.'"). Fashion is what we agree upon, the thing we share besides Amy (who does not look at fashion magazines unless maybe there was a special issue on man-tailored suits). "That's a darling heel!" Mrs. Norquist will say. "It would be good in a dark suede," I reply. It's honest communication. We are both ourselves when we talk about clothes, telling each other, for once, the whole truth.

When I saw myself in the mirror in that blue gown with its graceful silhouette and giddy flowers, I could hear Mrs. Norquist gasping and saying, "Isn't that gorgeous!" It was my secret wish that she would look at it and see in our lives sparkle instead of shame. It was my secret wish that if my party about love was as flawless as the gowns in that store, it would subsume the humiliation of its own existence . . . subsume the horror of my homosexuality.

"What do you care what other people think?" is what my own mother would say, of course — has said, many times over the course of my life. And that is the difference between us. My mother is a woman who moved to Cape Cod on a whim. Who has giant green marbles stuck in the plaster of her walls for decoration and an extensive collection of Buddha-like objects she has amassed in her travels through China, Tibet, and the gift shops of the lower Cape. She wears pajamas to work and is nicknamed Rocky and was, in her day, a pretty serious practitioner of non-monogamy. My mother is (still) a badass, because she just doesn't give a shit what anybody else thinks. I care what everybody thinks. So does Mrs. Norquist. I am not sure which one of them I find more mysterious.

I'm not going to lie to you: my gay wedding rocked. My oldest friend, Jesse, played "Crimson and Clover" on his electric guitar when we walked down the mountain, and I can still feel the sound of that song reverberating in my chest. My mother wore high heels and makeup for the first time I can remember and danced until one in the morning. There were these amazing pink margaritas everyone kept drinking. Mrs. Norquist gave Amy the handkerchief her mother gave her on her wedding day: "Something blue," she said, and that's all she said on the subject. That and "Isn't that gorgeous!" when she saw my gown. She still can't quite bring herself to call what happened in September a wedding. But then, for a long time, neither could I.

The dress is still hanging in my closet, which has less to do with my being sentimental than it does with eBay's being really complicated. I can't imagine that I'll ever wear it again, partly because mine is not a black-tie life, and also because I doubt very much that I could get back into it. (When conservatives discuss the perils of gay marriage, they fail to mention its most pernicious consequence: gay marriage, like all marriage, is extremely fattening.) One of these days I'll sell it, though: that thing cost a fortune, and who could feel okay about keeping something so expensive hanging in a garment bag? Amy I'm keeping.

Salamanca

FROM *Transition*

THE COUPLE WALKED IN through the door hand in hand, she leading him, like a pair of children who had just stepped out of one of those fables my mother used to read to us when we were small. These two had obviously grown quite at odds with each other. She was a tiny wizened figure in her seventies, while he had shot up in height rather than age, sprouting from the ground like some magical beanshoot. A tower rising into the sky, a tall, half-naked genie — his only concession to the ways of the city being a skimpy pair of red shorts with the number eight on one leg. The white woman led him along like an overgrown child, her prize. Behind them they trailed a string of curious followers scattered like human breadcrumbs dotting their route. They thronged the doorway, shoving one another aside. A couple of lithe boys managed to extricate themselves from the crush and tumbled to a halt just inside the entrance, mouths agape, their boxes of chewing gum and strings of lollipops all but forgotten, hanging limply from senseless fingers. The rest contented themselves with pressing their faces intently to the window, hands cupped to their foreheads against the glare, as if they were praying.

In the few years since it had opened, my mother's shop had become something of a refuge for strangers. It exercised a mysterious attraction. People walked in and buried themselves in the jumbled chaos of the interior as if they had lived there all their lives. They would turn up to pass a few hours drinking hot tea or gulping down frothy glasses of cold *limoon* summoned from Bimbo's café around the corner, and chatter about their lives. They were, for the most part, expatriate wives looking for ways to bridge the barren gulf that stretched across mid-morning toward lunchtime, when the children were due home from school and they could all go to the swimming pool or the club to cool off and wait for sunset and cocktail hour. The shop had become a reference point, one of those stopping-off places downtown when you needed to get out of the sun or had time to kill.

They came in all shapes, sizes, and colors, and my mother, a sociable person by nature, had the ability to make all these wanderers feel at home. In the evenings Sudanese couples would drop by on their promenade around town — normal people did not wander around during the day without good reason. And maybe it was the heat, or the fact that they were so far away from home, or something about finding an Englishwoman in the midst of this foreign landscape that made it attractive to this odd collection of exiles. They included diplomats and their wives, engineers, visiting professors, technocrats, volunteer teachers, the directors of secretive foundations, sharp-tongued novelists, deposed monarchs from mountain kingdoms you couldn't find in an atlas, would-be Lawrences who had just wandered into town on a camel, amateur artists, journalists, photographers, all looking for someone to help make sense of what they had found here. They came and went with the seasons and she listened to them all. Even Wasool, the Chicago-born African American whom everyone suspected of being a CIA agent even though he didn't look the part. Rabbit-toothed and lanky with large ears that popped out from beneath the crown of his *tagiya* skullcap, he resembled a distant relation of Goofy's. He had settled in Omdurman and married a Baggara woman who spoke not a word of English. All they had in common was love and the power of faith, which Wasool wielded like a baseball bat to thwack any "whiteys" in sight. Islam was his saving grace, he would say cryptically. His past was a closely shrouded mystery from which names such as "Angela" and "Bobby" would leap cryptically. His commitment to the struggle certainly did not explain why he spent so much time nowadays in the company of middle-aged white women. "He's a scream," my mother would declare whenever Wasool delivered one of his sermons. Everything about him was mixed up, including his name. The story was that when he converted, at an obscure mosque in a distant icy ghetto, he was told the name meant "prophet," so now he is forever known as "the arrival" — like an airport terminal. The irony was lost on Wasool that his African side was far outweighed by the American and that a white woman, my mother, had become his main source in unveiling the complex ethnographic intricacies of his adopted ancestral homeland, which is what he was doing on the day the minuscule German lady and her Nuba wrestler made their one and only visit.

I had just come back from school and was waiting for the order to start locking up. Nebiat, our Eritrean helper, was wandering around wearing his beret, which meant that he had places to go. Nebiat's student days were cut short by the war. He had recounted the story of his personal tragedy, of his epic trek to get here, countless times. Any gap in the conversation or a slack moment would prompt him to begin again, stressing the importance of walking strictly in single file, say, or diving toward the point of impact when a shell exploded — apparently the one place where shrapnel will not come down. We took him on good faith, despite his shaky grasp of guerrilla tactics. He liked us because we accepted him as an intellectual, not just another refugee, which is what he was to most people, hence the beret. It set him apart. Now he had an appointment. Nebiat always had more important places to be.

"Is that who I think it is?" Wasool whispered wide-eyed across the table as my mother got to her feet, gaze fixed on the stooping figure. By now all we knew about the odd-looking visitor was that she was German, because she was talking to herself as she moved about.

Wasool, piqued that his question had gone unanswered, turned to me. I was pressed into the gap between the shelves, painted cream and orange, that led through to the back. I shrugged and Wasool nodded as if this was all the confirmation he needed.

I have no idea when my parents first got the idea of opening a shop, but for as long as I could remember it had been a source of domestic strife. Right from the start it seemed fated to fail. In the beginning, they had envisaged a kind of health food center to provide for diabetics (my father was one) and people concerned about their weight. Khartoum was full of affluent ladies worried that their husbands might lose interest for long enough to find themselves a younger, slimmer wife. The solution offered was a machine that came all the way from shiny England. It had little round pads and Velcro straps to fix them to the offending fleshy parts that — hey presto! — by the miracle of modern science would disappear. That, at least, was the idea. On most days I would walk over from school and sit in the back doing my homework. The bulky women would squeeze through the narrow gap and disappear into the shaded booth. I would listen to their snores competing with the unperturbed hum of the machine. But since they never looked any less plump when they emerged, it was perhaps not surprising that most husbands tended to grow tired of paying for treatment that had no discernible diminishing effect on anything but their wallets. The machine was our star attraction, but we had other products, such as diet biscuits that replaced a meal. People would pick these up and turn them over slowly in their hands. It doesn't look like much of a meal, they grumbled. They were right. We kids were fed the broken packets, the ones with little teeth marks on the cellophane where a desperate mouse had tried to get in. And they had no effect on our appetites other than to make us feel rather sickly when we overdid it. The despairing ladies of Khartoum would waddle in and slump into the big wicker chair reserved for customers, wipe the sweat from their brow, and implore my mother to find a cure for them. She offered them Greek spaghetti that contained no starch and tasted of gritty string. As my father declared whenever a damaged packet found its way onto our table, you would be better off boiling the cardboard they came in. There were preserves and marmalade that contained no refined sugar. These proved popular, not least with the customs officials in Port Sudan, who delayed every shipment long enough for a few cases to go missing.

The sign over the doorway displayed the name painted on white glass in red and blue, along with the silhouette of a rather svelte female form — the image of perfection, the goddess whom the good wives of our sleepy river town came to worship. It read "Slimming" in English. It wasn't much of a name, but it was, as my mother remarked, to the point. There is no letter corresponding to *g* in the Arabic language. *Qaf* was deemed the closest substitute. "Salamanca," declared my father, half in jest, as he tried to explain to the weary sign painter how to render this unyielding word. "Salamanca . . . It has a ring to it." It was a dreamy sound that evoked far-off mysterious places, such as Samarkand or Camelot. It had nothing to do with anything, but it definitely had a ring to it.

But legends are sometimes not enough, and with time it became clear that people were not overly concerned about their weight, or at least not a sufficient number of them were. Heart disease and diabetes were plentiful, but being plump was a sign of well-being. Only poor people were thin, and there were enough of those to confirm the fact. Gradually the expensive, imported products gave way to local handicrafts aimed at the more discerning traveler.

And it was these that had drawn our latest visitor. The fierce little septuagenarian was digging her way furiously through every item, with my mother in hot pursuit. She did not take lightly to having her goods handled in such cavalier fashion and was clearly having a hard time restraining her tongue as a cascade of leather boxes, clay pots, necklaces made of glass beads and amber, hefty Bedouin silver bracelets, all came flying her way. The energetic little lady made her way through the shop like a furious demon, disturbing everything, ricocheting from one side to the other, knocking over lamps, copper bowls, stacks of colored baskets.

Nebiat, meanwhile, had decided it would be unfair of him to abandon his post at this time and so busied himself with clearing the onlookers from the doorway. There was some resistance, as if they were being ejected from a cinema before the film was over, and Nebiat's faith in the brotherhood of man and the revolution was being sorely tested. He shooed them ineffectively while they glared back nonchalantly in their grubby galabias, as if there was nowhere in the world they belonged more than here.

"Hitler," murmured Wasool, mouthing the word rather than speaking it.

"Here?" I frowned, completely at sea.

"She worked for him!" he hissed.

Whatever Wasool said had to be chewed over carefully. He was American, and nothing he said ever made complete sense. I was coming to the conclusion that the only Americans I understood were the ones in the movies. The rest of them were always at odds with the world, as though the only form in which Americans could really exist was up there on the screen.

I looked back at the woman who was still digging things up like a manic archaeologist, examining them briefly before tossing them aside. She looked a little frantic, but *Hitler?*

"Not this. *Nein!* None of it. It is not authentic!"

Hitler or no Hitler, my mother had dealt with difficult customers before. "It's all made by people in the villages where these things come from," she explained patiently, as though her decades of living in this country were being called into question.

"No no no." The woman was having none of it. "Ah. Maybe something here," she exclaimed, burrowing into the clothes rack like a ravenous rodent. Shoving hangers aside, she scrabbled through the collection of galabias and dresses. All "unique," all made locally for tourists looking for something colorful and, well, authentic. Then, to our astonishment, she began pulling her dress off over her head.

"Oh, my God!" cried my mother in horror. "What are you doing?"

There were muffled cries from inside the floral print dress. Something had become snagged, and our intrepid traveler now went staggering about the floor frantically. The gathered audience howled in response, their patience rewarded. They clutched one another and fell about. Others went shrieking down the street. Wide-eyed kids turned to stone, wads of gum tumbling from gaping jaws, not quite sure what they were witnessing as my mother tried to guide the headless white body, naked but for an enormous pair of sad gray underpants, out of sight. A strange flower topped by the bell of an inverted dress from which there issued odd yelps, strangled sounds in a language unknown to any of us. I stepped neatly out of the way as she crashed blindly into the shelves before making it through the gap into the back room.

"You really can't do that kind of thing here," we heard my mother chastising her loudly and in no uncertain terms. "People don't like it. You can't just start taking your clothes off." Subdued murmurs of what might have been apology could be heard.

I glanced over at the German lady's companion. The tall Nuba wrestler stood aloof in one corner of the shop like a piece of furniture that no one could quite place. He looked around him as though seeing nothing of what was there. Nebiat, the revolutionary in the Che Guevara beret, who had seen war and God knows what else, was looking perplexed, shaking his head as he spied the building's porter, an old soldier named Jubayr, whose bushy mustache and gnarled face was usually the portent of some form of complaint. He waved his staff at the boys and demanded to know what was going on.

"Madame," old Jubayr called from the door. He never came inside. "We can't have this kind of goings-on here. This is a respectable building. What are people going to say?"

My mother went out to calm him down. Of course it wouldn't happen again. In the meantime, the German woman had made her choice and now appeared wearing a long and very dignified caftan. She gave a little pirouette in front of her boyfriend, who remained impassive. Impatient to conduct her business and be on her way, the woman produced a purse and shook it under my nose.

"How much? How much? *Bikum?*" she added for good measure, obviously used to dealing with the natives. I muttered something, and she frowned the way you might frown at an idiot. There was some debate over the price, but all that mattered was ending this transaction as quickly as possible, and my mother, who normally drove a hard bargain, gave way without a fight. And then it was all over and the odd couple vanished through the doorway forever, their entourage yapping at their heels, waving cigarettes and caramels under their noses.

"She was a film star in the thirties," Wasool explained as we got ready to leave. It was lunchtime and the metal shutters were clattering down with relief all around us. "Hitler took a shine to her. She made films for him. *Triumph of the Will?* The Nuremberg rally?"

He was right, of course, but at the time none of us had ever heard of Leni Riefenstahl, nor could we have made the connection between that distant place in history and our little corner of the world. One of those strange jump cuts when time seems to fold in on itself like a fan closing. Usually history lay dormant in black-and-white photographs in our schoolbooks. There he is, riding along with the top down, hand held high in stiff-armed salute. And here she is in living color, a little old lady. It was like staring at an electric spark, frightening and fascinating all at once.

Wasool ambled out, chuckling to himself and shaking his head. Hyuck hyuck.

"So," my mother said, arching her eyebrows mischievously, "the real question is, how did he know who she was?"

LOUIS MENAND

Notable Quotables

FROM *The New Yorker*

SHERLOCK HOLMES NEVER SAID "Elementary, my dear Watson." Neither Ingrid Bergman nor anyone else in *Casablanca* says "Play it again, Sam"; Leo Durocher did not say "Nice guys finish last"; Vince Lombardi did say "Winning isn't everything, it's the only thing" quite often, but he got the line from someone else. Patrick Henry almost certainly did not say "Give me liberty, or give me death!"; William Tecumseh Sherman never wrote the words "War is hell"; and there is no evidence that Horace Greeley said "Go west, young man." Marie Antoinette did not say "Let them eat cake"; Hermann Göring did not say "When I hear the word 'culture,' I reach for my gun"; and Muhammad Ali did not say "No Vietcong ever called me nigger." Gordon Gekko, the character played by Michael Douglas in *Wall Street,* does not say "Greed is good"; James Cagney never says "You dirty rat" in any of his films; and no movie actor, including Charles Boyer, ever said "Come with me to the Casbah." Many of the phrases for which Winston Churchill is famous he adapted from the phrases of other people, and when Yogi Berra said "I didn't really say everything I said" he was correct.

So what? Should we care? Quotable quotes are coins rubbed smooth by circulation. What Michael Douglas did say in *Wall Street* was "Greed, for lack of a better word, is good." That was not a quotable quote; it needed some editorial attention, the consequence of which is that everyone distinctly remembers Michael Douglas uttering the words "Greed is good" in *Wall Street,* just as everyone distinctly remembers Ingrid Bergman uttering the words "Play it again, Sam" in *Casablanca,* even though what she really utters is

"Play it, Sam." When you watch the movie and get to that line, you don't think your memory is wrong. You think the movie is wrong.

"For lack of a better word" spoils a nice quotation — the speech is about calling a spade a spade, so there *is* no better word — and "Play it again, Sam" is somehow more affecting than "Play it, Sam." But not all emendations are improvements. What Leo Durocher actually said (referring to the New York Giants baseball team) was "The nice guys are all over there, in seventh place." The sportswriters who heard him telescoped (the technical term is "piped") the quote because it made a neater headline. They could have done a better job of piping. "Nice guys finish seventh" is a lot cleverer (and also marginally more plausible) than the non-utterance that gave immortality to Leo Durocher. But Leo Durocher doesn't own that quotation; the quotation owns Leo Durocher, the way a parasite sometimes takes over the host organism. Quotations are in a perpetual struggle for survival. They want people to keep saying them. They don't want to die any more than the rest of us do. And so, whenever they can, they attach themselves to colorful or famous people. "Nice guys finish last" profits by its association with a man whose nickname was the Lip, even if the Lip never said it, just as "Winning isn't everything" has a higher market valuation because of the mental image people have of Vince Lombardi. No one has a mental image of Henry (Red) Sanders, the coach who used the phrase first.

The adaptive mechanism benefits both parties. The survival of the quotation helps ensure the survival of the person to whom it is misattributed. The Patrick Henry who lives in our heads and hearts is the man who said "Give me liberty, or give me death!" Apparently, the line was cooked up by his biographer William Wirt, a notorious embellisher, who also invented Henry's other familiar quotation, "If this be treason, make the most of it!" But a Patrick Henry who never said "Give me liberty, or give me death!" or "If this be treason, make the most of it!," a Patrick Henry without a death wish, is just not someone we know or care about. His having been said to have said what he never said is a condition of his being "Patrick Henry." Certain sayings, like "It's déjà vu all over again," are Berraisms, whether Yogi Berra ever said them or not. "*Je ne suis pas marxiste,*" Karl Marx once complained. Too late for that. Like Yogi, he was the author of a discourse, and he lives as long as it does.

Karl Marx has 13 quotations (plus eight for which he shares credit with Friedrich Engels, who, interestingly, never felt it necessary to say "*Je ne suis pas engeliste*") in the compendious, enjoyable, and expensive *Yale Book of Quotations* (Yale, $50), edited by Fred Shapiro. Groucho Marx (no relation) has 51 quotations. The big winner is William Shakespeare, with 455, topping even the Yahwist and his coauthors, the wordsmiths who churned out the Bible but managed to come up with only 400 quotable passages. Mark Twain has 153 quotations, Oscar Wilde 123. Ambrose Bierce edges out Samuel Johnson in double overtime by a final score of 144 to 110. And Woody Allen has 40, beating out William Wordsworth, Rudyard Kipling, and both Roosevelts.

Shapiro, a librarian at the Yale Law School, is an attribution hound, as is Ralph Keyes, a quotation specialist and the author of *The Quote Verifier* (St. Martin's, $15.95). "Misquotation is an occupational hazard of quotation," Keyes advises, and both he and Shapiro have gone to considerable trouble to track down the original utterances that became famous quotations and their original utterers. Keyes finds that quotations tend to mutate in the direction of greater pith. He offers the original words of Rodney King as an instance: "People, I just want to say, you know, can we all get along? Can we get along? Can we stop making it, making it horrible for the older people and the kids? . . . Please, we can get along here. We all can get along. I mean, we're all stuck here for a while. Let's try to work it out. Let's try to beat it. Let's try to beat it. Let's try to work it out." This is the rambling outburst that became the astringent and immortal "Can't we all get along?" Keyes calls the process "bumper-stickering." It worked well for Rodney King.

Shapiro gives us results of similar detective work, and he offers additional scholarly fruit in the form of citations for the first appearance of many well-known terms, slogans, and catch phrases. "This book takes a broad view of what constitutes a quotation," he explains. The Internet has helped him out, and a lot of the stuff he has come up with is pretty irresistible. It is extremely interesting to know, for instance, that the phrase "Shit happens" was introduced to print by one Connie Eble, in a publication identified as *UNC–CH Slang* (presumably the University of North Carolina at Chapel Hill), in 1983. "Life's a bitch, and then you die," a closely related reflection, dates from 1982, the year it appeared in the *Washington Post.* "Been there, done that" entered the public discourse in 1983, via the *Union Recorder,* a publication out of the University of Sydney. "Get a life": the *Washington Post,* 1983. (What *is* it about the 1980s, anyway?) "Size doesn't matter," a phrase, or at least a hope, that would seem to have been around since the Pleistocene, did not see print until 1989, rather late in the history of the species, when it appeared in the *Boston Globe.*

There are some neat finds and a few surprises (to me, anyway) in the Yale book. I did not know that Billy Wilder was the person who said that hindsight is always 20/20. "There ain't no such thing as a free lunch" is attributable to a journalist named Walter Morrow, writing in the *San Francisco News* in 1949. We owe the useful phrase "Sue the bastards!" to Victor J. Yannacone Jr., identified as a U.S. lawyer and environmentalist. It was Jack Weinberg, of the Berkeley Free Speech Movement, who first said "You can't trust anybody over thirty." Joey Adams gets the credit for "With friends like that, who needs enemies?" The phrase "You can't go home again" was given to Thomas Wolfe by the writer Ella Winter. It was the wonderful story writer John McNulty, and not Yogi Berra, who was responsible for "Nobody goes there anymore. It's too crowded." "I'm not really a Jew. Just Jew-ish": Jonathan Miller, in *Beyond the Fringe.* And the first person to call a spade a spade? That's right, it was Erasmus.

Shapiro has a good ear for the quote bites of contemporary celebrity culture, and the courage to set out on this endless sea. Donald Trump appears twice, for "Deals are my art form" and (in a section headed "Television Catchphrases") "You're fired!" Cherilyn Sarkisian LaPierre, known to most of us as Cher, is included for the lines "Mother told me a couple of years ago, 'Sweetheart, settle down and marry a rich man.' I said, 'Mom, I am a rich man.'" (The great Sonny Bono, on the other hand, is sadly missing and deeply missed. What about "The beat goes on"? "I got you, babe"? Jingles that got us through some unhappy hours.) Zsa Zsa Gabor, asked how many husbands she has had, said, "You mean apart from my own?" Tug McGraw, asked what he would do with the salary he was making as a pitcher, said, "Ninety percent I'll spend on good times, women, and Irish whiskey. The other ten percent I'll probably waste." "I ate a whole chocolate bar" was Claudia Schiffer's comment after her retirement from the catwalk. There are separate sections in the Yale book for *Star Trek* (ten items, including "Live long and prosper" and "He's dead, Jim"; Gene Roddenberry has a section of his own), for "Advertising Slogans" (immediately following the section for Theodor Adorno, who would have grimly appreciated the irony and probably composed an incomprehensible aphorism about it), for "Sayings" ("No more Mr. Nice Guy": *New York Times,* 1967), for "Political Slogans," and for "Film Lines." I'm not sure that the sentence spoken by L. Paul Bremer III upon the capture of Saddam Hussein, "Ladies and gentlemen, we got him," is all that deathless, but I'm quite pleased with the single quotation attributed to Richard B. Cheney, identified as a U.S. government official, and dated May 30, 2005: "The insurgency is in its last throes."

It is tiresome to encounter, for the millionth time (J. Joyce), George Santayana's tiresome mot "Those who cannot remember the past are condemned to repeat it" (manifestly untrue any way you look at it). And it is annoying to reread Alfred North Whitehead's pompous *bouleversements:* "There are no whole truths; all truths are half-truths"; "Everything of importance has been said before by somebody who did not discover it." But if sententious paradoxes get endlessly circulated, that is not the editor's fault. Wilde was an epigrammatic genius, it's true, but too large a dose may cause stomach upset. Shapiro is interested in the sociology of knowledge (which is precisely where the study of quotation belongs), so there are quotations from Robert K. Merton, George Sarton, and Talcott Parsons, but relatively less attention is given to other academic figures. (Stanley Fish does not appear, though it can't be for lack of material. Edward Said does.) There is inevitably a problem in the case of people who are the quotation equivalent of vending machines. Charles Dickens, for example, or Bob Dylan, who is represented by a list of twenty-seven quotations that will seem, to anyone who is a Dylan listener, hopelessly arbitrary. It should all be here, every line!

In fact, though it is ungracious to say, a lot of the fun of this fun book is in second-guessing the editor. Virginia Woolf's quotations include the first sentence of *Mrs. Dalloway* ("Mrs. Dalloway said she would buy the flowers herself") but not the equally famous last sentence of *To the Lighthouse* ("I have had my vision"). Franz Kafka, a deep mine of quotability, has just eleven entries, and it is disappointing that one of them is not "It is enough that the arrows fit exactly in the wounds that they have made." There are two quotations from William James on the subject of truth, but not the most elegant of his formulations: "The true is the name for whatever proves itself to be good in the way of belief." Guy Debord, a brilliant aphorist who coined the phrase "society of the spectacle," is represented only by a late and dubious quotation about quotations. ("Quotations are useful in periods of ignorance or obscurantist beliefs.") The section for Justice Oliver Wendell Holmes Jr. — like his father an inexhaustible fount of one-liners — lacks the always apt reminder that "certitude is not the test of certainty." The philosopher Sidney Morgenbesser, whose offhand remarks were celebrated enough to have been collected, is here only for his famous retort to a speaker who had said that although there are many cases in which two negatives make a positive, he knew of no case in which two positives made a negative ("Yeah yeah"). Samuel Beckett has only nine quotations, most of them from *Waiting for Godot*. We miss his remark about what it will be like in the afterlife: "We'll sit around talking about the good old days, when we wished that we were dead." Goethe has twenty-six entries, including one that was new to me (the attribution, not the sentiment): "He can lick my ass" (1773). But a line from *Wilhelm Meister* that has given me resolve is not here: "Action is easy; thought is hard." We miss Henri Bergson's gnomic observation "The universe is a machine for the making of gods." There is a large woodpile of Robert Frost lines, but the couplet that ends "The Tuft of Flowers" — "Men work together, I told him from the heart, / Whether they work together or apart" — is not in it.

Poetry is, admittedly, an insuperable problem for quotation compilers. The feeling that the top of your head has been taken off, a definition of what makes a quote quotable that Shapiro takes from Emily Dickinson (who took it, basically, from Kant and Burke, who took it from Longinus — a nice example of the sociology of quotation), is a feeling that readers of poetry expect from every poem they read. They are in the game to look for the strong line. But — and now we are getting to the theoretical heart of the Problem of Quotation — the experience of sublimity is subjective and associational. For some reason, a string is plucked and it never stops vibrating. Who knows why, exactly? Everyone has a list. "My glass is full, and now my glass is run." "But one man loved the pilgrim soul in you." "In the gloom, the gold gathers the light against it." "Led by a blind and teachit by a bairn." "The waste remains, the waste remains and kills." "I bleed by the black stream / For my torn

bough." "There's a stake in your fat black heart." "This shaking
keeps me steady. I should know." "Drive, he said." "Sheer plod
makes plow down sillion shine." "You must change your life." None
of these are in the Yale book, but why would I expect them to be?
They're from my book.

"You can get a happy quotation anywhere if you have the eye,"
the younger Holmes once wrote. He thought that you could find
wisdom and felicity even in advertisements if you knew how to
tweak them properly. And when you start taking phrases out of
context and recasting them as quotations, you begin to feel (Shapiro must have undergone this sensation) a little vertiginous. What
is not, potentially, a quotation? The dullest instructional prose,
with the right light thrown on it, can acquire the gleam of sugges-
tiveness or insight. "Objects in the rear-view mirror may appear
closer than they are": that one has been appropriated many times.
Whenever I take a plane, I am struck by "Secure your own mask before assisting others" as advice with wide application. And I have often found myself imagining ways of fitting tab A into slot B.

Public circulation is what renders something a quotation. It's
quotable because it's been quoted, and its having been quoted
gives it authority. Quotations are prostheses. "As Emerson/Chur-
chill/Donald Trump once observed" borrows another person's
brain waves and puts them to your own use. (If you fail to credit
Emerson et al., it's called plagiarism. But isn't plagiarism just the
purest form of quotation?) Then there is a subset of quotations
that are personal. We pick them up off the public street, but we put
them to private uses. We hoard quotations like amulets. They are
charms against chaos, secret mantras for dark times, strings that vi-
brate forever in defiance of the laws of time and space. That they
may be opaque or banal to everyone else is what makes them precious: they aren't supposed to work for everybody. They're there to
work for us. Some are little generational badges of identity. Some
just seem to pop up on a million occasions. Some are razors. "I see
a red door and I want it painted black." "*Devenir immortelle, et puis,
mourir.*" "Much smaller piece." "You're two tents." The quotation I
have found most potent in warding off evil spirits is the motto of
the Flemish philosopher Arnold Geulincx (1624–1669): "*Ubi nihil
vales, ibi nihil velis.*" "Where you are worth nothing, you should
want nothing." That's mine. You can't use it.

Solipsism

The theory that the self is the only thing that can be known and verified. Maybe this is memoir after all.

Even this note on the title is an apparent lifeline out from solipsism: a mark for you to follow, if you're a reader who likes to do these things, who follows orders well, and a kind of hand-hold from one part of the text to another.

Ander Monson

Me. Me. Me. Me. Me. Me. Me. Me. Me.
Me. Me. Me. Me. Me. Me. Me. Me. Me.
Me. Me. Me. Me. Me. Me. Me. Me. Me.
Me. Me. Me. Me. Me. Me. Me. Me. Me.
Me. Me. Me. Me. Me. Me. Me. Me. Me.
Me. Me. Me. Me. Me. Me. Me. Me. Me.
Me. Me. Me. Me. Me. Me. Me. Me. Me.
Me. Me. Me. Me. Me. Me. Me. Me. Me.
Me. Me. Me. Me. Me. Me. Me. Me. Me.
Me. Me. Me. Me. Me. Me. Me. Me. Me.
Me. Me. Me. Me. Me. Me. Me. Me. Me.
Me. Me. Me. Me. Me. Me. Me. Me. Me.
Me. Me. Me. Me. Me. Me. Me. Me. Me.
Me. Me. Me. Me. Me. Me. Me. Me. Me.
Me. Me. Me. Me. Me. Me. Me. Me. Me.
Me. Me. Me. Me. Me. Me. Me. Me. Me.
Me. Me. Me. Me. Me. Me. Me. Me. Me.
Me. Me. Me. Me. Me. Me. Me. Me. Me.
Me. Me. Me. Me. Me. Me. Me. Me. Me.
Me. Me. Me. Me. Me. Me. Me. Me. Me.
Me. Me. Me. Me. Me. Me. Me. Me. Me.
Me. Me. Me. Me. Me. Me. Me. Me. Me.
Me. Me. Me. Me. Me. Me. Me. Me. Me.
Me. Me. Me. Me. Me. Me. Me. Me. Me.
Me. Me. Me. Me. Me. Me. Me. Me. Me.
Me. Me. Me. Me. Me. Me. Me. Me. Me.
Me. Me. Me. Me. Me. Me. Me. Me. Me.
Me. Me. Me. Me. Me. Me. Me. Me. Me.
Me. Me. Me. Me. Me. Me. Me. Me. Me.
Me. Me. Me. Me. Me. Me. Me. Me. Me.
Me. Me. Me. Me. Me. Me. Me. Me. Me.
Me. Me. Me. Me. Me. Me. Me. Me. Me.
Me. Me. Me. Me. Me. Me. Me. Me. Me.
Me. Me. Me. Me. Me. Me. Me. Me. Me.
Me. Me. Me. Me. Me. Me. Me. Me. Me.
Me. Me. Me. Me. Me. Me. Me. Me. Me.
Me. Me. Me. Me. Me. Me. Me. Me. Me.
Me. Me. Me. Me. Me. Me. Me. Me. Me.
Me. Me. Me. Me. Me. Me. Me. Me. Me.
Me. Me. Me. Me. Me. Me. Me. Me. Me.
Me. Me. Me. Me. Me. Me. Me. Me. Me.
Me. Me. Me. Me. Me. Me. Me. Me. Me.
Me. Me. Me. Me. Me. Me. Me. Me. Me.
Me. Me. Me. Me. Me. Me. Me. Me. Me.
Me. Me. Me. Me. Me. Me. Me. Me. Me.
Me. Me. Me. Me. Me. Me. Me. Me. Me.
Me. Me. Me. Me. Me. Me. Me. Me. Me.
Me. Me. Me. Me. Me. Me. Me. Me. Me.
Me. Me. Me. Me. Me. Me. Me. Me. Me.
Me. Me. Me. Me. Me. Me. Me. Me. <u>Me.</u>

At one point, say, the late 1800s, just before Dr. Thaddeus Cahill invents the electric typewriter, this would have meant more than it does today. That is, the 575 instances of Me.—and don't forget the single space after each period which means another keystroke for each instance—would have meant significantly more in 1895 than it does today. Physically speaking, the work required to generate the 575 instances above on a manual typewriter, where you'd have to press each key hard enough to get the system of levers moving the type-bar through an inked ribbon to hit the paper, was far greater than the work it required to generate this page on a computer. One reason people get carpal tunnel now is because the physical act of typing (itself lessened by about 95% in electric typewriters as compared to it did then, so it's easier for the hands to become lazy and just rest, and not for us to arch our fingers enough, etc.

It would have taken me, in eighth grade, when I typed 54 words per minute in our class just recently rechristened keyboarding instead of the older typing, approximately 10.65 minutes to generate that page, possibly longer when you think about the fatigue that sets in typing the same letters over and over—no variety of motion at all, just simple repetition—and of course this was on an electric typewriter, not even one of the old manual machines.

For me now it took less than thirty seconds to compose that text. I typed "Me. Me. Me." on my Titanium 15" Powerbook keyboard, which isn't all that comfortable, really, though I've gotten used to it because of the ease it otherwise affords, and then highlighted in Dreamweaver, copy-and-pasted a few times until I had a few lines, then copy-and-pasted that a few times, and came up with a good solid page of text, all text about me with a capital M in front trailed by a period and space. It's almost nothing. I didn't have to think about it, the Me. or the actual Me much. It's easy to do. You try it.

So how much does it mean? What work does it do given that it took vastly fewer minutes, calluses, and calories?

Useful Adjectives and Adjectival Phrases to Describe Ander Monson (from his PR website):
1. phenomenal 2. maverick 3. self-involved 4. trickeration-loving 5. asinine 6. straight-shooting 7. family-betraying 8. law-breaking 9. ne'er-do-well 10. bad boy 11. future addict 12. serious and accomplished 13. brainy but beautiful 14. more than likely delusional 15. poetry-ish 16. encyclopedic 17. whale-kicking 18. profane 19. piratical 20. regretful 21. sympathetic 22. criminal 23. pensive 24. bright but misguided 25. hurt, badly, baldly 26. good

Work is equal to force times distance, remember.

Invents is a fuzzy verb of course—often so-called inventions aren't a lightning-strike kind of moment but the latest in a series of incremental increases in existing technologies just significant enough to be seen as something completely, more or less inarguably, new.

Many of us learned to type on typewriters, with two spaces after each period or terminal punctuation mark. With the advent of typing on computers, which mostly use proportional-space fonts (fixed-width fonts, like courier, use the same amount of space for an i as they do for an m, which is obviously much wider. So sentences tended to look more spread out, and were not as easy to read. As such, we were told to use two spaces between sentences so the sentence breaks would be more obvious. Proportional fonts like this one, Arial (or maybe

I make broadsides, mostly pretty artistic, fine-press sorts of productions, for poetry and fiction readings at Grand Valley State University, the college that currently employs me. I don't know if anyone really cares that these broadsides get made or not as a condition of my employment, so I do them out of a love of the artifact of the broadside, the mementos that they are, and the simple beauty of elegantly typeset lines of prose or verse. Mostly I do these by offset printer or by laser printer in my office. I don't handset the type for a Vandercook letterpress, though I have done that too. When you're handsetting every letter, pulling them out of the type cases, which are sort of strangely arranged, and setting them in lines, you have a lot of time to think about the process of production, and about the words you are laboring over. The type, of course, appears reversed on the page from how it appears to you, so certain letters are very easy to confuse, so it's a maddening and painstaking, somehow beautiful process to print like this. You get to experience the physical act of print production, and this kind of letterpress work is now an extravagance, incurring significant expense. Try to get your wedding invitations letterpressed and you'll find out.

I do most of my design in Adobe InDesign which takes care of a lot for you. For instance it automatically kerns (spaces) prose, and handles line breaks and widows and orphans, mostly, and the sorts of details typographers love, like ligatures and old style figures, and all of that. I can turn on those options if I'm using a good OpenType typeface and let it do its thing. I print these broadsides, 50–500 normally, depending, for writers like Charles Wright, Charles Baxter, and I hope someday to do Charles Yu, thus completing my trilogy of Charleses. Sometimes I'll finish them with a deckle or ragged edge, or by burning the edges of the broadsides for effect. I always wanted to put a set in a stack, bring it to a firing range, and shoot through it for a really cool effect. I might use some spray-on fixer or a cheaper analogue like hairspray to keep the toner from dusting off on hands and slacks. I have thrown red wine across broadsides for effect. And applied rubber stamps. Spray painted. Even printed with my own blood. The list goes on.

(hence the saying "mind your p's and q's")

(printing press)

Also Rita Dove, Sonia Sanchez, David Means, and so on.

Helvetica, or something else depending on what fonts are on your computer system—the web works in this way with a looser hold on typography), are better-formatted for ease of reading, and as such one should only use one space between sentences. Anything more makes the textblock look loose. **Write this down.**

Commit it to memory, if your muscle memory allows it. And this is a minor point to be sure, but important in typographical terms, the terms that allow the construction of language on the page, and these tiny points are still sharp, are still worth considering in the technology that guides, supports our art.

all those accumulated hours of typing with the space-space after periods amount to a lot of habit, so it will be tough to break, like an addiction)

Ain't I *fancy*? Is this essay about me? Is all nonfiction about the me, the I, <u>the eye</u> trained in on the self?

I have a lot of semi-thought-out theories about the mechanisms of production writers have used, and about how (or whether) the <u>technologies</u> they used affected the work they did. I'm a little too lazy to go very far with that conceit in terms of busting out my close reading and LitCrit chops and such, but it's a salient point.

(longhand, dictation, typewritten, Microsoft Word, Pagemaker, Dreamweaver, InDesign, Flash, etc.)

(For one, I think we could probably do something with Marxist criticism and this idea of work: maybe an essay for another day.)

As for me, I am writing this essay in a program that specializes in bringing together these different formats of items (images: GIF, JPEG, PNG; interactive stuff like Flash and Shockwave buttons; sound; movie clips; text; hyperlinks; javascript and other programming elements) in a <u>WYSIWYG</u> format.

What you see is what you get is how the acronym works, a technology not really possible until word processing programs like Microsoft Word, originally called "Multi-Tool Word", began to be able to display fonts onscreen as they would actually appear, which takes a surprising amount of processing power and still does not work flawlessly.

I wonder how this affects the words I am writing—do they mean less, or more, or something different?

What if I process my words through a Shockwave digital effect so they can flash or something?

Does that change the words and make them something different, something beyond words?

Words marked up with formatting?

And what does writing consist of, exactly?

Think of this as performance, then, and not just my normal tendency to wrap myself up in myself. I remember first hearing the word *solipsism* in college, others applying it to my work on occasion—as a critique, probably, but I never understood the problem with being solipsistic. It seemed good—to make and inhabit a world, though perhaps hermetic and overly heady—and it sounded kind of sciency and nasty in the way that literary criticism has tried to bring other disciplines to bear on literature as if they were engineers applying new technologies to a particularly tricky mining problem.

I am taking advantage (sort of—note the dearth of multimedia crap on this page, no javascript kicking ass, no techy trickeration taking place) of the possibilities of the software. It allows me to generate more words, these worlds, and to try to metabolize the ways in which writing has meant in the past.

I type everything, though I have a set of journals, steno books mostly, not a Moleskine or whatever, that I use when I can't have my laptop in my lap warming me like a cat. Occasionally I'll start something longhand in a steno pad (I love the steno pad, that quick-flip technology designed for shorthand transcription) and try to work it out on the page before transferring it to Word or InDesign or Dreamweaver. And the work changes, almost immediately. It's really weird to watch if you

Especially weird is the thought that this essay is being created with no thought of 8.5″ x 11″ paper (or in Europe the A4 sheet) with the standard margins that Word thinks acceptable, or the other constraints (or pleasures—this goes both ways, as many people don't like reading longer texts onscreen, and love the feeling of crisp new paper in their hands) of the page. I am also not editing it in the same way, given that it is available on the website for free. You didn't pay for this. It's an extra. A promotional item, maybe. Or an attempt to extend the idea of what a book can do in an explicit way. And as it's here for you, it's like the opposite of solipsism, a piece of writing explicitly intended as communication. It's like getting your own personalized email from me to you, except that I don't have your email address, and you'd probably just delete it out of hand as spam anyhow.

Or maybe it's a bonus for the portion of readers who go online to get more out of a book, having been burned before by the lameness of promotional websites for books that should have great websites, like Mark Z. Danielewski's *House of Leaves*—I am writing this for you, dear reader that just wants more. Or maybe it's like the bonus materials / special features you find on DVDs that mostly—let's admit it now—suck, are useless, in spite of the promises made by proponents of the technology.

Now DVDs have this space, and viewers do expect the extras. Sometimes they are great, like Peter Jackson's work on the *Lord of the Rings* trilogy, or in my awesome (and I mean that—it inspires watch closely.

What if I was writing everything in InDesign, which lets you do a pile of amazing effects with type on the page, on a path, curlicuing along a vector curve? And at the same time, what is lost in this, in the technology that, in trying to make things easier, reduces your options. It's not that you can't do it, but the software doesn't anticipate it, doesn't encourage that sort of play, that particular kind of construction or creative impulse. Which is probably mostly fine. I mean, how much has the ideogram or concrete poetry really done for the world? I like Apollinaire as much as the next guy, but when it comes down to it I like my horizontal lines of text, running left to right (not boustrophedon, as the ox plows, back and forth) across the page and beginning again at the left margin, a kind of magic—these rules are complicated enough when it comes to language, to the way I think of writing.

And most people appear to agree with this —we mostly like our poetry straight, at least the we of us who like poetry at all.

Thus far, 8 out of 17 paragraphs in the essay

start with

(see the Word autocorrect and what it does to the first letters of lines in my poems when I try to work on it; just try to write a line and then write the next at a ten-degree angle up, radiating from the center of the page)

awe, even in the packaging) *Alien Quadrilogy* DVD set (9 DVDs, 2 cuts of each movie plus a pile of bonus stuff, and amazing fold-out packaging—the artifact of it is sexy as all hell, a design miracle). And sometimes they are not. But consumers want those extras. And now CDs that come packaged with videos, multimedia stuff, some live tracks, an extra DVD for fans who care enough not to simply download them on the internet. So technology has created this space, a kind of vacuum that waits to be filled.

I am trying to fill it up with words, with words that make some kind of meaning.

I am trying to make this mean something to you, more than just the physical act of its creation, all these words being clicked out by my keyboard through electrical impulse to the screen.

You get to watch me shuck and jive.

I am putting the **me** back in **me**moir here for you. Not that I think of this exactly as a **me**moir, but it is tied up (abattoired?) in **me**moir, as all writing is, in **me**mory and starlight light and the chain links of our pasts.

I suspect **I** am always going to be revisiting this question, re-solving (if not resolving) this problem. As a plus, since it's on the web, it is ephemeral—I can wipe this out at a later date and there will be no record of it here (aside from the ghostly trails in Google or websites that archive all old sites, the secret memory cache of the world).

Except with **you**, if **you** got here at all, if you got this far into the netherworld. Which makes this a bit of a risk, but not the usual risk associated with publishing, committing one's words to 5000 (if you're lucky) paperback copies forever.

I'm not sure what this says about me.

A note on the technology of this work's composition: composed initially, as is implied, for the *Neck Deep* website, and composed (or "written," whatever that word exactly suggests at this point in time) in Macromedia Dreamweaver (and finally edited now for the page in Word, soon to be transformed through Quark or In-Design for the journal's layout) it's weird even to transpose the thought process of this essay from screen to page.

I wonder if the essay changes meaning because several of its ideas are rendered impotent by virtue of this fixing of toner or ink to page, the tying down of this language to this single, definitive iteration.

Can I no longer revise it for the website since it has been "published"?

It is nonfiction. It is about the world, but the world reflected slash refracted in the lens. It is about the past tense and present tense, and maybe the f u t u r e tense.

I've come a long way to here. And there's much left to do.

So, for now—for the now that is captured, frozen here, somewhere between me and you—enjoy.

Which is the definitive "publication"?

Does the devotion of more physical resources to the production of this edited glossy codex, *The Pinch*, with its set of production values and editorial processes, its surrounding writers and artwork, and its mailing or bookstore-shelving, make it more valid or less? At the least it offers another layer of meaning and transformation to consider, which is pretty fun, I think. Still, check out the website for more on this—and maybe this will even have undergone another transformation or revision back to the website by the time it is printed.

Thus rendering it gloriously, flagrantly, interestingly obsolete.

RICK MOODY

On Celestial Music

FROM *Salmagundi*

1. Otis Redding as Purveyor of Celestial Music

Music has soul. We operate as though it does. In fact, music is one of the few areas of human endeavor where the word "soul," even among secular types, is liable to go unchallenged. All kinds of music are occasionally imputed to have soul. Even music that doesn't have anything but volume or a tiresome double-kick drum sound. Ray Conniff, to a listener somewhere, has soul. Who am I to say otherwise? Soul in these cases perhaps indicates earnestness, rhetorical force, and/or vocal polyps. Nevertheless, there are persuasive indications that the word "soul" does indeed manifest itself in music, and so maybe it's useful here at the outset to point to a recording that demonstrates why music belongs in any discussion about heaven. So, along these lines, I'm going to describe briefly the mechanics of one example of *soul music*, namely, a live recording by Otis Redding entitled "Try a Little Tenderness."[1]

Lyrically speaking, "Try a Little Tenderness" starts as an exhortation to do better at peeling away the layers of defensiveness in a lover, a woman (in this case) who is not only *weary*, in the general sense, but maybe particularly weary of the traditional role of woman. Her only job at the song's opening is selflessness. Her condition is more than apparent, for example, in the limpid lyrical perception, "I know she's waiting, just anticipating, the thing that she'll never possess." What to make of this? What exactly is "the thing she'll never possess"? Is it love? Is it justice, in the prejudicial

landscape of the USA in the middle and late sixties? Or, as with the
weariness in the first line, is some more general dissatisfaction implied? One thing it's obvious Otis Redding intends, in his role as
purveyor of celestial music: to make us conscious of our human
frailty, our lack, our incompleteness. And he does so here not only
with the lyrics but with perfect phrasing and with the kind of vulnerability that's all but absent from music in these troubled times.

Still, this is to avoid mention of the dynamically satisfying *freak
out* at the end of the song. The big ending! If celestial music is the
music of the spheres, then the big ending of "Try a Little Tenderness" proves that music here on earth can also be tuned to the in-
terstellar realms, especially when the rhythm section kicks in, and
the horns start, and Otis begins his passionate exhortation as to
how, exactly, tenderness is meant to be practiced (holding, squeezing, never leaving), and the horns work their way up the scale, likewise the rhythm guitar, chromatically, while Redding commences
his soul shouting, and the crowd goes wild, hoping that he'll play
through the chorus just one more time! Yes, *try a little tenderness!*
How could we resist! We have not tried sufficiently! So many areas
of our lives remain unexplored! So many virtues seem to lie dormant in us! So much is failure and halfheartedness! Tenderness as
opposed to oppressing the poor and disenfranchised, tenderness
as opposed to military intervention in foreign countries! Tenderness as opposed to the amassing of money, power, and real estate!

What I mean to say is that this live performance of Otis Redding
enacts the attempt at tenderness he promotes, and in this way his
song proves itself, proves the validity of *soul* in music, by *exercising*
the soul, and if you are not convinced by my recitation of these
facts, get the *Monterey Pop* DVD and watch it, because I swear just as
you can be absolved of your malfeasances by watching the pope on
television, you can be made a better person by watching Otis
Redding deliver this song; you will go into the next room, and you
will look at your husband, or your wife, or your child, you will look
at the people whom you have treated less well than you might have,
and you will kneel in front of these people and you will beg for the
chance to try a little harder and to make their burdens a little less
burdensome. If those five minutes of grace are not an example of
what lies out there, beyond what we daily understand, if those five
minutes are not like unto a candle that glimmers in the unending
darkness of life on earth, then I have no idea what paradise is.

2. *Heaven and Premium Stereo Equipment*

Music is of God, that is, and music is with God, and music is how God expresses Him- or Herself, and music is everywhere, and music is a crafty art and is completed in places inside us, in the impossible-to-locate precincts wherein there is access to feelings that we might otherwise ignore. Or: the abstraction of music is how God conceals His or Her complicated plan. Or: the abstraction of music, its connection to deep feeling, has all the traces of the Holy Ghost, so it seems to me, and if I didn't understand this logically as a kid, I at least understood how moving music was when I was first going to church in the suburbs.

Back then, I wanted to lay eyes on things. Because when you're a kid you're open to ideas, but you trust what's in front of your face. I remember feeling that the praying part of the religious service was deeply suspect. People would get this expression on their faces, something near to earnest self-regard. I was supposed to overlook this earnest mien, and I was meant to know intuitively the precise organization of hands for prayer, and then I was supposed to know what to murmur and to whom. And then there was the posturing *after* church. Forget about it! That was not what I associated with God, heaven, the sublime, the celestial. There was some talk during Sunday school about heaven, and it was always of the old-guy-with-beard variety, and I never believed any of that. I had a bullshit detector where ideology was concerned. I resisted what I was told, even if it was good for me, even if it made the world a better place.

What moved me was the music. Music filled me with this intense feeling about the state of things, from my earliest recollections. Not only the organ music before and after services. The organ music was sublime, even when I didn't know anything about harmony and counterpoint. Organ music scared me and demanded something of me by virtue of its grandiosity. (This would perhaps be the moment to say the obvious, that if earthly music is played in heaven, then J. S. Bach really must be the Kapellmeister.) There was also the choir singing during church service. My mom was known to sing in the choir (later on, I did a bit of it myself), and there was a lot of singing going on around my house generally. The human voice, raised in song, was important, was unearthly, gave access to the numinous. And obviously there are indications of this across the centuries of recorded time, almost wherever you look. In David's psalms, for example: "O sing to the Lord a new song; sing his praise in the congregation of the faithful."[2] I wouldn't have had any idea what this meant back when I was first in church. But I knew I liked the singing.

At about the same time, my mother became highly partisan regarding the popular recording artists known as Simon and Garfunkel. We had a lot of their LPs. In fact, we had all of them. I could make a good argument about the sublime and the song known as "The Sounds of Silence," which would then lead to a discussion of John Cage and the theological importance of silence, but I'm putting that off for another time. Instead, I want to talk about a mostly forgotten Simon and Garfunkel tune on the album *Wednesday Morning, 3 A.M.*, entitled "Sparrow." This song, in the folk genre that characterized early Simon and Garfunkel recordings, unfolds as a series of sympathetic questions about a sparrow, addressed to the other preoccupied living things of the world: Who will love a little sparrow? Who will speak to it a kindly word? A swan is posed this question, a field of wheat, an oak tree, and yet all of these eminences decline the opportunity to become stewards of the common sparrow, himself adrift on the callousness of the world, where it is the fate of tenderness to be crushed. Then in the last verse the earth steps in, having been asked the same question. The earth responds with a forceful affirmative in regards to the sparrow, quoting from Scripture, "From dust were ye made and dust ye shall be."

This little song shook my earthly foundations back in Connecticut, where my early music-appreciation lessons were taking place. Not only because it had that mysterious, unearthly quality that English folk music had about it. Not only because of the harmonies, which were always pretty extraordinary in the Simon and Garfunkel corpus. Above all, the song moved me because it depicted so much loss and so much weariness, and because the sparrow, it seemed to me, *had to die*. These days, "Sparrow" might sound a bit quaint to the average listener, owing to its self-evident allegorical scaffolding. But this is also what makes folk songs profound, that they are simple, unadorned, and eager to confront religious, philosophical, and political questions. They are modal, polysemous, difficult to pin down, they are fairy tales with melodies. This makes folk music ideal for a kid who's six or seven. Moreover, I didn't have any defense against the emotional freight of a song. What was "Sparrow" about for me? "Sparrow" was about loving the forgotten, the marginalized, the sick, homely, and despised, and it was about how everything has to die, and if heaven is a locale wherein the injustice of earthly mortality is repaired, uh, for *eternity*, then "Sparrow," in its radical acceptance of the spurned little bird, points in the direction of heavenly music, what it might *do*, how it might make the case for the equalizing force of paradise.

I guess I'm covering up if I'm not saying that I admired this particular song at a troubling time, the time when my own parents were divorcing. I suppose it's obvious that I was identifying with the sparrow, feeling, like him, as though refuge from heartache was hard to come by. In this way, many of the songs I liked then seemed *sad*. For example: another song I cherished was "Golden Slumbers" by the Beatles. It's the lullaby on a very complex, protean album, *Abbey Road*. Let me explain where I listened to it. My parents had this new stereo system, in a big wooden cabinet in the living room. It was a *hi-fi*, in the classic sense of the term, and it was maybe the expensive hi-fi that they bought to convince themselves, through amplification, that they were more allied and resilient than they were. My father, who never seemed to be home, was not there while we were making dinner, and so he probably wouldn't remember my mother putting on *Abbey Road*, whereupon we would dance around to the rock numbers, like "Mean Mr. Mustard" and "Come Together." Nor was he there when we sang along with "Golden Slumbers" and "Here Comes the Sun."

Eventually, an evening came to pass that I understood as the moment during which my parents were discussing how to tell us they were separating. They were enclosed in that family room with the expensive hi-fi. The louvered drawing room doors were closed. There was an unsettling silence in the house. We (my sister, brother, and I) looked at these closed doors from up the staircase, between the dowels supporting the banister. Something lasting and grim was taking place. It was obvious. And soon my mother came to break us the news. Ever after, when I imagined this scene, I heard in my head, chief among other songs, "Golden Slumbers." Once, as the song suggests, there *was* a way to get back home. In the past tense. The song still calls forth that loss in me, that time after certainty. Does this melancholy reside in the lyrics, because the relationship between the singer of the song (Paul McCartney) and the children to whom he sings, is, arguably, not dissimilar to the relationship between the divine (from a perch in heaven) and His beloved flock here on earth?

Probably, I liked "Golden Slumbers" because no one sang me lullabies as a kid. I had no idea about *agape* and *caritas.* I had no idea about heaven. I was skeptical. A lullaby, from my point of view, would have been like a happy ending in a movie. Happy endings were for people who believed any nonsense that came along. So I liked "Golden Slumbers," from the newly released *Abbey Road,* because I secretly wanted somebody to sing a lullaby to me. Admitting such a thing makes me uncomfortable. And yet it was from unfulfilled longing that I formulated some ideas of that *elsewhere* of paradise, the place where no longing goes unfulfilled.

3. The Heavenly Jukebox

So far it sounds like I'm making a playlist for a heavenly jukebox. What would be the selections on such a jukebox? Is this jukebox any good? From an earthly point of view, I imagine that if there is music in heaven, it should celebrate virtues and ideals. Does the heavenly jukebox therefore contain only songs by Pat Boone or Deborah Gibson? Does God, whatever He/She/It is, have some amazing celestial version of iTunes where you can hear the songs you like all day long as long as you have, as a virtuous individual, gained admission to the celestial realms? Could I, for example, hear "The Spirit of Radio" by Rush in heaven (assuming I'm virtuous), even though I won't allow myself to listen to it on earth because it is simply too embarrassing? What if hearing Rush would (arguably) make me happy for all eternity? Do people in this kingdom of the worthy get to play Whitesnake around the clock just because they are good and deserving? Or have they transcended Whitesnake, having passed beyond the earthly realms? Do they allow Metallica in heaven? What about that Finnish band where the lead singer wears satanic horns? Maybe he's a really hard-working guy, despite wearing the horns, and is just trying to provide for his

Finnish wife and child? Will he be admitted into heaven and be able there to play a gig with Jimi Hendrix sitting in?

Does God allow celestial broadcasts of Led Zeppelin's "Stairway to Heaven"? Or "Heaven Is a Place on Earth" by Belinda Carlisle? Or "Just Like Heaven" by the Cure? Or "Heaven" by the Talking Heads; or "Pennies from Heaven," or the oft-covered "Knockin' on Heaven's Door," which seems to imply that the doorway to heaven is constructed of such a lightweight material that you *could* knock on it. These songs all have "heaven" in the title, but I don't think they are all good songs, except maybe the Dylan composition, and they don't teach me anything about what kind of music exists in heaven.

And what kind of musical instruments *do* they have in heaven? In the old days, they had trumpets and lutes. Many accounts substantiate this point. Are we to believe that heavenly instrumental groups stopped innovating a thousand years ago? Unlikely! So are there, in fact, electric guitars in heaven, or things that sound like electric guitars? Are there didjeridoos in heaven? What about synthesizers or digital samplers? Do they have the latest plug-ins for computer-based music in heaven? Does one have to clear his or her samples in heaven (because stealing is a venial sin), or can you go ahead and pilfer copyrighted music to your heart's content? What about all those exotic, *foreign* instruments? Tibetan bowls? Mouth harps? Are these instruments available to all who need them for the sake of expression?

Well, it's a real stretch to posit a jukebox in heaven, and I don't think God is a jukebox, and you cannot take your iPod with you when you are gone, and there is no digital sampler and no mixing board to connect it to. Music in heaven probably would not have lightweight lyrics, or even unimpeachably useful lyrics like "All You Need Is Love," and since it's unlikely that we will reach heaven in our corporeal forms, we may not have ears with which to listen to music, nor voices with which to sing it.

4. The Groove in Heaven

Common time is said to be the time signature that most closely resembles the human heartbeat, and 4/4 is also the time signature with the best opportunity for the *groove*. If in my early life I might have advanced the notion that the music in heaven would be noteworthy for lyrical exegesis on subjects like compassion and love, in my teens I would have thought it was all about the groove. Bass and drums, those were the things that made music heavenly, as when you are a teenager or a young adult, and you like the endless groove, for example, in "Sister Ray" by the Velvet Underground, and you are willing to hear that groove go around and around, and you do not exactly care what the lyrics say, if indeed you are able to decipher them. The view from rock club floors and dance clubs and mosh pits is that music is ecstatic, that the groove is ecstatic, and if music is ecstatic then heavenly music should be the acme of this ecstasy. It should be all about union and the sense of community, things that are self-evident at concerts and clubs. When I am in the groove, the groove is good. Thus, the teenage version of myself imagined that heaven, or paradise, was where there was always a good groove, and all kinds of people could dance around to it together for light-years at a time. When I was in the groove, wallowing in the one-four chord progression, let's say, during a song by Funkadelic, then it was all about how many people you could get playing at one time, and the entire audience was on its feet chanting along with some line like "Get up for the down stroke! Everybody get up!" even if many listeners were not exactly sure what the down stroke was nor why they should get up on it. At one time, I would have said that if heaven could not deliver on these things, on the promise of community, and on a music that had a good groove to it, then I didn't think heaven was heavenly.

Meanwhile, it would be logical and easy to make the argument that the groove, generally speaking, has a sexual cast about it, and that people respond to the groove because it is suggestive of the pace and rhythm of sexuality. If this is the case, then again we might have to disqualify this music from heaven, on the basis that there is no corporeal resurrection, in my view, and thus no need for music that appeals to the carnal (or procreative) ecstasy of the flesh. For similar reasons, Cotton Mather frowned upon dancing: "Their Children dance, and They go down the Grave into Hell."

In the vicinity of this notion of the sexual cast of the groove for me would be the related notion of intoxication in heaven gener-

ally. There is no need for intoxication in heaven. I suppose this is
kind of obvious. Why would you need to be intoxicated there? In
heaven, you have not fallen short, you are not in a condition of
wanting, you are theoretically happy, and so you are not looking
for the music or drugs or spirits to intoxicate you in any way. You
don't need to be bludgeoned by the music in heaven, you don't
need to dance until you are exhausted, you don't need one more
rousing chorus, because you don't need to be roused, and you are
not going to get banged up in the mosh pit, nor are you going to
suffer hearing loss, and no one is going to cough during the most
beautiful part of the aria, and no one is going to climb over you to
get to their seat during the opening measures of the second movement of the symphony.

5. Music for Canyons

I bring up this fact of intoxication because of how quitting drinking improved and defined my own spiritual life. I didn't have any
genuine conviction about heaven, or God, or spirituality, or an afterlife, or anything else, really, between the ages of fifteen and
twenty-six, when I was often busy doing other things, most of them
not very good for me. This came to an end in 1987,[3] after which it
occurred to me to go back to church out of gratitude for my reprieve and for the remission of the considerable pain I'd been living with.

At this point, music came back into my life in a number of ways.
First, I started dabbling in it again. I'd taught myself guitar as a
teenager, and so I bought a guitar anew and began practicing it,
and I began writing songs, which I had also done when young. I
also started listening to things in a new way. I can chart the subsequent metamorphosis in my musical taste with a number of recordings I first heard on a local new music program that was broadcast
each night in New York City.

First among the discoveries of that time was the music of Arvo
Pärt. While I can't remember exactly which piece I first heard by
Pärt, I can remember the first album I bought, which was the ECM
release called *Tabula Rasa*. On this recording, both the piece called
"Cantus in Memory of Benjamin Britten" and the orchestral piece

"Fratres" genuinely moved me in ways that "serious" music rarely had. These pieces, which are said to have been composed as a way out of the dead end of serial music and academic atonality, are frankly spiritual and completely tonal, using elements of early music, like plainsong, for their raw material. Elsewhere, Pärt set liturgical texts. For these reasons, and because the pieces are so simple, there is some grumbling in classical music circles about Pärt's work. He's not serious, he's conservative, etc.

I didn't care about any of this when I first heard these recordings, and I still don't. Pärt's compositions split me open like I was an oyster, and the way they did it was by exploiting the simple harmonies of ancient Western music, the kind of dignity and stateliness that I associated with the music of the church as I first heard it. I can't explain what it is about this simplicity and tonality that was so moving to me. And I'm not sure I want to. "Tintinnabuli" is the term that Pärt has in the past used to describe these pieces, meaning that they sound like bells or have the unadorned grace of bells. That description is enough for me.

Pärt led me to other things. Not just spiritually inclined classical music, but to kinds of music that were organized along similar principles, where there was simplicity and elemental harmonics, and where the devotion was to serenity and austerity and to the notion of music itself. That is, I wasn't as interested in the noise that was very moving to me as a young person, nor was I interested in virtuosity for its own sake. Rather, I was after a somewhat baroque idea that tonality *was* spiritual, and even divine. I was therefore moved by minimalism, by LaMonte Young, by Meredith Monk, by chamber music like the Penguin Café Orchestra, by early music, by Hildegard von Bingen, William Byrd, Purcell. It also seemed that anything contemporary that I liked had a lot of echo in it, as if music that was made in canyons was somehow better than music that was made anywhere else. Music that celebrated or was illustrative of sound and nature and the physicality of things.[4]

Maybe in this way I'm beginning to answer the question about *why music in heaven at all?* One thing that everybody always talks about in heaven is the *light.* Dante talks a lot about the light in *Paradiso.* Such a pleasing light! When other chroniclers have made it up there and reported back, there's always ecstatic light in their description. No paintings, no sculptures, no epic poems. No one in heaven is busy making installations or performing performance art. But in addition to light, there *is* music.

This goes all the way back, I imagine, to when there was music to the planets themselves, the heavenly bodies. It's an old perception, the music of the spheres, you find it as far back as Cicero (in *De Re Publica*), and if he was writing it down, he probably wasn't the first to have remarked on the subject: "This music is produced by the impulse and the motion of these spheres themselves. The unequal intervals between them are arranged according to a strict proportion, and so the high notes blend agreeably with the low, and thus various sweet harmonies are produced." Music, according to this argument, is an essential quality of creation, and we might mention especially the sublimity of harmony. And, as Cicero further observes, along with the ubiquity of heavenly music goes the tendency of men to want to imitate it: "Skillful men reproducing this celestial music on stringed instruments have thus opened the way for their own return to this heavenly region, as other men of outstanding genius have done by spending their lives on Earth in the study of things divine."

Why music then? Because when we sing it and play it, we are not only imitating the things that are, but we are praising them, praising the things that are, and praising is good, and you find it, too, in almost any account of heaven. The angels sing their praises, and when we sing, according to, among others, the Levites, we are imitating the angels.

6. Heaven and Non-Being

Still, in the end, any discussion of heaven hinges on the injustice of non-being, and whether you are worried about this injustice. This seems to me the weakest link in the argument about heaven. Must there be some reward for living through this life in the first world? For living through the war and greed and hypocrisy and selfishness? Maybe there *is* no reward, really, but having done a good job here! Maybe that is its own reward! The reward for living in a dignified way in the first world is dignified life in and of itself. Who isn't full of longing for a better place? Who, driving through Elizabeth, New Jersey, or Omaha, Nebraska, or Indianapolis, Indiana, wouldn't long for an idealized heaven? And if the longing is good and human, what need for heaven? Longing and compassion and tenderness *are* heavenly, and they make you better than you otherwise were. Isn't that enough?

If the whole belief in heaven depends on a fear of non-being, then it's no more satisfying than the notion of naked people sitting around on clouds playing lutes. Myself, I have no fear of non-being. I fear mortal pain, which so often seems to precede non-being, but otherwise I don't fear the end of the author of these particular sentences, and I don't require, for his sake, everlasting life. There's enough hassle involved with temporary life. Everlasting life would be closer to hell, for me, than any fiery lake clogged with politicians. Because what would one *do* with eternity?

Unless, for the sake of argument, we are simply talking about energy. Unless we are talking about the little spark calved off the big creative first cause. Maybe we are simply talking about our ability to unite with that first cause. Maybe we are talking about a union that might take place, in which I can be, ideally, some little spark, some match light in the mostly dark and empty universe, the thirteen dimensions of it, and my eternal match light would not necessarily require consciousness or lutes. And along with being this spark, I can imagine that I have a tone, and if I were going to pick one, I would pick something high, in the treble clef, something I couldn't reach when I was a baritone pretending to be a tenor. As this note, or some other note, I can imagine a heaven where I get to play this tone, and to collide with other notes, as if I were a constituent in a John Cage piece, and here there are no entrances and exits, and I don't have to have perfect rhythm, nor do I have to know my scales, because I am all scales. Therefore I have no responsibilities, as a note, I just *am*, because I can't be entirely eliminated, because that doesn't happen — energy gets reused — and in this piece of music you can come in anywhere, and you can be a part of it, or not a part of it, and this composition has a long duration, an eternal duration, but you don't have to worry about this, because you are no longer a perceiving entity, you are just the note and the note is a good thing to be in this composition, which has all the characteristics that good things have, namely it causes no harm, and believes only in its iteration as goodness, which is harmony and sublimity. And all kinds of other music are apparent in this music, even though they are lost, all possible music is contained in this infinite music, so Otis Redding is in there, and Simon and Garfunkel, and Funkadelic, and Arvo Pärt, maybe even Rush, because everything is in there, and in this way I am gone and gone is good, but I am also a very excellent musician and no one is any better, except the artful arranger of all sounds.

Notes

1. From, e.g., *The Stax/Volt Revue, Vol. 2: Live in Paris,* Atlantic Records, 1991.

2. And especially in Psalms 146–150: "Praise him with the blast of the trumpet; praise him with the harp and lyre. Praise him with timbrel and dances; praise him upon the strings and pipe. Praise him with ringing cymbals; praise him upon the clashing cymbals. Let everything that has breath praise the Lord. Alleluia."

3. Committed to psychiatric hospital, got sober, etc.

4. I am not, however, a partisan of the music known as New Age. I do not endorse bland sheets of wallpaper over a machined bed of "exotic" percussion, even if I am in a spa or a yoga studio.

HUGH RAFFLES

Cricket Fighting

FROM *Granta*

1

On the way to the cricket fight, Mr. Wu slipped us a piece of paper. It looked like a shopping list. "More numbers," said Michael, my translator. He read:

THREE REVERSALS
EIGHT FEARS
FIVE FATAL FLAWS
SEVEN TABOOS
FIVE UNTRUTHS

It was Mr. Wu's answer to a question I'd asked him earlier that day in the private banquet room upstairs at the Luxurious Garden Restaurant in Minhang, an enormous industrial suburb in southwest Shanghai. Ask him anything you want, Michael said. But when I told Mr. Wu that I didn't understand the Three Reversals, he looked straight through me without a smile.

Michael, a Shanghai college student, had signed on to work with me as a translator but had quickly become my full-fledged collaborator. Together we were learning about cricket fighting, a centuries-old pastime that seemed to be undergoing a revival. We followed crickets all over the city and found ourselves in places new to both of us as we met traders, trainers, gamblers, event sponsors, entomologists, all kinds of experts. By the time we sat down to eat in the Luxurious Garden, we already knew two of the Reversals and wanted only to confirm the third. But like so many other people we met in Shanghai, Mr. Wu wanted us to know how much deeper the world of Chinese cricket fighting was than we, or even he, could ever hope to understand.

2

We first met Mr. Wu in the back room of a factory social club full of men playing card games. He had jagged stitches in his palm and winced when we shook hands. He was a little nervous: although cricket fighting is legal, gambling is not, and recent crackdowns in the city have even led to executions. Nonetheless Mr. Wu was willing to help and promised to take us to a serious cricket fight. A few nights later he led us to a warren of rundown apartment blocks, through an open front door and into a brightly lit side-room just big enough for a TV, a fish tank, and a gold plastic love seat.

Mr. Wu was close with the father of Boss Xun, the sponsor of the cricket casino we were going to. Boss Xun not only provided the premises but also handled the local police, guaranteed a referee to arbitrate the fighting and the cash, and made available a secure and well-organized public house in which the animals were deposited before the fight. For all this, he and his partner, Boss Yang, took five percent of the winnings. Mr. Wu was a cricket lover of the first order and, we would find out, a gifted judge of cricket form, but he was only a small gambler and not a full member of this underworld, and this, he later explained apologetically, was why he was nervous.

Boss Xun, however, was relaxed and welcoming. He wore track pants, a T-shirt, plastic flip-flops, and a gold chain; his gray hair was close-cropped, and his nails were carefully manicured. "Please feel at home," he said. But Mr. Wu was chain-smoking and on edge. I remembered the instructions he'd given us in the cab: no smoking during the fight, no alcohol, no eating, no cologne, no scent of any kind, no talking, no noise of any kind. "We will be like the air," Michael assured him. But it was hard to be unobtrusive. Boss Xun insisted on seating us at the head of the long, narrow table next to the referee, with the best possible view of the crickets and directly opposite the only door. The casino was basic — a bare white-washed room — and its simplicity was a measure of transparency. As the gamblers entered, they could take in everything, the room and its occupants, at a glance. A few nights earlier, Michael and I had watched a TV exposé of a cricket gambling den, complete with hidden cameras and pixilated interviewees, so we expected a darkened cellar full of shadowy dealings. But Boss Yang and Boss Xun's casino was lit by an antiseptic fluorescent strip that threw its glare into every corner, and their table was covered by a white cloth on which sterile implements were laid out on either side of the clear plastic arena.

This was a secure zone — the windows were stuffed with thick cushions to keep noises in and noses out — but it was also a place of entertainment. Boss Xun worked the room with self-contained charisma. The referee called the bets with finesse, moving everything along swiftly and managing friction with boisterous humor, despite the large amounts of money flying across the table.

"Who will call first?" he began, addressing the two trainers, one on either side of him. Their motions were slow and deliberate. They pulled on white cotton gloves supplied by the house, lifted the lids from the pots to examine their animals, stirred them with long straws of yard grass, and delicately transferred them to opposite sides of the arena. One of the trainers was clumsier than the other; he faltered as he eased his fighter out of the transfer case, nervous in the knowledge that most of the bets are placed before the animals are even visible, that many people wager on the trainers more than on the insects. As the crickets emerged under the lights, everyone leaned in, eager for that moment when the animal's spirit, power, and discipline would be revealed.

For several minutes, the bets mounted on one animal, then the next, stopping only when the second pile of cash in front of the referee had grown to equal the first. Men with fistfuls of 100-yuan notes clamored to have their bets acknowledged by the referee or, once the house bets closed, called odds to entice others with whom they might make side bets. The referee's voice boomed above the rest, building up the crickets and the stakes. Some men offered a loud commentary on the animals and the wagers. Others simply watched.

And then, at the instant the referee directed the trainers to prepare their crickets, the room fell silent. The two trainers began again to gently stroke their animals (back legs, abdomen, jaws) with the yard grass. The crickets didn't move. If you were close enough, you could see the beating of their hearts. The referee called, "Open the floodgate!" and lifted the panel that divided the arena. The silence intensified. It was obvious that these animals were far more combative than any Michael and I had seen before. A sudden assault, a dart, a lunge at an opponent's jaw or leg, and the room emitted a sharp, involuntary gasp.

This was a typical gambling house in the industrial zone, Mr. Wu told us later as everyone poured out of the building into the empty streets of the housing estate. Downtown, the sponsors rent hotel suites and hand-pick their high-rolling punters, and at those places the minimum bet is 10,000 yuan — a low but not unusual annual wage in Shanghai — and total stakes can exceed a million. Tonight in Minhang, though, the referee opened the bidding with modest encouragements: "Bet what you like, we're all friends here, even a hundred is fine tonight." Still, at one point during the evening, as the stakes climbed over 30,000 yuan, a gambler who had traveled here from Nanjing showed his hand for the first time and, with no change of expression — almost, it seemed, absent-mindedly — tossed a bankroll of 6,000 yuan into the middle of the table. He watched impassively as the referee delegated an observer to count and recount the cash until the gate was lifted in the arena and the crickets aggressively locked jaws, wrestling, and flipping each other over, again and again, in a blur of bodies. And then — as if abruptly losing interest — the animals disengaged, walking away into opposite corners and refusing their trainers' attempts to entice them back into the fray. Even the referee's effort to stimulate them by eliciting singing from the two crickets kept for this purpose in pots beside the arena had no effect. It was a draw, a rare outcome that provoked a contemptuous clucking from Mr. Wu, who stage-whispered to us that really good crickets fight to exhaustion, that though athletic and well matched, these animals were poorly trained.

If the crickets appear to tire, if they hang back, or if one turns away, the referee lowers the gate to separate the fighters, resets the sixty-second timer, and invites the trainers to tend to their insects. Like corner men at a boxing match, the trainers try to restore their charges' fighting spirit, but often one cricket simply slumps, his opponent puffs up and sings, and the referee calls an end to the fight. Then, all at once, the cash again begins to fly in the casino — large notes out to the winners, five percent in small bills coming back to the referee.

The winning cricket is returned carefully to his pot, ready for the journey home or back into the public house to prepare for another fight. The loser, no matter how valiant or how physically unscathed, has finished his career. The referee collects him in a net and drops him into a large plastic bucket behind the table, for release "into nature," everyone told me. It was okay, Michael added, I shouldn't worry, the animal would be all right; the curse on anyone who harms a defeated cricket guaranteed it.

3

In Linnaean terms, the fighting crickets kept in Shanghai are mostly *Velarifictorus micado,* a black or dark brown species that grows to between thirteen and eighteen millimeters long and is highly territorial and aggressive in the wild, or, in smaller numbers, the equally bellicose *V. aspersus.* They appear in early August, at *Li qiu,* the division in the lunar calendar that marks the start of autumn and the moment when crickets in eastern China undergo their seventh and final molt. The crickets are now mature and sexually active, and males are able to sing and, as their color darkens and they grow stronger, ready to fight. *Li qiu* is also the signal for tens of thousands of cricket lovers, from Shanghai, Hangzhou, Nanjing, Tianjin, and Beijing, to head for railway stations. They pack the trains to Shandong province, which has established itself over the past twenty years as the source of the finest fighting crickets. People told us that the travelers to Shandong usually bet more than 100 yuan on a fight. Small-time gamblers like Mr. Wu are more likely to wait for the cricket markets in Shanghai to fill with insects from the provinces.

As the fighting season approaches its height in November, the line of pots creeps farther along the table and the contests stretch deeper into the night. But that evening of our first visit to Boss Xun's casino was in late September, and there were just a handful of fights. After they were over, Boss Xun asked if we wanted to visit the public house.

The public house is designed to counter some of the more underhanded tactics said to be popular among cricket trainers. The most sensational of these is doping, especially with ecstasy. Although a tripped-out cricket is likely to be a winning cricket, the drug's real target is the opposition: crickets are acutely sensitive to stimulants. They rapidly detect when their adversary is chemically enhanced, and they respond by turning tail, so forfeiting the contest.

Every cricket slated for Boss Xun's casino spends at least five days undergoing detox in his public house. Part maximum-security zone, part clinic, it was a four-room apartment stripped and retooled. Three rooms had multiply-padlocked steel gates; the fourth was a social space equipped with couch, chairs, TV, and PlayStation, its whitewashed walls decorated with color close-ups — glamour shots — of crickets. Nobody drank or smoked. Two of the gated rooms were bolted storage areas lined with shelves on which I made out stacks of cricket pots. The third was unlocked and, like the casino, brightly lit. Boss Xun led us inside, and I saw a long table and a row of men — owners and trainers there to care for their insects — each tending to a pot. Two assistants, men I recognized from the casino, were stationed across the table. One of them fetched the labeled pots from a cabinet behind him while the other closely observed the visitors. But what made the scene momentarily disorienting was that the men lined up at the table, silently intent on their crickets, were dressed identically in white surgical gowns and matching white masks.

Bio-security is everything. It is well known that trainers dip their yard grass in solutions of ginseng and other substances, which, like smelling salts in a boxing corner, can revive even the most battered fighter; they try to contaminate the food and water of their competitors' animals; they try to engulf them in poisonous gas. They'll even insert tiny knives in their yard grass and put poison on their fingertips, hoping to get close enough to the opposition.

Nonetheless, the public house isn't foolproof. One chink in the armor is when the insects first enter. This is when they're fed and then weighed on an electronic scale. This weight is recorded on the side of the pot, along with the date and owner's name, and it then becomes the basis on which insects are allocated to fighting pairs. Great care is taken to match crickets as precisely as possible. Weights are recorded in *zhen*, a Shanghainese cricket-specific measure now used nationally for this purpose. One *zhen* is around a fifth of a gram, and there should be no more than a 0.2 *zhen* difference between paired fighters. Trainers have become adept at manipulating their insects' weight. In the past, they would subject the animals to an extended sauna to extract liquid just before the weigh-in. Nowadays, it's more common to use dehydration drugs, impossible to detect and, by all accounts, with few ill effects. Once fed, weighed, and admitted, the animal has at least five days under the care of the public house staff and his visiting trainer to recover his strength, and if all goes according to plan, he'll ultimately fight below his weight — imagine Mike Tyson versus Sugar Ray Leonard . . .

4

The speed of urban growth and transformation in Shanghai is stunning. In less than one generation, the fields that gave the crickets a home have all but gone. Now, dense ranks of giant apartment buildings, elongated boxes with baroque and neoclassical flourishes, stretch pink and gray in every direction, past the ends of the newly built metro lines, past even the ends of the suburban bus routes. The spectacular neon waterfront of Pudong, the symbol of Shanghai's drive to seize the future, is only ten years old but already under revision. I marveled at the brash bravery of the Pearl Oriental Tower, a multicolored rocket ship that dominates the dazzling skyline, and thought how impossible it would be to build something so bold yet whimsical in New York. Michael and his college-age friends laughed. "We're a bit tired of it, actually," Michael said. But they also know nostalgia. Only ten years ago, in what seems like another world, they helped fathers and uncles collect and raise crickets in their neighborhoods. They moved in and out of each other's homes and alleyways, sharing a daily life that the high-rise apartments have now banished. Downtown, remnants of that life are visible in pockets not yet rebuilt or thematized. Sometimes, though, residents are merely waiting, surrounded by their neighbors' rubble, holding out against forced relocation to distant suburbs as the government clears more housing in time for the city to host Expo 2010.

Eleven miles from the city center and a crowded fifteen-minute bus ride from the huge metro terminus at Xinzhuang, the township of Qibao is a different kind of neighborhood. An official heritage attraction, a stroll through a past violently disavowed for its feudalism during the Cultural Revolution but now embraced as a part of national culture, Qibao is newly elegant with canals and bridges; its narrow pedestrianized streets are lined with reconstructed Ming and Qing Dynasty buildings. There are storefronts selling all kinds of snack foods, teas, and craft goods to Shanghainese and other visitors, a temple with Han, Tang, and Ming Dynasty architectural features, a weaving workshop, an ancient teahouse, a famous wine distillery, and — in a house built specifically for the sport by the great Qing emperor Qianlong — Shanghai's only museum dedicated to fighting crickets.

All these crickets were collected here in Qibao, said Master Fang, the museum's director. He stood behind a table laden with hundreds of gray clay pots, each containing one fighting male and, in some cases, its female sex partner. Qibao's crickets were famous throughout East Asia, a product of the township's rich soils, he told us. But since the fields here were sold off in 2000, crickets have been harder to find. Master Fang's two white-uniformed assistants filled the insects' miniature water bowls from pipettes, and we humans all drank pleasantly astringent tea made from his recipe of seven medicinal herbs. Master Fang was an animated storyteller, and Michael and I were drawn to him immediately. "Master Fang is a cricket master," confided his assistant, Ms. Zhao. "He has forty years' experience. There is no one more able to instruct you about crickets."

Everyone at the museum was caught up in preparations for the Qibao Golden Autumn Cricket Festival. The three-week event includes a series of exhibition matches and a championship, with all fights broadcast on closed-circuit TV. The goal is to promote cricket fighting as a popular activity distinct from the gambling with which it is now so firmly associated, to remind people of its historical and cultural origins, and to extend its appeal beyond the demographic in which it now seems caught: men in their forties and above.

Twenty years ago, before the construction of the new Shanghai gobbled up the landscape, when city neighborhoods were still patchworks of fields and houses, people lived more intimately with animal life. Many found companionship in cicadas or other musical insects, which they kept in bamboo cages and slim pocket boxes, and young people, not just the middle-aged, fought crickets. They learned how to judge a likely champion and train the fighters to their fullest potential and how to use the pencil-thin brushes made of yard grass or mouse whisker to stimulate the insects' jaws and provoke them to combat. They also learned the Three Rudiments around which every cricket manual is structured: judging, training, and fighting.

Cricket fighting is experiencing a revival in China. Even as it loses out to computer games and Japanese manga with the young, it is thriving among older generations. Yet it's an insecure return that few aficionados are celebrating. For even as the cricket markets flourish and the gambling dens proliferate, much of this enthusiasm is accompanied by a sense that this is another feature of daily life that, like so much else, is already as good as gone.

Master Fang pulled a cricket pot from the shelf behind him and ran his finger over the text etched on its surface. In a strong voice, he began to recite, drawing out the tones in the dramatic cadences of classical oratory. These are the Five Virtues, he announced, five human qualities found in the best fighting crickets, five virtues that crickets and humans share.

The First Virtue: "When it is time to sing, he will sing. This is trustworthiness."

The Second Virtue: "On meeting an enemy, he will not hesitate to fight. This is courage."

The Third Virtue: "Even seriously wounded, he will not surrender. This is loyalty."

The Fourth Virtue: "When defeated he will not sing. He knows shame."

The Fifth Virtue: "When he becomes cold, he will return to his home. He is wise and recognizes the facts of the situation."

On their tiny backs crickets carry the weight of the past. The loyalty of the Third Virtue, for example, is no ordinary loyalty; it is the loyalty one feels for the emperor, the willingness to lay down one's life, and not to shirk one's ultimate duty. These are not simply ancient virtues, they are points on a moral compass. As anyone will tell you, these crickets are warriors; the champions among them are generals.

The passage on Master Fang's pot is taken from the thirteenth-century *Book of Crickets*, the earliest surviving manual for cricket lovers and perhaps the world's first book of entomology. Its author, Jia Sidao (1213–1275), is still remembered as imperial China's "cricket minister," the sensual chief minister in the dying days of the Southern Song Dynasty, so absorbed in the pleasures of his crickets that he allowed his neglected state to tumble into wrack, ruin, and domination by the invading Mongols.

Jia Sidao was the first to document the complex system by which cricket lovers classify their animals. He identified and ranked four body colors: first yellow, then red, black, and finally white. The authoritative xishuai.com cricket lovers' website now adds purple and green. Each color corresponds to a broad category of behavior. However, most of the cricket experts I met in Shanghai describe only three colors: yellow, green, and purple. Yellow crickets are said to be the most aggressive, but not necessarily the best fighters, because green insects, although quieter, are more strategic and — according to the annual illustrated list of cricket champions — include a greater number of generals.

Below these gross distinctions is a further set of divisions into individual "personalities," whose total number is often put at seventy-two. Trainers use a system based on physical variables and complex clusters of characteristics. Length, shape, and color of the insect's legs, abdomen, and wings are all systematically parsed, as is the shape of the head — current manuals might include seven or more possibilities — and differences in number, shape, color, and width of the "fight lines" that run front-to-back across the crown. Experts also consider the energy of the antennae, the shape and color of the animal's "eyebrows" (which should be "opposite" in color to the antennae), the shape, color, translucence, and strength of the jaws, the shape and size of the neck plate, the shape and resting angle of the forewings, the sharpness of the tail tips, the hair on the abdomen, the width of the thorax and face, the thickness of the feet, the animal's overall posture. The insect's "skin" must be "dry," that is, it must reflect light from inside itself, not from its surface; it must also be delicate, like a baby's. The cricket's walk must be swift and easy; it should not have a rolling gait. In general, strength is more important than size. The jaws are decisive.

Judging a cricket's quality requires deep knowledge. Nonetheless, judging is only one of the three rudiments of cricket knowledge, and for Master Fang, it is less important than training.

Master Fang told us that the trainer's task is to build on the cricket's preexisting natural virtues to develop its fighting spirit. This indispensable quality is revealed only at the moment the insect enters the arena. Though a cricket might look like a champion in all respects, it can still turn out to lack spirit in competition. This, Master Fang insisted, has less to do with the individual cricket's character than with its care. It is the task of the trainer to build up the cricket's strength with foods appropriate to its stage of growth and individual needs, to respond to its sicknesses, develop its physical skills, cultivate its virtues, overcome its natural aversion to light, and habituate it to new surroundings. A cricket knows when it is loved and cared for, and it responds with loyalty, courage, obedience, and the signs of quiet contentment.

Master Fang removed the lid from one of his pots, took his yard-grass straw, and barked orders at the cricket as if at a soldier ("This way! That way! This way! That way!"), and the insect, to Michael's and my real astonishment, responded unhesitatingly, turning left, right, left, right, a routine of exercises that Master Fang explained increased the fighter's flexibility, made him limber and elastic, and showed that man and insect understand each other through the language of command as well as beyond it.

5

A few days later, Michael took me to Wanshang, the largest flower, bird, beast, and insect market in Shanghai. The main hall was filled with traders — mostly women — recently arrived in Shanghai from Shandong and other provinces of eastern China. They sat in rows with their crickets laid out neatly in small pots before them. Around the edges of the hall, permanent stalls were occupied by Shanghainese dealers, also newly returned from buying crickets in the rural districts, their clay pots arrayed on tables, the insects' origins chalked up on a blackboard behind them.

Michael showed me the same pattern at cricket markets throughout the city. At Anguo Road, in the grim shadow of Tilanqiao, Shanghai's largest jail, Shanghainese sellers sit at tables while traders from the provinces squat on stools in their own distinct areas, their pots laid out on the ground.

Even though the provincial traders at these markets don't plan to stay in Shanghai, and even though they are likely to be relatively prosperous in their home districts, once in the city they are migrants, subject to harassment, discrimination, and expulsion. Nonetheless, most expect to do well. By minimizing their outgoings, traveling with relatives, going home infrequently, carrying as much stock as possible when they return, and sleeping in cheap hotels close to the market, they can make considerably more in the three months of the cricket season than in the entire rest of the year.

Shanghainese traders don't sell female crickets. Females don't fight or sing and are valued only for the sexual services they provide to males. It's the provincial traders who deal in these, selling them in bulk, stuffed into bamboo sections in lots of three or ten, depending on their size (bigger is better) and coloring (a white abdomen is best). Females are cheap, and, at first glance, it seems as if these traders only sell cheap animals, female and male.

The signs in front of the provincial traders said 10 yuan for each male, sometimes two for 15 yuan. The buyers filed past their pots, browsing the rows with an air of detachment, occasionally lifting the lids to peer inside, taking the grass brush, stimulating the insect's jaws, perhaps shining a flashlight to gauge the color and translucence of its body, trying to judge not only its physical qualities but its fighting spirit. Despite their studied indifference, they were often drawn in, quickly finding themselves bargaining for an insect priced anywhere between 30 and 2,000 yuan. Only children, novices like me, the elderly, the truly petty gamblers who play crickets for fun, and bargain hunters who believe their eye is sharper than the seller's would buy the cheap crickets, it seems.

But how do you judge an insect's spirit without seeing it fight? Groups of men crowd around the Shanghainese stalls. Eventually, someone moved aside to share the view: two crickets locking jaws inside their tabletop arena. The stallholders tended to the animals like trainers at a real fight. But they were seated in chairs, pots piled around them, and as the match progressed they delivered relentless patter like auctioneers, talking up the winner and attempting to raise its price.

This is a risky sales strategy. No one buys a loser, so the defeated are quickly tossed into a plastic bucket. And if, as often happens, the winner isn't sold either, he has to fight again and may be beaten or injured. The seller relies on his ability to inflate the winner's price enough to compensate for the losses. But the woman from Shanghai who eagerly waved us over as she spooned tiny portions of rice into doll's-house-size trays, told us that the Shanghainese insisted on watching the crickets fight before they'd put their money down, that they liked to shift the risk to the seller.

"Provincial traders don't dare fight their crickets," the woman said. She was lively and straightforward and generous, too, inviting us to share her lunch and giving me a souvenir cricket pot, disappointed I wouldn't take the insect as well. She expounded on her neighbors, traders from Shandong province. "They sell their crickets as brand-new to fighting," she said, so casually it almost slipped past, and it was only thanks to Michael's quickness that I discovered she was telling us that crickets circulate throughout the market, unconstrained by social division; they pass not only from trader to buyer but also from trader to trader, from Shanghainese to Shandongese, and from Shandongese to Shanghainese. And, as they travel through these crowded spaces, they gain and even recover value; they're born again: losers become ingénues, cheap crickets become contenders.

For a few weeks, the crickets are everywhere. On working-class street corners, groups of men cram themselves around an arena, watching the battles unfold. In the newspapers, it's high culture and lowlife, elite sponsorship and police raids. The crickets bring the gambling houses to life. They light up the stores that sell the elaborate implements every cricket trainer needs: tiny food and water dishes, wooden transfer cases, "marriage boxes," grass and whisker brushes made of duck down, tiny long-handled metal trowels and other cleaning implements, pipettes, scales (weighted and electronic), technical manuals, specialized foods and medicines. And, of course, cricket pots in enormous variety, some old (and often fake), some new, most of clay but some of porcelain, some to commemorate special cricket events, some large, some small, some with inscriptions or mottoes or stories, some with intricate images, some (perhaps the most beautiful of all) plain.

6

Dr. Li Shijun of Jiao Tong University invited us to his home. A few journalists, some cricket experts, and a university colleague or two would also be there. We must be sure to show up as planned.

I was keen to meet Dr. Li. I'd seen him interviewed on a TV program included on a DVD I'd picked up at one of Shanghai's many cricket markets. The reporter was enthusiastic about the professor's campaign to promote cricket fighting as a high-culture activity free of gambling, a project in line with state policy. "Gambling," she said in the final voice-over, "has ruined the reputation of cricket fighting. Cricket fighting is like Beijing Opera — it is the quintessence of our country. Many foreigners regard it as the most typically Oriental element of our culture. We should lead it to a healthy road." Just a few days before I arrived in Shanghai, Dr. Li had again featured prominently in the media, this time in a newspaper article on a gambling-free tournament he had staged downtown. The newspaper journalist identified Dr. Li as the "Cricket Professor." The TV reporter called him the "Venerable Cricket Master."

Dr. Li's apartment was tucked away in a corner of a low-rise housing complex close to the university campus. He was a charming host, warm and welcoming, a youthful sixty-four-year-old with a mane of silver hair. Several people were already there when we arrived, and he swiftly corralled us into his office, all the while pointing out the prizes from his lifelong passion: the cricket-themed paintings, poems, and calligraphy created by himself and his friends that enlivened the walls and bookcases, the large collection of southern cricket pots that formed the focus of one of his four published books on cricket-related matters.

Dr. Li grew up in Shanghai and, like other men of his generation, his fascination with crickets was sparked and nurtured by an older brother. He described passing the large (now long gone) cricket market at Chenghuangmiao every day on his way to school in the late 1940s; he remembered using his pocket money to buy crickets and the circle of "insect friends" that grew around him — boys his own age and the adults who would stop to play with them.

At the end of his book *Fifty Don'ts of Cricket Collecting* (don't buy a cricket with rounded wings, don't buy a cricket with just one antenna, don't buy a cricket that is half male, half female, etc.), Dr. Li remarks that it's no mystery that society looks down on cricket fighting; whereas at the university he teaches in a suit and tie, at the insect market, surrounded by "low-level people," he has to wear a T-shirt, shorts, and slippers like everyone else. The lack of cultivation — evident in the smoking, cursing, and spitting all around him — was not simply a personal matter: "If you want others to treat you with respect you must first act decently," he insisted. It wasn't just a question of deportment either. For Dr. Li there is a crisis of civility in Chinese society, and cricket fighting is part of the solution. With its ancient traditions and scholarly demands, cricket fighting is a rare practice, closer to tai chi than mahjong. But it is a practice debased by gambling.

Campaigns against gambling have been a feature of the People's Republic since 1949. But despite periodically aggressive policing and especially since the post-Mao reforms, the government has had little success in controlling its expansion. Unlike the failed attempt to outlaw mahjong during the 1980s, the assault on crickets has been indirect and, in this respect, has paralleled policy during the Ming and Qing dynasties, when imperial prohibitions ran up against the emerging professional network of urban cricket houses, but legislation continued to target gambling rather than crickets.

Dr. Li told us about his scheme to promote development in Henan province by helping local farmers enter the Shanghai cricket market in competition with traders from Shandong, Anhui, and elsewhere. He was spending significant sums of his own money on this project and investing a great deal of his considerable energy, even traveling to the countryside to donate equipment and teach villagers how to distinguish between different insect species. The village he was working with was on the same latitude as Shandong, and he had every reason to expect its crickets to be as strong. The pilot project had produced promising results. It was now only a question of convincing the buying public.

He led us into a large sitting room in which he had laid out a variety of pots and implements. Selecting two pots, he carried them over to a low coffee table positioned in front of a couch. He transferred the crickets into an arena on the table and invited me to sit beside him. He put a yard-grass straw in my hand and, as people often did, encouraged me to stimulate the insects' jaws. I was clumsy with the brush and always felt as if I was tormenting the insect, who, more often than not, simply stood still and suffered my attentions. But I was jiggling my wrist as best I could when I looked up to find that all the other people present, with the exception of Dr. Li, who continued to stare intently at the crickets as if he and I were alone in the room, had produced digital cameras and were lined up in formation, snapping away at close range like paparazzi at a premiere. And now Dr. Li turned creative director, instructing me how to position the grass, how to hold my head, what to look at, how to sit . . .

A few days later an article appeared in the *Shanghai Evening Post* under the headline ANTHROPOLOGIST STUDYING HUMAN-INSECT RELATIONS, U.S. PROFESSOR WANTS TO PUBLISH A BOOK FOR CRICKETS. Its author was Li Jing, a smart young reporter I had met at Dr. Li's house. Li Jing subtly traced Dr. Li's erudition. She noted his eager recourse to the yellowing books on his shelves and his willingness to take me on as his acolyte as well as his friend ("Questions flew out of his mouth like bullets," she wrote of my reaction to the crickets). In offering me guidance, Dr. Li was *chuandao jie huo,* a Confucian term for the teacher's task of passing on the knowledge of the ancient sages and resolving its interpretive difficulties. She let her readers know that his pro-cricket, anti-gambling campaign was a matter of culture, that it reached out from the whirlpool of the present to a higher ground that was both an available safe haven of the past and an anchor for the future. The photo caption, adapting a well-known saying, read, "United by their love of crickets, these two strangers immediately became friends."

7

Centuries before anyone thought of placing crickets in pots and provoking them to fight each other, their evocative singing and their presence in the home gave them a special place in Chinese life. In this poem from the *Shijïng* (*The Book of Songs*), an anthology compiled around three thousand years ago, the cricket seeks out human company and finds its way into the heart of the household:

> It is in the wild in the seventh month,
> Under the eaves in the eighth month,
> In the house in the ninth month,
> and under my bed in the tenth month.

There is a long history of cricket friends — people who become friends through crickets, and crickets who become friends with people. Jia Sidao recommends trainers chew sesame seeds before feeding them to their insects, just as mothers sometimes do before feeding them to their babies. But crickets are friends, not babies. And this is something that cricket lovers (unlike some pet lovers) are unlikely to forget. Because, as well as the Five Virtues, they have the Three Reversals.

If the Five Virtues show the similarity between crickets and people, the Three Reversals recognize the differences.

The First Reversal: A defeated cricket will not protest the outcome of a fight; he will simply leave the arena without complaint.

The Second Reversal: A cricket requires sex before a fight and performs better for the stimulation it provides; rather than having an enervating effect on athletic performance (as, according to this reversal, it does in men), among crickets, pregame sex promotes physical prowess, mental focus, and fighting spirit.

The Third Reversal: Crickets have sex with the female on the male's back — a position functionally impossible for people (without complicated equipment). Moreover, as the entomologist L. W. Simmons points out in what we might think of as a decisive commentary on Reversal Three: "Since the female must actively mount a courting male, there is little if any opportunity for forced matings by males."

The last time I saw Boss Xun, he invited me to travel with him the following year to Shandong. We would spend two weeks there collecting crickets, he said. He knew everyone and had excellent relations with the local authorities. His offer tugged at me strongly — to be around cricket friends, human and insect, once more. Michael was enthusiastic, too. Perhaps, he said, we could spend the entire season with the crickets. That, we agreed, would really be something to come back for.

DAVID SEDARIS

This Old House

FROM *The New Yorker*

WHEN IT CAME TO decorating her home, my mother was nothing if not practical. She learned early on that children will destroy whatever you put in front of them, so for most of my youth our furniture was chosen for its durability rather than for its beauty. The one exception was the dining room set, which my parents bought shortly after they were married. Should a guest eye the buffet for longer than a second, my mother would notice and jump in to prompt a compliment. "You like it?" she'd ask. "It's Scandinavian!" This, we learned, was the name of a region — a cold and forsaken place where people stayed indoors and plotted the death of knobs.

The buffet, like the table, was an exercise in elegant simplicity. The set was made of teak and had been finished with tung oil. This brought out the character of the wood, allowing it, at certain times of day, to practically glow. Nothing was more beautiful than our dining room, especially after my father covered the walls with cork. It wasn't the kind you use on bulletin boards but something coarse and dark, the color of damp pine mulch. Light the candles beneath the chafing dish, lay the table with the charcoal-textured dinnerware we hardly ever used, and you had yourself a real picture.

This dining room, I liked to think, was what my family was all about. Throughout my childhood, it brought me great pleasure, but then I turned sixteen and decided that I didn't like it anymore. What happened was a television show, a weekly drama about a close-knit family in Depression-era Virginia. The family didn't have a blender or a country-club membership, but they did have one another — that and a really great house, an old one, built in the twenties or something. All their bedrooms had slanted clapboard walls and oil lamps that bathed everything in fragile golden light. I wouldn't have used the word "romantic," but that's how I thought of it.

"You think those prewar years were cozy?" my father once asked. "Try getting up at five A.M. to sell newspapers on the snow-covered streets. That's what I did and it stunk to high heaven."

"Well," I told him, "I'm just sorry that you weren't able to appreciate it."

Like anyone nostalgic for a time he didn't live through, I chose to weed out the little inconveniences: polio, say, or the thought of eating stewed squirrel. The world was simply grander back then, somehow more civilized, and nicer to look at. Wasn't it crushing to live in a house no older than our cat?

"No," my father said. "Not at all."

My mother felt the same: "Boxed in by neighbors, having to walk through my parents' bedroom in order to reach the kitchen. If you think that was fun, you never saw your grandfather with his teeth out."

They were more than willing to leave their pasts behind them, and reacted strongly when my sister Gretchen and I began dragging it home. "The *Andrews* Sisters?" my father groaned. "What the hell do you want to listen to them for?"

When I started buying clothes from Goodwill, he really went off, and for good reason, probably. The suspenders and knickers were bad enough, but when I added a top hat he planted himself in the doorway and physically prevented me from leaving the house. "It doesn't make sense," I remember him saying. "That hat with those pants, worn with the damn platform shoes . . ." His speech temporarily left him, and he found himself waving his hands, no doubt wishing that they held magic wands. "You're just . . . a mess is what you are."

The way I saw it, the problem wasn't my outfit but my context. Sure I looked out of place beside a Scandinavian buffet, but put me in the proper environment and I'd undoubtedly fit right in.

"The environment you're looking for is called a psychiatric hospital," my father said. "Now give me the damn hat before I burn it off."

*

I longed for a home where history was respected — and, four years later, I finally found one. This was in Chapel Hill, North Carolina. I'd gone there to visit an old friend from high school — and because I was between jobs, and had no real obligations, I decided to stay for a while and maybe look for some dishwashing work. The restaurant that hired me was a local institution, all dark wood and windowpanes the size of playing cards. The food was okay, but what the place was really known for was the classical music that the man in charge, someone named Byron, pumped into the dining room. Anyone else might have thrown in a compilation tape, but he took his responsibilities very seriously, and planned each meal as if it were an evening at Tanglewood. I hoped that dishwashing might lead to a job in the dining room, busing tables, and, eventually, waiting on them, but I kept these aspirations to myself. Dressed as I was, in jodhpurs and a smoking jacket, I should have been grateful that I was hired at all.

After getting my first paycheck, I scouted out a place to live. My two requirements were that it be cheap and close to where I worked, and on both counts I succeeded. I couldn't have dreamed that it would also be old and untouched, an actual boarding house. The owner was adjusting her "Room for Rent" sign as I passed, and our eyes locked in an expression that said, "Hark, stranger, you are one of me!" Both of us looked like figures from a scratchy newsreel: me the unemployed factory worker in tortoiseshell safety glasses and a tweed overcoat two sizes too large, and her, the feisty widow lady, taking in boarders in order to make ends meet. "Excuse me," I called, "but is that hat from the forties?"

The woman put her hands to her head and adjusted what looked like a fistful of cherries spilling from a velveteen saucer. "Why, yes it is," she said. "How canny of you to notice." I'll say that her name was Rosemary Dowd, and, as she introduced herself, I tried to guess her age. What foxed me was her makeup, which was on the heavy side and involved a great deal of peach-colored powder. From a distance, her hair looked white, but now I could see that it was streaked with yellow, almost randomly, like snow that had been peed on. If she seemed somewhat mannish, it was the fault of her clothing rather than her features. Both her jacket and her blouse were kitted out with shoulder pads, and when they were worn together she could barely fit through the door. This might be a problem for others, but Rosemary didn't get out much. And why would she want to?

I hadn't even crossed the threshold when I agreed to take the room. What sold me was the look of the place. Some might have found it shabby — "a dump," my father would eventually call it — but, unless you ate them, a few thousand paint chips never hurt anyone. The same could be said for the groaning front porch and the occasional missing shingle. It was easy to imagine that the house, set as it was, on the lip of a student parking lot, had dropped from the sky, like Dorothy's in *The Wizard of Oz,* but with a second story. Then there was the inside, which was even better. The front door opened into a living room, or, as Rosemary called it, "the parlor." The word was old-fashioned, but fitting. Velvet curtains framed the windows. The walls were papered in a faint floral pattern, and doilies were everywhere, laid flat on tabletops and sagging like cobwebs from the backs of overstuffed chairs. My eyes moved from one thing to another, and, like my mother with her dining room set, Rosemary took note of where they landed. "I see you like my davenport," she said, and, "You don't find lamps like that anymore. It's a genuine Stephanie."

It came as no surprise that she bought and sold antiques, or "dabbled" in them, as she said. Every available surface was crowded with objects: green glass candy dishes, framed photographs of movie stars, cigarette boxes with monogrammed lids. An umbrella leaned against an open steamer trunk, and, when I observed that its handle was Bakelite, my new landlady unpinned her saucer of cherries and predicted that the two of us were going to get along famously.

And for many months we did. Rosemary lived on the ground floor, in a set of closed-off rooms she referred to as her chambers. The door that led to them opened onto the parlor, and when I stood outside I could sometimes hear her television. This seemed to me a kind of betrayal, like putting a pool table inside the Great Pyramid, but she assured me that the set was an old one — "My 'Model Tee Vee,'" she called it.

My room was upstairs, and in letters home I described it as "hunky-dory." How else to capture my peeling, buckled wallpaper and the way that it brought everything together. The bed, the desk, the brass-plated floor lamp: it was all there waiting for me, and though certain pieces had seen better days — the guest chair, for instance, was missing its seat — at least everything was uniformly old. From my window I could see the parking lot and, beyond that, the busy road leading to the restaurant. It pleased Rosemary that I worked in such a venerable place. "It suits you," she said. "And don't feel bad about washing dishes. I think even Gable did it for a while."

"Did he?"

I felt so clever, catching all her references. The other boarder didn't even know who Charlie Chan was, and the guy was half Korean! I'd see him in the hall from time to time — a chemistry major, I think he was. There was a third room as well, but owing to some water damage Rosemary was having a hard time renting it. "Not that I care so much," she told me. "In my business, it's more about quality than quantity."

I moved in at the beginning of January, and throughout that winter my life felt like a beautiful dream. I'd come home at the end of the day and Rosemary would be sitting in the parlor, both of us fully costumed. "Aha!" she'd say. "Just the young man I was looking for." Then she'd pull out some new treasure she'd bought at an estate sale and explain what made it so valuable: "On most of the later Fire King loaf pans, the trademark helmet is etched rather than embossed."

The idea was that we were different, not like the rest of America, with its Fuzzbusters and shopping malls and rotating showerheads. "If it's not new and shiny, they don't want anything to do with it," Rosemary would complain. "Give them the Liberty Bell and they'd bitch about the crack. That's how folks are nowadays. I've seen it."

There was a radio station in Raleigh that broadcast old programs, and sometimes at night, when the reception was good, we'd sit on the davenport and listen to Jack Benny or *Fibber McGee and Molly*. Rosemary might mend a worn WAC uniform with her old-timey sewing kit, while I'd stare into the fireplace and wish that it still worked. Maybe we'd leaf through some old *Look* magazines. Maybe the wind would rattle the windows and we'd draw a quilt over our laps and savor the heady scent of mothballs.

I hoped that our lives would continue this way forever, but inevitably the past came knocking. Not the good kind that was collectible but the bad kind that had arthritis. One afternoon in early

April, I returned home from work to find a lost-looking white-haired woman sitting in the parlor. Her fingers were stiff and gnarled, so rather than shake hands I offered a little salute. "Sister Sykes" was how she introduced herself. I thought that was maybe what they called her in church, but then Rosemary walked out of her chambers and told me through gritted teeth that this was a professional name.

"Mother here was a psychic," she explained. "Had herself a tarot deck and a crystal ball and told people whatever stupid malarkey they wanted to hear."

"That I did," Sister Sykes said, chuckling.

You'd think that someone who occasionally wore a turban herself would like having a psychic as a mom, but Rosemary was over it. "If she'd forecast thirty years ago that I'd wind up having to take care of her, I would have put my head in the oven and killed myself," she told me.

When June rolled around, the chemistry student graduated, and his room was rented to a young man I'll call Chaz, who worked on a road construction crew. "You know those guys that hold the flags?" he said. "Well, that's me. That's what I do."

His face, like his name, was chiseled and memorable, and, after deciding that he was too handsome, I began to examine him for flaws. The split lower lip only added to his appeal, so I moved on to his hair, which had clearly been blow-dried, and to the strand of turquoise pebbles visible through his unbuttoned shirt.

"What are you looking at?" he asked, and before I had a chance to blush he started telling me about his ex-girlfriend. They'd lived together for six months, in a little apartment behind Fowler's grocery store, but then she cheated on him with someone named Robby, an asshole who went to UNC and majored in fucking up other people's lives. "You're not one of those college snobs, are you?" he asked.

I probably should have said "No," rather than "Not presently."

"What did you study?" he asked. "Bank robbing?"

"Excuse me?"

"Your clothes," he said. "You and that lady downstairs look like those people from *Bonnie and Clyde,* not the stars but the other ones. The ones who fuck everything up."

"Yes, well, we're individuals."

"Individual freaks," he said, and then he laughed, suggesting that there were no hard feelings. "Anyway, I don't have time to stand around and jaw. A friend and me are hitting the bars."

He'd do this every time: start a conversation and end it abruptly, as if it had been me who was running his mouth. Before Chaz moved in, the upstairs was fairly quiet. Now I heard the sound of his radio through the wall, a rock station that made it all the harder to pretend I was living in gentler times. When he was bored, he'd knock on my door and demand that I give him a cigarette. Then he'd stand there and smoke it, complaining that my room was too clean, my sketches were too sketchy, my old-fashioned bathrobe was too old-fashioned. "Well, enough of this," he'd say. "I have my own life to lead." Three or four times a night this would happen.

As Chaz changed life on the second floor, Sister Sykes changed it on the first. I went to check my mail one morning and found Rosemary dressed just like anyone else her age: no hat or costume jewelry, just a pair of slacks and a ho-hum blouse with unpadded shoulders. She wasn't wearing makeup, either, and had neglected to curl her hair. "What can I tell you?" she said. "That kind of dazzle takes time, and I just don't seem to have any lately." The parlor, which had always been just so, had gone downhill as well. Now there were cans of iced-tea mix sitting on the Victrola, and boxed pots and pans parked in the corner where the credenza used to be. There was no more listening to Jack Benny, because that was Sister Sykes's bath time. "The queen bee," Rosemary called her.

Later that summer, just after the Fourth of July, I came downstairs and found a pair of scuffed white suitcases beside the front door. I hoped that someone was on his way out — Chaz, specifically — but it appeared that the luggage was coming rather than going. "Meet my daughter," Rosemary said, this with the same grudging tone she'd used to introduce her mother. The young woman — I'll call her Ava — took a rope of hair from the side of her head and stuck it in her mouth. She was a skinny thing, and very pale, dressed in jeans and a western-style shirt. "In her own little world," Sister Sykes said.

Rosemary told me later that her daughter had just been released from a mental institution, and though I tried to act surprised, I don't think I was very convincing. It was like she was on acid almost, the way she'd sit and examine something long after it had lost its mystery: an ashtray, a dried-up moth, Chaz's blow dryer in the upstairs bathroom — everything got equal attention, including my room. There were no lockable doors on the second floor. The keys had been lost years earlier, so Ava just wandered in whenever she felt like it. I'd come home after a full day of work — my clothes smelling of wet garbage, my shoes squishy with dishwater — and find her sitting on my bed or standing like a zombie behind my door.

"You scared me," I'd say, and she'd stare into my face until I turned away.

The situation at Rosemary's sank to a new low when Chaz lost his job. "I was overqualified," he told me, but as the days passed his story became more elaborate, and he felt an ever-increasing urge to share it with me. He started knocking more often, not caring that it was 6 A.M. or well after midnight. "And another thing . . . ," he'd say, stringing ten separate conversations into one. He got into a fight that left him with a black eye. He threw his radio out the window and then scattered the broken pieces throughout the parking lot.

Late one evening, he came to my door, and when I opened it he grabbed me around the waist and lifted me off the floor. This might sound innocent, but his was not a celebratory gesture. We hadn't won a game or been granted a stay of execution, and carefree people don't call you a "hand puppet of the Dark Lord" when they pick you up without your consent. I knew then that there was something seriously wrong with the guy, but I couldn't put a name to it. I guess I thought that Chaz was too good-looking to be crazy.

When he started slipping notes under my door, I decided it was time to update my thinking. "Now I'm going to *die* and come back on the same day," one of them read. It wasn't just the messages but the writing itself that spooked me, the letters all jittery and butting up against one another. Some of his notes included diagrams, and flames rendered in red ink. When he started leaving them for Rosemary, she called him down to the parlor and told him he had to leave. For a minute or two, he seemed to take it well, but then he thought better of it and threatened to return as a vapor.

"Did he say 'viper'?" Sister Sykes asked.

Chaz's parents came a week later, and asked if any of us had seen him. "He's a schizophrenic, you see, but sometimes he goes off his medication."

I'd thought that Rosemary would be sympathetic, but she was sick to death of mental illness, just as she was sick of old people, and of having to take in boarders to make ends meet. "If he was screwy you should have told me before he moved in," she said to Chaz's father. "I can't have people like that running through my house. What with these antiques, it's just not safe." The man's eyes wandered around the parlor, and through them I saw what he did: a dirty room full of junk. It had never been anything more than that, but for some reason — the heat, maybe, or the couple's heavy, almost contagious sense of despair — every gouge and smudge jumped violently into focus. More depressing still was the thought that I belonged here, that I fit in.

For years, the university had been trying to buy Rosemary's property. Representatives would come to the door, and her accounts of these meetings seemed torn from a late-night movie: "So I said to him, 'But don't you see? This isn't just a house. It's my home, sir. My home.'"

They didn't want the building, of course, just the land. With every passing semester it became more valuable, and she was smart to hold out for as long as she did. I don't know what their final offer was, but Rosemary accepted it. She signed the papers with a vintage fountain pen, and was still holding it when she came to give me the news. This was in August, and I was lying on my floor, making a sweat angel. A part of me was sad that the house was being sold, but another, bigger part — the part that loved air conditioning — was more than ready to move on. It was pretty clear that as far as the restaurant was concerned, I was never going to advance beyond dishwashing. Then, too, it was hard to live in a college town and not go to college. The students I saw out my window were a constant reminder that I was just spinning my wheels, and I was beginning to imagine how I would feel in another ten years, when they started looking like kids to me.

A few days before I left, Ava and I sat together on the front porch. It had just begun to rain when she turned and asked, "Did I ever tell you about my daddy?"

This was more than I'd ever heard her say, and before continu-

ing she took off her shoes and socks and set them on the floor beside her. Then she drew a hank of hair into her mouth and told me
that her father had died of a heart attack. "Said he didn't feel well
and an hour later he just plunked over."

I asked a few follow-up questions, and learned that he had died
on November 19, 1963. Three days after that, the funeral was held,
and while riding from the church to the cemetery Ava looked out
the window and noticed that everyone she passed was crying. "Old
people, college students, even the colored men at the gas station
— the soul brothers, or whatever we're supposed to call them
now."

It was such an outmoded term, I just had to use it myself. "How
did the soul brothers know your father?"

"That's just it," she said. "No one told us until after the burial
that Kennedy had been shot. It happened when we were in the
church, so that's what everyone was so upset about. The president,
not my father."

She then put her socks back on and walked into the parlor, leaving both me and her shoes behind.

When I'd tell people about this later, they'd say, "Oh, come on,"
because it was all too much, really. An arthritic psychic, a ram-
shackle house, and either two or four crazy people, depending on
your tolerance for hats. Harder to swallow is that each of us was
such a cliché. It was as if you'd taken a Carson McCullers novel,
mixed it with a Tennessee Williams play, and dumped all the sets
and characters into a single box. I didn't even add that Sister Sykes
used to own a squirrel monkey, as it only amounted to overkill.
Even the outside world seems suspect here: the leafy college town,
the restaurant with its classical music.

I never presumed that Kennedy's death was responsible for Ava's
breakdown. Plenty of people endure startling coincidences with
no lasting aftereffects, so I imagine that her troubles started years
earlier. As for Chaz, I later learned that it was fairly common for
schizophrenics to go off their medication. I'd think it strange that
the boarding house attracted both him and me, but that's what
cheap places do — draw in people with no money. An apartment
of my own was unthinkable at that time of my life, and, even if I'd
found an affordable one, it wouldn't have satisfied my fundamen-
tal need: to live in a communal past, or what I imagined the past to

be like — a world full of antiques. What I could never fathom, and still can't, really, is that at one point all those things were new — the wheezing Victrola, the hulking davenport. How were they any different from the eight-track tape player, or my parents' Scandinavian dining room set? Given enough time, I guess, anything can look good. All it has to do is survive.

SAM SHAW

Run Like Fire Once More

FROM *Harper's Magazine*

THE RUNNERS SLOG past a bivouac of plastic card tables and folding chairs, past electric-green Port-O Lets ripe with disinfectant, past indifferently groomed hedges and the red brick façade of Thomas A. Edison Vocational and Technical High School. At the corner of 168th Street, they cut north to the Grand Central Parkway, the course rising gently as trucks and cars rocket by. The concrete apron is a blinding white line. They pass illegally parked cars, wipers festooned with tickets. Trash has blown into the grass of Joseph Austin park, named for Mario Cuomo's childhood baseball coach. Here are silent handball and basketball courts, and a playground where sprinklers throw a flume across a midway empty of children. Alone or in twos or threes, the runners pass the hydrants and trash cans of 164th Place, moving southward to Abigail Adams Avenue and thence east a half-block under shade trees to the row of card tables, where women jot notes on clipboards, like a delegation of Green Party poll watchers. At a comfortable pace, you can walk the loop in about ten minutes. The course of the world's longest footrace measures .5488 mile.

I first walked it myself on a balmy day last June, then found a seat at Base Camp among a half-dozen volunteers, bright-eyed European women and men with the lost-boy quality of scoutmasters. A giant digital clock was perched atop a pair of milk crates. Every few minutes one of the racers passed by, and we all applauded.

At 3 P.M., amid a crackling of police bullhorns, two thousand mostly black and Hispanic teenagers emptied out of Edison High. They pumped their legs, lampooning the runners' form, sometimes diverting the race into traffic. "The first couple years, the kids threw things at us," a volunteer told me.

Such were the hazards last summer in Jamaica, Queens, at the tenth running of the Self-Transcendence 3,100. The fifteen participants — all but two of them disciples of the Bengali Guru Sri Chinmoy, who has resided in the neighborhood for forty years — hailed from ten countries on three continents. They ran in all weather, seven days a week, from 6 A.M. to midnight, or until their bodies compelled them to rest. If they logged fewer than fifty miles on a given day, they risked disqualification. By their own reckoning, the runners climbed eight meters per lap, mounting and descending a spectral Everest every week and a half. They toiled in this fashion for six to eight weeks, however long it took them to complete 5,649 circuits — 3,100 miles — around a single city block.

Before any concerns aesthetic or spiritual, the loop serves the practical function of enabling the Base Camp crew to attend to the physical requirements of runners traveling at all speeds. (By the sixth week of the race, nine hundred miles would separate course record holder Madhupran Wolfgang Schwerk, of Solingen, Germany, from Suprabha Beckjord, in last place.*) But in another, more ethereal sense, the Self-Transcendence Race could not exist on any other course. Here was a kind of living koan, a race of invisible miles across a phantom plain wider than the continental United States. For fifty days, breathing miasmal exhaust from the Grand Central Parkway, the runner traversed a wilderness of knapsack-toting teenagers, beat cops, and ladies piloting strollers. Temperatures spiked. Power grids crashed. Cars also crashed — into the chain-link fence around Joe Austin park or into other cars. There was occasional street crime. One summer a student was knifed in the head. The runner endured. He crossed the finish line changed. It was said to be the most difficult racecourse in the world. Point-to-point racing is gentler on the spirit, and concrete is ten times more punishing than asphalt. Such hurdles were more than necessary evils; they were central to the nature of the race. As

---

* The fifty-year-old proprietor of the Washington, D.C., gift shop Transcendence-Perfection-Bliss of the Beyond, Beckjord is the only female competitor in the race's history and the only ten-time participant, having returned to Jamaica every June since the inaugural running. She has logged enough miles around Edison High to circle the equator.

one of the disciples told me, grinning and drawing air quotes with his fingers, "It's 'impossible.'"

I fell into step beside Abichal Watkins, a forty-five-year-old Welshman with a keen, appraising squint. After only five days, he looked like a man who had wandered out of the desert with a story to tell. "There are so few things for the mind to dwell on here," Abichal said. "It loses its strength." Relative to most of the racers, Abichal — born Kelvin and rechristened in 1999 by Sri Chinmoy — came to distance running late in life. That tale begins in the mid-1990s, when Chinmoy announced the completion of his millionth "Soul Bird" painting (artworks expressing the "heart's oneness"), and his disciples resolved to match the feat by running, collectively, a million miles. Abichal pledged an even thousand. Within a year, Chinmoy had painted another million Soul Birds, and the running project was scuttled, but Abichal kept it up. In Wales he edits a magazine and a website devoted to multiday ultramarathons. He had finished the Self-Transcendence Race twice before; a third attempt failed when his visa expired 2,700 miles in.

We passed Edison High, progressing counterclockwise up 168th Street toward the Grand Central Parkway. (The runners switch direction every day, not for the sake of novelty but to ensure that the toll of rounding corners is borne equally by both legs.) Abichal does not consider himself an athlete. "The race is a metaphor for life." He gestured, lassoing the whole of Jamaica around us. "People in the neighborhood, we'll see them year after year. They stop by, say hi. They ask, 'How do you do that?'" He laughed. This was the first interview I conducted while power-walking. It was awkward. My pen kept slipping in my hand.

Abichal wore an iPod clipped to his waist, jarring my notion of the Chinmoy disciples as latter-day ascetics. I wondered what he had been listening to. "'Fix You,'" he said, "by Coldplay." For more than a hundred miles, Abichal had been listening to the track on a continuous loop. ("Lights will guide you home," the chorus intones, "and ignite your bones.") He gazed philosophically at his iPod. "There's something special about this song."

As we neared 164th Place, a white town car pulled gently to the curb. With the speed and nonchalance of a dope dealer, a man in the passenger seat reached through the window and deposited something into Abichal's hands. Sri Chinmoy. The sight of him tripped me up. Here was the Guru himself, gold-complected, resplendently bald. Dressed as if for a day at the public pool, in shorts and a cotton shirt, he did not look like a man who had inspired seven thousand followers in sixty countries to forswear alcohol, tobacco, meat, and sex. I wanted to stop, but the race paused for no man, not even an avatar of divine consciousness.

A few paces ahead, Abichal studied the objects he'd received: two strawberries, cupped in his palms like bulbous, red communion wafers. "I don't know why he gave me two," he said. He turned to me, suddenly serious. "I think one of them is for you." Our fables, stretching back to the myth of Persephone and Genesis 3:6, teach circumspection in receiving gifts of fruit. Abichal nodded, and I ate the Guru's strawberry. Within a few weeks, the runners would be hobbled by distance, gorging ice cream and butter to stem the loss of body weight. We passed the giant digital clock, and the women applauded. Two thousand eight hundred and thirty miles to go.

The specter of death has hung over long-distance running since Robert Browning published his *Dramatic Idylls* in 1879. In a flight of lyric fancy widely mistaken for truth, the poem "Pheidippides" describes an ill-starred footman sprinting from Marathon to Athens with news of a surprise Greek victory in an early battle of the Persian Wars.

> So, when Persia was dust, all cried, "To Akropolis!
> Run Pheidippides, one race more! the meed is thy due!
> 'Athens is saved, thank Pan,' go shout!" He flung down his shield
> Ran like fire once more: and the space 'twixt the Fennel-field
> And Athens was stubble again, a field which a fire runs through,
> Till in he broke: "Rejoice, we conquer!" Like wine through clay,
> Joy in his blood bursting his heart, he died — the bliss!

Never mind that the story is plainly apocryphal, a pastiche of Herodotus, Plutarch, and Lucian. When Pierre de Coubertin organized the first modern Olympic Games, his friend the philologist Michael Breal urged him to include a distance race in tribute to the doomed runner. Today, in spite of the fact that hundreds of thousands of Americans run marathons,* the long-distance athlete

---

* The ultramarathon (any race exceeding 26.22 miles), which attracts a smaller and more fanatical community of athletes, gained brief notoriety in January 2004, when a member of the Colorado running cult Divine Madness banked 207 miles in

in popular culture is typically a Jobian figure, tortured and solitary. Iconic Nike ads of the 1990s cast him in grainy black-and-white, doubled over and unleashing a stream of vomit onto his shoes. The hero of William Goldman's *Marathon Man* gets his teeth drilled by a Nazi. Always, the runner is haunted. His race is a form of flight — from himself, from the mediocrity of society, from a lugubrious backstory.

Browning reimagined Pheidippides at the height of the so-called Golden Age of Pedestrianism. In 1878, the Crimean War veteran, baronet, and amateur sports promoter Sir John Dugdale Astley launched a series of six-day exhibition footraces, held along ellipse tracks before throngs of delirious spectators. The winner crawled away with a cash purse and a small fortune in gate fees, as well as a silver-and-gold belt valued at £100 and bearing the legend LONG DISTANCE CHAMPION OF THE WORLD.

In June 1879, Edward Payson Weston strode 550 miles in six days along a wooden track in London's Agricultural Hall, beating 10-to-1 odds to become the first American-born Astley Belt champion and an international sensation. "There were Weston shoes, Weston hats, and Weston coats," rhapsodized *Harper's Weekly.* "Musicians composed Weston marches, and young ladies danced to Weston Waltzes." His "clean-cut and shrewd" face gazed nobly from photographs "in thousands of private dwellings as well as in most public places." The dandyish Rhode Island native was a star, and he behaved like one, preening and sulking, issuing crackpot statements to the press, and hobnobbing with deep-pocketed strangers.

That August, Weston sailed from Liverpool to New York City on the steamship *Nevada,* but his triumph was partial and short-lived. The steamer *Harlem,* engaged to intercept the great pedestrian in New York Harbor with six kegs of beer, two cases of wine, and a basket of sandwiches, failed to arrive on schedule, and his admirers greeted him instead in a tugboat. Dressed in a priestly black suit, Weston griped to reporters about a prize watch he had been promised by the mayor of Newark that had never materialized. "If I

---

the forty-eight-hour race Across the Years and then dropped dead. Farther afield, the "Marathon Monks" of Japan's Mount Hiei have practiced spiritual running in a ritual that dates to the eighth century. At the culmination of seven years of training, the aspirant logs two back-to-back marathons per night for three months, carrying a length of rope and a knife so that he can hang or disembowel himself if he fails to complete a run.

owned a house in perdition and another in Newark," he said, "I'd rent the Newark house."

At a time when a pound of mutton cost fourteen cents, some seventy-five thousand spectators paid a dollar apiece for admission to the next Astley Belt match, at Madison Square Garden. Loiterers choked 26th Street. They scaled drainpipes and shinnied up ropes to the low windows of the theater, where sentries lay in wait with sharpened sticks. The Englishman Charles Rowell covered 127 miles within the first day and night of the race. His early lead left scant doubt as to the eventual outcome, but the circus inside the Garden roiled on with a Boschian grandeur. Bands played "Yankee Doodle," "Tommy Dodd," and "Marching Through Georgia." Rowell sucked on a sponge while his countryman George Hazael cut a simian figure with his fumbling headlong stride. "The question is often asked, 'What is that thing?' when Hazael goes around," a reporter wrote with jingoistic cruelty, "but the questioner is always awed into silence when told that that is one of the best runners in England." Ever the showman, Weston burlesqued the gaits of his rivals, stopping now and then to spritz himself with eau de toilette from an atomizer he toted around the loop. The other contestants shuffled more or less suicidally toward the grail of 450 miles, short of which they would not see a nickel. It was a scene befitting the venue, raised by P. T. Barnum as a hippodrome for mock-Roman chariot exhibitions. Rowell took ill in the last days of the race, but his advantage was overwhelming. Amid a flurry of rumors that he had been mickeyed with a cluster of poisoned grapes, he completed his 530th mile and repaired to his tent with Weston's prize belt and a share of the gate receipts totaling $25,000 — roughly the equivalent of $500,000 today.

The winner of the Self-Transcendence Race would return to his home country with a plastic trophy and a scrapbook. Each contestant forked over an entry fee of $1,250 — an investment none would recoup. Self-transcendence, it seemed, was not a lucrative career. In late June, Kuranga Peele of Neusiedl, Austria, flew home. In 2004, Peele had finished second, with the seventh-best time in race history. This year he had logged just over 660 miles. "Kuranga didn't feel up to it," Abichal explained. "You have to be totally committed, or the mind can get in the way."

As the fourteen remaining contestants sauntered around the

block, it was impossible to tell at any given moment who was winning and who was losing. Madhupran Wolfgang Schwerk, with a lead of more than a hundred miles two weeks into the race, was heavily favored. Nobody at the racecourse expressed much surprise — Madhupran held the course record. I shadowed him past the playground with a mixture of admiration and unease. His gait called to mind pistons and crankshafts, the famous efficiency of German engineering. Just looking at him made me thirsty for a Coke. Short of a bunch of poisoned grapes, it was hard to imagine anybody closing the gap. This might have had something to do with Madhupran's support team. He was the only runner to have imported a full-time handler, Helmut Schieke, himself a former trans-America record holder, who hailed Schwerk whenever he finished a lap, often with a plastic cup of diet cola or tea or a slice of honeydew melon. He was also alone in having landed a corporate patron. Lanxess, a German producer of plastics and rubbers, had fronted his airfare, along with his registration fee. In exchange, he arrived each morning dressed in a crisp Lanxess singlet, matching shorts, and sneakers.

Cars passed Base Camp at the requisite school-zone crawl, and the drone of a lawn mower filled me with a strong Pavlovian urge to lie down in a hammock. On the refreshment table an argosy of chips, raisins, granola bars, olives, cookies, ice cream, and butter lay open to would-be saboteurs, but who would tamper with a race whose profits are tallied in the coinage of the soul?

On the corner of 168th Street, a man in a baseball cap was squinting through a hand-held video camera at the pageant of runners drifting southward. "The footage isn't very good," he confessed, wagging his head. His name was Daniel, and he had flown to New York to report on the race for RTL, a German television station. A second German news team was supposed to arrive tomorrow, and Daniel planned to beat them to the story. Suprabha ambled past, talking on a cell phone. "The problem is, they don't really run," Daniel said. "They jog, they stop, they walk. I need running. I need sweat streaming down faces."

If the scene on Abigail Adams Avenue disappointed Daniel, the trouble was partly semantic. The Self-Transcendence Race was not, strictly speaking, a sporting event. It was spiritual detox. For two months the athletes paid no bills, ran no errands, conducted no business. They lived in a state of Thoreauvian simplicity. "The mind says it's stupid to go around and around," I was told by a volunteer named Aklanta, one of a squadron of chiropractors at the racecourse. "But it's not stupid on a higher plane." The race revealed the "true nature" above one's "base nature," he said. "You find out what your true nature wants. What does it want? Not what advertisements on television tell you you want. That's manipulation. I don't want to be manipulated. You need joy in your life. Otherwise, it's just stimulation — up and down, nothing constant."

A middle-aged man approached Base Camp. With his white mustache and straw boater, he recalled Edward Payson Weston walking through Confederate Maryland in 1861, disguised, in Weston's own words, by "Messrs Brooks, Brothers, clothing dealers" as a "Susquehanna Raftsman on a bender." He stopped on the sidewalk, watching the runners shuffle past with the dazed look of a man who had just been sprung from jail. And so he had — it was summer vacation. His furlough would stretch until the last week of August, when he would return to his post as a laboratory specialist at Edison High. "Essentially, a test-tube washer, I help to purchase — or to prevent the purchase of — equipment. Mercury used to be a thing you played with," he said with nostalgia. "Now it's a deadly poison."

A credential sticking out of his shirt pocket identified the speaker as one M. Cogan. He wore his nametag religiously, a precaution dating to the years he worked at Bellevue Hospital. "Someone had to die for that," he explained. Europeans in high-performance sportswear parted around us as he related a long, grim story about a psychiatric patient in a stolen lab coat butchering a female doctor. "I'm not sure if he raped her before he dissected her or after or a little of both." On another occasion, he told me, a paraplegic escaped from the prison ward and disappeared across the border into Mexico. The thought of this wheelchair-bound fugitive thriving under Latin-American skies seemed to cheer him up. "They're good neighbors," he said of the Self-Transcendence crew. "That's all I know. Chinmoy seems to attract a nice crowd. But I haven't got to the point where I want to join." He had first encountered the group on an afternoon in the 1970s when a bald-headed stranger reproached him for lighting a cigarette in a local restaurant. The stranger was Sri Chinmoy. "I guess it's a clean-living cult sort of thing. Like the Mormon Church." Not long thereafter, noticing Chinmoy's name in a letter submitted to the *New York Times* by the composer Leonard Bernstein, Cogan realized the Guru was a famous and important man.

We strolled together past the line of Port-O Lets to the refreshment table, where Cogan stopped and told a spindly German volunteer that he intended to run a race of his own, albeit one of humbler length. He seemed an unlikely candidate for cardiovascular exercise, but in this climate of burgeoning goodwill, with songbirds flicking through the trees and rival German news teams trolling Joe Austin park, all things seemed possible. Cogan beamed at the disciples, "You've inspired me."

What, exactly, had Leonard Bernstein written to the *Times?* I never found the letter Mike Cogan remembered, but an item in an April 1979 "Notes on People" column described a recently formed "mutual admiration society" comprising the Guru and the flamboyant composer of *West Side Story:*

> Sri Chinmoy, whose followers say he has written 3,000 songs, dropped by Mr. Bernstein's Manhattan apartment a few weeks ago, and brought with him a choral group that sang a new Chinmoy number called, "Leonard Bernstein." It went, in part:
>
> > Leonard Bernstein, Leonard!
> > Eternity's singing bird! Beauty truth,
> > Truth beauty,
> > Nectar oneness your divinity.

Bernstein had responded in kind, presenting the Guru with an original work for sitar, flute, tabla, bass, and drone. Until recently, all I had known of the Guru I owed to an LP called *Love, Devotion, Surrender,* a 1973 jazz-rock fiasco by Carlos Santana and John McLaughlin, both former Chinmoy disciples.*

---

* The music critic Robert Christgau describes its artwork thus: "On the back cover is a photograph of three men. Two of them are dressed in white and have their hands folded — one grinning like Alfred E. Neuman, the other looking like he's about to have a Supreme Court case named after him: solemn, his wrists ready for the cuffs. In between, a man in an orange ski jacket and red pants with one white sock seems to have caught his tongue on his lower lip. He looks like the yoga coach at a fashionable lunatic asylum. Guess which one is Sri Chinmoy."

Born on August 27, 1931,* in East Bengal, India, and orphaned at twelve, the Guru spent his adolescence and early adulthood studying meditation at the Sri Aurobindo Ashram, where he earned the title Fastest Runner twelve years in a row. In 1964 he emigrated to New York and took a job as an assistant in the passport-and-visa section of the Indian consulate. These were lean years for the Guru. According to his memoirs, he lunched on potato chips or candy bars, often in a telephone booth outside his office, but already he was laying the foundation for his spiritual mission, playing free concerts and lecturing on Hinduism. In the ensuing decades, the Guru's self-transcendence empire fanned across six continents, spurred by a distinctly American flair for public relations.

He has performed original tribute songs for a motley assortment of public figures, including Sting, Jane Goodall, Carl Lewis, Kofi Annan, and Quincy Jones, whose cryptic endorsement "Sri Chinmoy is such a brave musician!" appears on posters promoting the Guru's concerts. Besides Grammy winners and athletes, his disciples include Ashrita Furman, the manager of a Queens health-food store, who has set 148 Guinness World Records — a meta-record itself — most recently for backward bowling, egg-and-spoon racing, and lemon eating. Photographs posted on Chinmoy's official websites and displayed in the businesses operated by his disciples show the Guru, whose philanthropic network The Oneness-Heart-Tears and Smiles delivers medical supplies around the globe, glad-handing a varsity roster of world leaders — Princess Diana, Popes Paul VI and John Paul II, Mikhail Gorbachev, Mother Teresa. Nelson Mandela once called him an "outstanding soldier of peace."

In 1996, a district superintendent of the National Park Service approved a plan to install a brass plaque in the lobby of the Statue of Liberty that would officially designate the foremost icon of American democracy a Sri Chinmoy Peace Blossom site. Three hundred or so spectators attended the unveiling on the Guru's sixty-fifth birthday. Within a month, the Park Service reversed its decision, and the plaque was removed, but similar plaques identify

* The 3,100-mile distance of the Self-Transcendence Race celebrates Chinmoy's birth year; an earlier incarnation, held in 1996, measured 2,700 miles, in honor of his birthday.

more than nine hundred surviving Peace Blossoms around the world, including cultural centers (the Sydney Opera House), natural formations (the Matterhorn, the Great Barrier Reef), airports (Afonso Pena in Curitiba, Brazil), and political frontiers (the entirety of the Russia-Norway border). In 1994 the late king of Nepal officially christened an unclimbed four-mile-high Himalayan peak "Sri Chinmoy Peace Mountain."

I took to lunching a few blocks from the racecourse at Annam Brahma restaurant, where footage of Sri Chinmoy's sundry exploits airs continuously on a wall-mounted television. In 1985 he took up weightlifting; clips of the Guru hoisting all manner of eccentric burdens flashed across the screen while I sipped my *lassis*. With the aid of a special scaffold, he calf-raised people,* cars, the 1,495 volumes of his collected poetry and prose.† It brought to mind the omnipotence paradox: could God produce an oeuvre He couldn't lift? The footage resembled one of those supplemental tapes certain enterprising high school juniors append to their college applications. The Guru was a grind *and* a jock. He was the most prolific painter who ever lived. He had read poetry with Joyce Carol Oates and jammed with Carlos Santana. He claimed to have lifted 7,064 pounds and 7,040 pounds with his right and left arms, respectively. Not since Leonardo da Vinci had a single man been so well rounded.

---

* Since 1988, when he launched his "Lifting Up the World with a Oneness-Heart" campaign, Chinmoy has ceremonially hoisted more than seven thousand friends and celebrities, including Jesse Jackson; Cambodian Prime Minister Samdech Hun San; Ravi Shankar; Moorhead Kennedy, held hostage for 444 days in Iran; Mickey Thomas, lead vocalist of Jefferson Starship; and the actresses Mercedes Ruehl and Alyssa Milano.

† A selection of titles from the Chinmoy library attests to the breadth of the Guru's interests: *The Earth-Illumination-Trumpets of Divinity's Home, Part 1; I Play Tennis Every Day; The Ambition-Deer; Einstein: Scientist-Sage, Brother of Atom-Universe; Impurity: The Mad Elephant Mental Asylum; A Soulful Tribute to the Secretary-General: The Pilot Supreme of the United Nations; God Wants to Read This Book; Great Indian Meals: Divinely Delicious and Supremely Nourishing; Gorbachev: The Master-Key of the Universal Heart; Muhammad Ali and Sri Chinmoy Meditate; Come, My Non-English Friends! Let Us Together Climb Up the English Himalayas; The Mushroom and the Umbrella; My Heart's Salutation to Australia; A Mystic Journey in the Weightlifting World, Part One; Airport Elevation: Questions Answered by Master Sri Chinmoy at the San Juan International Airport, October 29, 1976; I Love Shopping, Part 1; My Ivy League Leaves: Lectures on the Spiritual Life; Niagara Falls Versus Children's Rise; Religion-Jugglery and God-Discovery; The Sailor and the Parrot; War: Man's Abysmal Abyss-Plunge, Part 1; Sleep: Death's Little Sister; Canada Aspires, Canada Receives, Canada Achieves; Yes, I Can! I Certainly Can!!*

Other videos were available for download on the Guru's websites. In one of them, the seventy-four-year-old Chinmoy purports
to curl a 256-pound dumbbell. The weight rests on a platform
above the Guru's left leg. He knits his face and hums. At the appointed moment, an assistant lowers the platform and the weight
sits motionless on Chinmoy's leg. After ten seconds, the assistant
replaces the platform, and the Guru smiles beatifically. The footage presented a kind of Rorschach test. Where some found proof
of the existence of God, others saw an old man supporting a dumbbell on his knee. I showed the video to friends. "I don't get it," they
said. "Did he lift the weight or not?" I kept silent. Here was the
pertinent question. Once you answered, there was no turning
back. For the moment, I preferred to live in a world of divine
strongmen.

In six decades of professional footwork, Edward Payson Weston endured all manner of setbacks and injuries. He sprained ankles and
toes. Fevers and stomach cramps dogged him, as well as creditors,
who took advantage of his highly publicized walks to have him arrested for unpaid debts. Once he was shot in the leg. Always Weston rallied. On the seventh day of the walk that made his name,
a pilgrimage from Boston to Washington, D.C., for Abraham Lincoln's 1861 inauguration, he broke for a predawn restorative of
sandwiches. This proved a tactical mistake, saddling the pedestrian
with chest pains, which he blamed on mustard. His companions
noted:

> He stopped every quarter of a mile and sat down to sleep; was exceed-
> ingly irritable, which caused the whole party to have the blues, of the
> "darkest kind." Mr. Weston concludes to go back half a mile, to a public
> house and sleep . . . He returns a few steps, when, suddenly throwing off
> his blanket, he exclaims: "*No, I wont go back!*" and, wheeling around,
> strikes into a four-mile gait.

Such theatrics, anticipating James Brown's stage show by a full
century, typified Weston's spirit on the road. Some of the same
mettle could be found in Jamaica, where ingrown nails on both of
Pranab Vladovic's big toes had become a topic of worried conversation. Slight and boyish, with close-cropped hair, Pranab sat on a
massage table considering the problem. His feet looked like they

had been dredged out of the East River — chalky white with a thick brownish discharge at the nail beds. "These are the cards you get," he announced with equanimity. A few disciples stood around the massage table while a podiatrist, sober and brusque in a tan nylon jacket and gray nylon pants, frowned at the suppurating digits. The diagnosis was bleak. If he left the nails intact, he explained, the infection might compromise the bone, and the toes would have to be removed. Pranab hugged his knees.

"Can he keep walking?" someone asked.

The question seemed to rattle the doctor. "That's his choice. I wouldn't do it. How much farther till he's done?"

"Two thousand miles."

The distance unfurled like a carpet spanning from Queens to Juarez, Mexico. I winced a little at the sound of the figure. "You got no shot," the doctor said.

The race, however, had a physic all its own. "You get scared beforehand," Abichal had told me. "Your body gets scared. It's like stage fright. Like moving into a different realm." For two months, the high school and ball courts and the abutting stretch of parkway became a shrine. Did I know about ley lines? Abichal asked. The theory, as articulated in the 1920s by one Alfred Watkins (no relation), posits a system of arcane pathways linking megaliths, tors, and other craggy points across Britain, and possibly the world. Largely ignored by science, ley lines have enjoyed a colorful life in the hinterlands of paranormalism, championed to various ends by psychics, pagans, dowsers, UFOlogists, dime-store novelists, and a few Nazi cranks who attributed a network of *heilige Linien,* or "holy lines," crisscrossing Europe to the ancient Teutons.

"There are rivers, superhighways of energy," Abichal told me, "and there are junctions where they meet." The junctions exert a spiritual tug. Stonehenge, for instance, or Sedona. "Sedona is a big energy vortex." So, too, the racecourse. "I get a good vibe here," he said, indicating a triangle of lawn behind the wrought-iron fencing of the high school. "It's open. It's green. There's some kind of energy vortex on this corner."

The Self-Transcendence runners being mostly European, July 4 went largely unremarked at the racecourse. The fields teemed with men engaged in various team sports. Flags hung limp in the cooling air as Madhupran and Abichal strolled past, each brandishing a Popsicle. A couple of Indian families spread blankets on the grassy margin by the bleachers in Joe Austin park, and chops on a clamshell barbecue threw gusts of meaty smoke into the paths of the vegetarian runners. At dusk, Sri Chinmoy arrived in a white jeep to dispense bananas.*

By moonlight, Joe Austin park was a place of desolate beauty. Traffic thrummed eastward undeterred, blanching the runners in a wash of halogen beams. On 168th Street, a man watered his lawn in the dark, while a few stray fireflies winked among the hedges of Edison High. I was given to understand that miracles sometimes visited Jamaica. A white woman in a sari told me that Sri Chinmoy had cured her of lupus. The runners, too, had recovered from injury and illness. "Shin splints that would stop an ordinary runner for weeks last only days," insisted one of the disciples, another chiropractor, on loan from Chicago. "The will of the — if you allow me to say — soul conquers the will of the physical." Witness Pranab, who clipped past me, murmuring into a dictaphone. He had left the racecourse for two hours to have his toenails removed, resuming the race at his usual pace as soon as he returned. "Now I have to soak my toes," he said. "It's a little more work." His date with the podiatrist's knife had cost him roughly eighteen miles.

Beyond the rooftops of Jamaica, the horizon throbbed with light, as of a millenarian firestorm engulfing Manhattan. Now and then a plume of colored sparks crested the tree line, Queens County's rejoinder to the thirtieth annual Macy's Fireworks Spectacular with Lionel Richie and the New York Pops. I decided to buy a proper pair of running shoes.

"Without preparatory training . . . the most fatal injuries may be committed in attempting pedestrian feats." Such was the counsel of *Beadle's Dime Hand-Book of Pedestrianism,* published in 1867. On the cover of the thirty-two-page tract, a man wearing a sporty hat and gaiters trots across a sketchily rendered countryside. Mysteri-

---

* The offering of sanctified food — called *prasad* — sometimes flummoxed visitors to the racecourse, as in late July, when the Guru made an offering of Granny Smith apples to a pair of emissaries from Russian TV. The reporter accepted with telegenic diplomacy, but the cameraman froze, plying his camera like a rifle trained on a buck. An hour later, both apples lay uneaten on a table cluttered with audiovisual equipment.

ously, he carries a riding crop. "In a mind upset by literary study," the author urges, "the best plan, if practicable, is to give up the reading and writing entirely, for a time." Duly warned, I toed the line by the weathered scoreboard on Joe Austin Way at a minute to six.

Ribbons of peach and pink banded the eastern horizon, giving the sky the look of a novelty cocktail. At dawn, the scene here was somber. The racers sat glumly on folding chairs or stretched against trees. Many of them doctored their feet with balms and tapes. Sri Chinmoy had returned from a trip to the Far East bearing gifts for the runners, ceremonial white bandannas emblazoned with the bloody sun of the Japanese flag. A few tied these souvenirs around their foreheads. They looked a little like bandages on a company of outnumbered and ill-equipped soldiers marching to certain death. One of the race directors called us to attention and we stood together, observing a moment of silence rendered incomplete by traffic sounds. Then we were off.

The pace was leaden. After five hours of stasis the body of the multiday runner locks up like a rusty transmission. Madhupran alone advanced at his usual clip, lunging and working his arms like an animatronic cross-country skier. Within fifteen minutes he had lapped me. Sri Chinmoy visited the course at around 6:20, and his arrival had an immediate restorative effect on the disciples. Wearing a preppy pink-striped shirt, he circled the block three times in a blue Smart car, goosing little fanfares from the horn when he passed a group of racers. It was oddly exhilarating to see the Guru operate a car, particularly one he could have parked in a walk-in closet. The runners bowed their heads, touched their hearts, or waved, quickening their pace. "It's the same as if you like the author of a book and then you meet him in reality," a disciple explained. It was difficult to imagine John Updike inspiring this sort of reverence.

The Guru's drive-by was only the opening act in a morning lineup of music, poetry, and cheerleading. Two female choral groups staked out stretches of Abigail Adams Avenue, clapping and singing. Meanwhile, the sun had broken through the clouds, and commuters were tumbling groggily into cars to ford the Grand Central Parkway. When I'd asked her how she felt about Jamaica, Suprabha had told me, "If you use your imagination, you can feel as if you're running on a beautiful country road. You tune out the traffic, the motorcycles." Helmut, Madhupran's handler, echoed her advice. "This is the hardest race you can find. Very hard concrete. You should have it in your mind like an endless road. Don't see it as it is, a dirty sidewalk. You must have the fantasy to see it another way — you must see flowers, a beautiful forest with trees."

I tried to conjure these pastoral mirages as I ran. Here was the broad green sign directing motorists to Queens's Utopia Parkway. The same brown Honda had been parked outside Edison High for weeks. Eventually the summer-school contingent straggled in, glassy-eyed and inured to the sight of nylon-clad wraiths hustling up the block. I wished one of the runners would tell me how to clear my mind of all this urban wrack. After a morning of continuous locomotion, my legs were confused. Each step reverberated up the tibiae, delivering an unhappy shock to my knees. My stomach, too, rebelled. To the aspiring pedestrian, *Beadle's* prescribed a midday smorgasbord of roast beef, mutton, partridge, pheasant, or venison, along with one or two potatoes. No other vegetable was permitted. Short on fresh game, I snacked on nectarines and granola. Even so, I spent a good deal of time locked in the piney, sauna-like seclusion of a Port-O Let.

At around 1:30, I finished my forty-eighth circuit of the block, and a volunteer informed me that I had surpassed 26.2 miles. "You've run a marathon!" she announced. Was this my first? I admitted it was. She clapped her hands. I had transcended myself! Was I excited? My time of seven hours, twenty-five minutes left room for improvement, I felt. Nonetheless, I traded high-fives with a few of the runners, who received the news variously with bemusement or wide-eyed gravity. Remembering Pheidippides, I took care to hydrate. Self-transcendence aside, I didn't intend to die in a pair of red nylon shorts.

By nightfall, I was circling Edison High in a trance. The sign for Utopia Parkway shone inscrutably in the darkness, beckoning me eastward toward parts unknown. As if afflicted by a kind of anatomical Stockholm syndrome, my legs bore me clockwise of their own accord, and I had the idea I could keep plodding forever. I was wrong. Blisters ruptured on the soles of both my feet, and every step became a slog through molten glass.

I drove home at geriatric speeds, unsure I'd be able to work the brake pedal in case of emergency. On the advice of a disciple, I sat for a long time in a scalding bath of Epsom salts. I had made eighty circuits of the block for a cumulative distance of 43.904 miles — six miles short of the required daily minimum. My base nature wanted aspirin and 10,000 BTUs of air conditioning. What did my true nature want? I couldn't say.

A sense of giddy anticipation attended Madhupran's final push on the morning of July 22. Lanxess had dispatched a coiffed and cheerful stringer, who sat in the van interrogating Helmut on the champion's progress and typing what I assumed was a press release on a laptop.

"If I want to say that his diet consisted of da, da, da —" she prompted.

"Rice, sweet potatoes, coconut milk," Helmut replied. "And he ate every day one honeydew. And dinkel bread. No wheat. So. Now comes my horse. Don't forget my horse."

Near the Port-O Lets, a violinist serenaded an empty swath of sports fields. By Madhupran's penultimate lap, the throng of acolytes, friends, and confused passersby at the racecourse numbered about two hundred. That morning, Sri Chinmoy had written three new compositions in honor of Madhupran's success. Xeroxed sheet music was handed out, and men and women gathered in scrums along Joe Austin Way to rehearse. A blue ribbon bearing the gold-embossed legend SELF-TRANSCENDENCE RACES was strung across the sidewalk opposite a gauntlet of camera-wielding disciples.

Madhupran accelerated through his final quarter-mile shouldering a victory flag fringed with gold tassels, each stride an object lesson in the kinetics of belief. He had knocked more than a day off his own world record. When he crossed the line, Sri Chinmoy led the crowd in a triumphal sing-along. "The champion of champions / Am I," proclaimed the chorus. "In God's limitless pride sky / I fly."

Like his many thousands of poems, the Guru's songs are nothing if not pithy. After the disciples repeated the first song several times, they proceeded to the next. "In the world's longest bravest distance run / Who waves the victory flag? / Madhupran! / Madhupran!" The Guru clapped a metronomic beat against his knee. Whenever the singers fell silent, he beckoned for more. The third song was the longest, and the most popular:

> I am the world's longest distance
> Daring and shattering runner
> My Supreme Lord's
> Sun-power Smile
> And his Moon-Bliss-Love
> Winner

Madhupran crooned along in his operatic baritone, clasping his plastic-sheathed bouquet like a beauty pageant winner. Sri Chinmoy dispensed vanilla creme cookies and individually wrapped Keebler Club & Cheddar Sandwich Crackers, and then he left. The crowd dispersed, and the runners who had quit circling the block to watch Madhupran enter the record books returned to the grind. Some had nine hundred miles ahead of them.

By the vans, an enterprising disciple scavenged for crumbs in an abandoned cardboard box. "They may be dregs," he said, smiling, "but they're the master's dregs." A kindly, heavyset Russian woman sat counting off laps. In the 1980s she had fled the "atheist state" of the Soviet Union for Texas, where she discovered transcendental meditation. Now she gazed mournfully up the block. She felt empty, she said. "It's always like this. You wait and wait for the event. Then in thirty minutes — it's history."

In the last days of July, the tempo of the race changed. Wind jostled the trees, while in the park a woman herded leaves with an electric blower. Endgame had arrived. Sometimes two runners reached 3,100 miles in a day. Each finish triggered music and applause, but the excitement of Madhupran's victory was never quite matched. We sang the Guru's songs again and again, like a touring cast of *Godspell* at the end of a fifty-city run.

The Self-Transcendence Race was supposed to end on August 1, but Sri Chinmoy granted a week's extension so the laggards could finish. The last miles would prove the crudest. Scattered power outages had afflicted Queens. To conserve energy in the stupefying heat of August, government buildings set their thermostats at a balmy 78 degrees, and the lights of Coney Island's totemic Parachute Jump went dark. So, too, NASDAQ's digital display in Times

Square. Summer school was officially pronounced "optional." Mayor Bloomberg declared a heat emergency; later, the city would confirm a heat-related death toll of 140. I worried about the four runners still circling Joe Austin park.

By day fifty-eight, deep red circles bloomed on Abichal's cheeks. "I think sometimes even the runners ask, 'What am I doing here?'" he confessed. Often he would orbit the block for hours without glimpsing another racer, a phenomenon he called "the dark side of the loop." At night he veered into the fence outside Edison High. He had numb toes and a strange vertiginous feeling, as if the ground were rolling beneath his feet. Sometimes he dreamed about the race. In the dreams somebody chased him around the block, or he was chasing someone else, he couldn't say which. He woke unrefreshed. "I just run all night," he said. "Round and round." The energy on the loop had changed. The race has a force, he explained, a power you feel at every level of your being. "Then when you cut the head off, it's gone."

Rathin Boulton from Australia crossed the finish line on August 7. He held his bouquet while a modest crowd sang and clapped. A few yards away the door of a white sedan hung open. Sri Chinmoy emerged wearing flip-flops, his striped shirt tucked into canary-yellow trunks, and made his halting way to the scoreboard.

Last year, Rathin had run 3,100 miles in fifty-six days, eleven hours. At the Guru's urging, one of the race directors read this figure aloud. Then he repeated Rathin's latest score of fifty-seven days and change. "This is — more?" the Guru asked.

There was nervous laughter from the gallery. Rathin had traveled 3,100 miles around a concrete block in Queens, but he had not transcended himself. The Guru sipped from a juice box while a disciple set up a microphone attached to a small public-address system. "How many years have you been on our path?" Chinmoy asked. "Ten years, Guru," Rathin answered. Chinmoy sat clutching his right knee, head bowed, as neighborhood kids passed by in jeans and baggy shorts. Then, in a warbling voice, he began to sing. "*Rathin, Rathin, Rathin, Rathin.*" I had the impression he was composing this number on the spot. Heedless of the roaring planes overhead, the disciples joined in, timidly at first but with mounting conviction, until the Guru produced a box of vanilla cookies and called them to order. It was snack time.

Afterward he indulged in a little postprandial lecturing. I dutifully recorded what I could, but the very first sentence confounded me. "Once upon a time," the Guru said, and a siren drowned him out. Whole paragraphs were lost in the muddle of ambient street noise, giving his remarks a Dadaist quality. I heard the phrases "unimaginable joy" and "peace blossoms." Chinmoy acknowledged a man who had helped him organize a trip to New Zealand, where he had lifted a thousand sheep. His voice was breathy and sweet. "I am playing a flute for a kangaroo. My only audience is a kangaroo." He spoke at length about Lord Krishna, breaking off to quiz his disciples on their mastery of the Bhagavad-Gita. "In which chapter does Lord Krishna show his divine form to humans?" he asked. "Eleven," someone shouted. Wind buffeted the microphone. I made out the words "bodyguards" and "karate chop." Now and then the Guru paused for a bite of creme cookie, and sounds of mastication crackled from the PA. My notes resembled a collection of haikus. Finally, the Guru stood and waved, padded to the white sedan still idling at the curb, and was spirited away.

On the loop, Abichal offered some perspective. The mind likes to grasp things, he told me; this is its nature. But reality cannot be grasped. A true master addresses the heart. To do so, he must short-circuit the student's intellect, a process sometimes calling for "special techniques." He speaks indirectly, in riddles, coaxing the student toward a more receptive state. It made a certain sense, but half the time I'd found the Guru simply inaudible. Abichal nodded. "It's like that for a lot of people," he said. "Even the disciples."

By the late 1880s, the pedestrian craze had cooled. "The public may occasionally lose its head," the *New York Times* concluded, "but it is unsafe to assume that it will do so more than once or twice in the same direction. It rushed to see Rowell trot over 500 miles of sawdust because long-distance pedestrianism was a new thing." Slave to the god of novelty, the great unwashed had forsaken distance footracing for such au courant conveyances as the bicycle and the roller skate. A century later, the pedestrian has wandered into cultural oblivion, his feats relegated to microfilm archives and a few out-of-print sports chronicles.*

Edward Payson Weston clung doggedly to fame well into his se-

---

* Notably John Cumming's *Runners & Walkers* and *Ultramarathoning: The Next Challenge* by Tom Osier and Ed Dodd.

nescence, but an accident brought his career to an unceremonious end in 1927. His glory days behind him, the great pedestrian was broke, sharing a Greenwich Village flat and begging for work in the pages of the *Times*. Eight days after he received a gift of $30,000 from Anne Nichols, author of the popular Broadway comedy *Abie's Irish Rose*, Weston was pasted in the streets of New York by a taxicab. He was eighty-eight years old. For decades he had railed against the evils of the motorcar, an invention for loafers and slobs. Weston spent the balance of his life confined to a wheelchair. The age of pedestrians was dead.

I returned the next day to watch Abichal cross the finish line. The heat wave had broken, and he circled the block with a look of resignation. He would finish a week later than he'd hoped. "I feel joy," he said, but I couldn't shake the sense that past races had meant more to Abichal. As we walked against the stream of traffic on the parkway, he told me about a particularly grueling race he'd run a few years back. "I was so looking forward to the end. Dying, dying, dying. Then on the last lap — it all fell away." He made a little magician's flourish with his hand. "What I thought would be the goal just vanished, like a mirage. There was no goal. It didn't exist. I realized that my mind had been playing this trick. It was just another lap, same as all the other laps." This summer, Abichal had not transcended himself in precisely the way he'd imagined, but he would run again.

As we neared the diminished Base Camp with its skeleton crew of volunteers, Abichal's thoughts turned to the future of his sport. There was an upcoming 1,200K in Germany, the Deutschlandlauf; 2006 would see new six- and seven-day races in France and Greece. A note of hope entered his voice. "They said the marathon was impossible. Now hundreds of thousands run them. Maybe this is it."

At 10:20 P.M., a few disciples gave up tossing a Frisbee to watch Abichal embark on his final lap. Someone had arranged two long files of tea candles leading to the finish line — the lights of Coldplay's "Fix You," come to guide him home. A bicycle horn bleated in the dark, and we called his name as he lumbered eastward bearing the Self-Transcendence banner in one hand and the Red Dragon of Wales in the other. An unexpected knot formed in my throat as Abichal walked gingerly across the line and accepted his flowers. After the usual singing, Abichal sat with a cake in his lap while friends filed past to shake his hand, and then we stood in silence. Altogether, the turnout was about a quarter the size of Madhupran's. "Speech," somebody called. The brake lights of a passing car flashed, and a mild electrical current passed through the crowd. "Guru," came a whisper behind me. There was a collective turning of heads. "Guru's here?" "Abichal, I think Guru's here." But the car sped down the block. Pink and blue balloons joggled above Abichal's bowed head. His time was fifty-eight days, sixteen hours, twenty-two minutes, three seconds.

The next week Abichal met me for lunch at Smile of the Beyond, a vegetarian diner managed by one of the race directors. Suprabha had crossed the finish line the previous Thursday, and now the racecourse was empty. Some of the runners had already returned to the jobs they had left behind in their home countries. Others planned to hang around Jamaica for the Guru's seventy-fifth-birthday party at the end of the month. The previous year, he had celebrated with a solo concert performance on seventy-four pianos. It would be difficult to top.

Abichal showed up twenty minutes late, his hair newly trimmed to a boyish wiffle — most likely at Perfection in the Head-World, the disciple-operated barbershop down the street. He looked ten years younger, but he walked on the legs of a senior citizen. It was strange to see Abichal in a restaurant. In the seven weeks I'd known him, I had almost never caught him sitting. Now that the struggle was past, he said, he felt a constant sense of freedom. The race was like a weight he'd been carrying for months. He was relieved: not physically — although his body was recovering — but psychically. He intended to edit a poetry anthology. There was also his magazine and website. In December he would fly to Arizona to run Across the Years, the race that killed a man in 2004. He hadn't decided whether he would return to Jamaica next June. "Have to wait and see," he said. On a television screen in the corner, Sri Chinmoy lifted an airplane.

After lunch, Abichal offered to walk with me to the racecourse. His thoughts followed a meandering path. "For many of us, the mind is limited," he said. "It's useful, we need to use it, but it grasps at bits. Then it uses those bits to form a picture and acts as if the picture is reality." We lingered at the verge of the racecourse. He looked mistily at a trash can heaped with ice cream wrappers and soda cans. "I still feel a connection to this bin. Sometimes it would be full to overflowing. Sometimes somebody would dump a big bag in." Abichal squinted up at the clouds. The light was different now, he said. The race starts just a week before the summer solstice, when the days are at their longest. We fell into a natural orbit around the block. "It's all the same," Abichal said. He pointed out features of the loop like a docent leading a cathedral tour. "Same bins, same cracks in the sidewalk." He nodded at a sapling by the high school. "This oak tree replaced a birch that was here a few years ago. You know what lives where. Blue flowers live at this corner. And a flower called a scarlet pimpernel, and yellow clover. This pine tree lives here. And little red flowers, too." Abichal crouched down to show me. Somebody had tossed an empty Newport box in the grass, alongside a foil printed with the words BOMB BAG. The flowers were minuscule, each blossom the size of a Q-tip. "There's still something here. I can feel my echo. Some trace of the experience." Abichal rounded the corner. "This is where the course flattens out. Now it starts to rise gently. In the past sometimes, I'd get a burst of energy here. You feel that you can run forever."

The Renegade

FROM *The New York Review of Books*

AS THE CURTAIN GOES UP, I'm sitting naked on the potty in my grandfather's backyard in a little village in Serbia. The year is 1940. I look happy. It's a nice summer day full of sunlight, although Hitler has already occupied most of Europe. I have no idea, of course, that he and Stalin are hatching an elaborate plot to make me an American poet. I love the neighbor's dog, whose name is Toza. I run after him carrying my potty in my hand, wanting to pull his tail, but he won't let me.

What would I not give today to have a photograph of Toza! He was a country mutt full of burrs and fleas, and in his wise and sad eyes, if we had known how to read them, we would have found the story of my and my parents' lives.

I had a great-uncle of whom nothing is known. I don't even know his name, if I ever did. He came to America in the 1920s and never wrote home. Got rich, my relatives said. How do you know that? I asked. Nobody knew how they knew. They had heard rumors. Then the people who'd heard the rumors died. Today there's no one left to ask. My great-uncle was like one of those ants who, coming upon a line of marching ants, turns and goes in the opposite direction for reasons of his own.

Ants being ants, this is not supposed to happen, but it sometimes does, and no one knows why.

This mythical great-uncle interests me because I resemble him a bit. I, too, came to America and, for long stretches of time, forgot where I came from or had no contact with my compatriots. I never understood the big deal they make about being born in one place rather than another when there are so many nice places in the world to call home. As it is, I was born in Belgrade in 1938 and spent fifteen eventful years there before leaving forever. I never missed it. When I try to tell that to my American friends, they don't believe me. They suspect me of concealing my homesickness because I cannot bear the pain. Allegedly, my nightmarish wartime memories have made me repress how much dear old Belgrade meant to me. My wartime memories may have been terrifying, but I had a happy childhood despite droning planes, deafening explosions, and people hanged from lampposts. I mean, it's not like I knew better and dreamed of a life of quiet strolls with my parents along tree-lined boulevards or playing with other children in the park. No. I was three years old when the first bombs fell and old enough to be miserable when the war ended and I had to go to school.

The first person who told me about the evil in the world was my grandmother. She died in 1948, but I recall her vividly because she took care of me and my brother while my mother went to work. The poor woman had more sense than most people. She listened to Mussolini, Hitler, Stalin, and other lunatics on the radio, and since she knew several languages, she understood the imbecilities they were saying. What upset her even more than their vile words was their cheering followers. I didn't realize it then, but she taught me a lesson that has stuck. Beware of the so-called great leaders and the collective euphorias they excite. Many years later I wrote this poem about her:

EMPIRES

My grandmother prophesied the end
Of your empires, O Fools!
She was ironing. The radio was on.
The earth trembled beneath our feet.
One of their heroes was giving a speech.
"Monster," she called him.
There were cheers and gun salutes for the monster.
"I could kill him with my bare hands,"

She announced to me.
There was no need to. They were all
Going to the devil any day now.
"Don't go blabbering about this to anyone,"
She warned me.
And pulled my ear to make sure I understood.

When people speak of the dark years after the war, they usually have in mind political oppression and hunger, but what I see are poorly lit streets with black windows and doorways as dark as the inside of a coffin. If the lone light bulb one used to read by in bed late into the night died suddenly, it was not likely to be replaced soon. Every year, we had less and less light in our house and not much heat in winter. In the evening, we sat in our overcoats listening to the rumblings of each other's empty stomachs. When guests came, they didn't even bother to remove their hats and gloves. We would huddle close, whispering about arrests, a neighbor being shot, another one disappearing. I wasn't supposed to hear any of this, in case I forgot myself in school and got everyone at home in trouble.

This was the first time I heard people say that we Serbs are numskulls. There was no disagreement. Who else among the nations in Europe was stupid enough to have a civil war while the Nazis were occupying them? We had the Communists, the royalists, and at least a couple of factions of domestic fascists. Some collaborated with Germans and Italians and some did not, but they all fought one another and executed their political opponents. I didn't understand much of it at the time, but I recall the exasperation and anger of the grownups.

Of course, the mood was most likely different in other homes where they welcomed the Communists. We were, after all, members of a mummified, impoverished, middle-class family that would have preferred that everything had remained the same. My mother and grandmother hated wars, distrusted national demagogues, and wanted the kind of government that left everybody alone.

In other words, they were the kind of people, as we were lectured in school, destined to be thrown on the garbage dump of history.

*

Occasionally, one of our visitors would start defending the Serbs. Our history is one of honor, heroic sacrifice, and endless suffering in defense of Europe against the Ottoman Empire, for which we never got any thanks. We are gullible innocents who always think better of our neighbors than they deserve. We sided with England and America when the rest of Europe was already occupied by the Nazis and it was suicidal to go against them.

Yes, my grandmother would say, we did that because we are conceited fools with exaggerated notions of our historical importance. A rabble of thieving and dimwitted yokels who were happiest under the Turks when they had no freedom, no education, and no ambition, except to roast a suckling pig on some holiday.

"Mrs. Matijevic, how can you talk like that?" our visitors would object. My grandmother would just shrug her shoulders. Her husband had been a military hero in World War I, a much-decorated colonel who had lost his enthusiasm for war. I recall being shocked when I first heard him say that Serbs should not have kicked out the government that signed the nonaggression pact with Hitler in 1941. Look what the war had brought us, he would say.

I wonder what my unknown great-uncle in America thought about all that. I bet he had his own ideas on the subject as he sat in some outhouse in Kansas or Texas reading in last month's papers how on March 27, 1941, the heroic Serbs walked the streets of Belgrade shouting "Better death than a pact" while Hitler threw a fit. I reckon he must have tried to explain to his wife now and then about Serbs.

If she were an Apache or a member of some other Native American tribe, she may have understood more quickly. Serbs are a large, quarrelsome tribe, he would have said, never as happy as when they are cutting each other's throats. A Serb from Bosnia has as much in common with a Serb from Belgrade as a Hopi Indian does with a Comanche. All together, they often act as if they have less sense than God gave a duck.

On second thought, he probably never brought up the subject. The Balkans, with its many nationalities and three different religions, is too complicated a place for anyone to explain or begin to make sense of, especially since each ethnic group writes its history only remembering the wrongs done to them while conveniently passing over all the nasty things they've done to their neighbors over the centuries.

When I came to the United States in 1954, I discovered that the conversation among the immigrant Serbs my parents saw now and then was identical to the one I had heard in Belgrade. The cry was still, How did we who are so brave, so honorable, so innocent end up like this? Because of traitors, of course. Serbs stabbing each other in the back. A nation of double-crossers, turncoats, Judases, snakes in the grass. Even worse were our big allies. England, America, and France screwed us royally. Didn't Churchill say to Eden at Yalta that he didn't give a fuck what happened to Yugoslavia after the Communists took over?

Much of this was true. A few sleazy political deals by world leaders did contribute to our fate. We, displaced persons, were living proof that the world is a cruel place if you happen to find yourself on the wrong side of history. Still, I didn't care for all that obsessive talk about betrayals and internal enemies. It reminded me too much of how the Communists back home talked.

"It's exhausting to be a Serb," my father would say after an evening like that. He was a cheerful pessimist. He loved life but had no faith in the idea that the human condition was meliorable. He had had sympathies for the Chetniks, pro-monarchy Serbian nationalists, at the beginning of the war, but no more. Nationalist claptrap left him cold. He was like his father, who used to shock family and friends by ridiculing Serbian national heroes. Both he and my father went to church and had genuine religious feelings, but they could not resist making fun of priests.

"There is nothing sacred for them," my mother would say when she got angry with the Simic family. Of course, she really wasn't any better. It's just that she preferred that appearances be kept up. Her philosophy was, let the world think we believe in all that nonsense, and we'll keep our real views to ourselves.

After my parents separated in 1956, I left home. I attended university at night and worked during the day, first in Chicago and then in New York City. If someone asked me about my accent, I would say that I was born in Yugoslavia, and that would be the end of it. I saw my father frequently, but though he liked to reminisce about his youth in the old country he had an equal and even greater interest in America, and so did I.

It was only when we went to visit his brother Boris that the eternal subject of Serbian national destiny came up. Boris was a successful trucking company executive who lived in a posh Westchester suburb, where he had a house, a wife, and three German shepherds. He loved to organize large dinner parties to which he'd invite his many Serbian friends, serve them fabulous food and wine, and then argue with them about politics till the next day.

Boris was a lefty in Yugoslavia, an admirer of the partisans, but as he grew older he became more and more conservative, suspecting even Nixon of having liberal tendencies. He had a quality of mind that I have often found in Serbian men. He could be intellectually brilliant one moment and unbelievably stupid the next. When someone pointed this out to him, he got mad. Never in my life had I heard so many original and idiotic things come out of the same mouth. He was never happier than when arguing. Even if one agreed with everything he said and admitted that black was white, he would find reasons to fight you. He needed opponents, endless drama with eruptions of anger, absurd accusations, near fistfights. Boris, everyone who knew him said, would have made Mahatma Gandhi reach for a stick. Compromise for him was a sign of weakness rather than of good sense. He was not a bad man, just a hothead when it came to politics. He died before Milošević came to power, and I have wondered ever since what he would have made of him and his wars.

Listening to Boris and his pals endlessly rehash our national history, I assumed this was just immigrant talk, old water under the bridge. Like many others, I was under the impression that Yugoslavia was a thriving country not likely to fall apart even after Tito's death. I made two brief trips to Belgrade, one in 1972 and another in 1982, had heard about ethnic incidents, but continued to believe, even when the rhetoric got more and more heated in the late 1980s after the emergence of the first nationalist leaders, that reason would prevail in the end. I had no problem with cultural nationalism, but the kind that demands unquestioning solidarity with prejudices, self-deceptions, paranoias of the collective, I loathed. I couldn't stand it in America, and even less so in Serbia.

The few friends and relatives I had in Belgrade were telling me

about the rise of a new leader, a national savior, called Slobodan
Milošević, whom they all seemed to approve of. I started reading
Belgrade papers and weeklies and having a huge monthly telephone bill trying to understand what was taking place. After more
than forty years in America, I became a Serb again, except, as many
would say, a bad Serb.

"We don't want to live with them anymore," friends would tell me.
They wanted a complete separation from Croats and Bosnians and
at the same time a Serbia that would include all the areas where
Serbs had lived for centuries. When I pointed out that this could
not be done without bloodshed, they got very upset with me since
they were decent people who didn't approve of violence. They simply would not accept that the leaders and the policies they were so
thrilled about were bound to lead to slaughter.

"How can you separate yourselves when you are all mixed together?" I would ask and not get a straight answer. I could recall
the ethnic mixture we had in our neighborhood in Belgrade and
could not imagine that someone would actually attempt to do
something so wicked. Plus, I liked the mix. I spent most of my life
translating poetry from every region of Yugoslavia, had some idea
what their cultures were like, so I could not see any advantage for
anyone living in a ghetto with just their own kind.

Of course, I was naïve. I didn't realize the immense prestige that
inhumanity and brutality have among nationalists. I also didn't
grasp to what degree they are impervious to reason. To point out
the inevitable consequences of their actions didn't make the slightest impression on them, since they refused to believe in cause and
effect.

The infuriating aspect of every nationalism is that it doesn't understand that it is a mirror image of some other nationalism, and
that most of its pronouncements have been heard in other places
and at other times. Smug in their ethnocentricity, certain of their
own superiority, indifferent to the cultural, religious, and political
concerns of their neighbors, all they needed in 1990 was a leader
to lead them into disaster.

How did I see what many others didn't? Or as the Serbs would say,
what made me an *odrod* (renegade)?

The years of the Vietnam War focused my mind. It took me a

while to appreciate the full extent of the prevarication and sheer madness in our press and television and our political opinion, and to see what our frothing patriots with their calls for indiscriminate slaughter were getting us into. The war deepened for me what was already a lifelong suspicion of all causes that turn a blind eye to the slaughter of the innocent.

"Go back to Russia," I recall someone shouting to the antiwar demonstrators in New York. So, it's like that, I recall thinking then. You opt for the sanctity of the individual and your fellow citizens immediately want to string you up. Even today our conservatives argue that we lost the war in Vietnam because the protesters undercut the military, who were forced to fight with one hand tied behind their backs. In other words, if we had gone ahead and killed four million Vietnamese instead of two million, we would have won that war.

Milošević struck me from the beginning, in the late 1980s, as bad news. I said as much in an interview with a Serbian paper. This provoked a reaction. I was called a traitor in the pay of Serbia's enemies, and many other things. This only spurred me on.

After the siege of the Croatian town of Vukovar in 1991, one didn't have to be Nostradamus to prophesy how badly it would all end for the Serbs. I wrote numerous pieces in Serbian and German newspapers arguing with the nationalists. Many others did the same in Serbia, and far more forcefully and eloquently than I did. We were in the minority. As is usually the case everywhere, a craven, corrupt intellectual class was unwilling to sound the alarm that war crimes were being committed, accustomed as they were under communism to being servants to power.

The belief in the independence of intellectuals, as so much of the twentieth-century proves, is nothing but a fairy tale. The most repellent crimes in the former Yugoslavia had the enthusiastic support of people whose education and past accomplishments would lead one to believe that they would know better. Even poets of large talent and reputation found something to praise in the destruction of cities. If they wept, it was only for their own kind. Not once did they bother to stop and imagine the cost of these wars, which their leaders had instigated, for everybody else.

*

Many of my compatriots were upset with me. Serbs always imagine elaborate conspiracies. For them every event is a sham behind which some hidden interest operates. The idea that my views were my own, the product of my sleepless nights and torments of my conscience, was unthinkable. There were innuendoes about my family, hints that for years there had been suspicions about us, that we were foreigners who had managed for centuries to pass themselves off as Serbs.

My favorite one was that the CIA had paid me huge amounts of money to write poems against Serbia, so that I now live a life of leisure in a mansion in New Hampshire attended by numerous black servants.

Incapable of either statecraft or a formulation of legitimate national interest, all Milošević and his followers were good at was fanning hatred and setting neighbor against neighbor. We now know that all the supposedly spontaneous, patriotic military outfits that went to defend Serbs in Croatia and Bosnia were organized, armed, and controlled by his secret services.

There is nothing more disheartening than to watch, year after year, cities and villages destroyed, people killed or sent into exile, knowing that their suffering did not have to happen. Once newspapers and weekly magazines became available on the Internet, I'd rise early every morning to read them and inevitably fall into the darkest despair by eight o'clock.

Serbs often say in their defense that they were not the only ones committing war crimes. Of course not. If everyone else were an angel, there would not be several hundred thousand refugees in Serbia today. Nonetheless, it is with the murderers in one's own family that one has the moral obligation to deal first.

This, as I discovered, was not how a patriot was supposed to feel. The role of the intellectual was to make excuses for the killers of women and children. As for journalists and political commentators, their function was to spread lies and then prove that these lies were true. What instantly became clear to me is that I was being asked by my own people to become an accomplice in a crime by pretending to understand and forgive acts that I knew were unforgivable.

It's not just Serbs who make such demands, of course. It is not much better in America today, but that, too, is not an excuse. The unwillingness to confront the past has made Serbia a backpedaling society, unable to look at the present, much less deal with difficult contemporary problems. It's like a family that sits around the dinner table each evening pretending that granny had not stabbed the mailman with scissors and dad had not tried to rape one of his little girls in the bathroom just this afternoon.

The worst thing is to be right about one's own kind. For that you are never forgiven. Better to be wrong a hundred times! They'll explain it later by saying that you loved your people so much. Among the nationalists, we are more likely to be admired if we had been photographed slashing the throat of a child than marching against some war they had fought and lost.

When I went back to Belgrade in 1972, after an absence of almost twenty years, I discovered that the window above the entrance of our apartment building, through which I had kicked a ball after the war, was still broken. In 1982 it was still not repaired. Last fall, when I returned, I discovered it had been fixed after the NATO bombing, which hit the TV studio close by and broke lots of windows in the neighborhood.

The reason it was not repaired earlier is that all the tenants in the building had quarreled and were not on speaking terms. My late aunt did not acknowledge the existence of some of her neighbors for forty years, so it was unthinkable that she would knock on their doors for the sake of a window or the many other things that needed to be done. That, to my mind, is pretty much the story of Serbs and Serbia — or so I intend to tell my great-uncle, whom I still hope to run into one of these days.

He'll be more than hundred years old, sitting in a rocking chair at a nursing home in rural Alabama, deaf and nearly blind, wearing a straw hat and a string tie over a Hawaiian shirt, but still looking like a Serb despite all the guises he devised in his long life to not look like one. From time to time he mutters some words in that strange language his nurses take to be just an old man's private gibberish. "All you ever need is a roof, a bowl of bean soup, and some pussy."

LAUREN SLATER

Tripp Lake

FROM *Swink*

AT THE AGE OF NINE, I went to my first and only camp, located in Poland, Maine, way up off 95, by a kidney-shaped lake where across the shore we could see the serrated lines of red roofs and, on sunny days, white sails walking along the water. The camp was called Tripp Lake and it was for girls, or so my parents said, who were especially competitive, girls like me, not yet pubescent, packed with all the power of a life that had yet to really unfold, that brought with it the hard parts, the shames, the sadnesses, none of that yet. I wore my hair in what was called a pixie cut, which was a nice way of saying it was short as a boy's — crewcut, really — and, at that age, white-blond so the stubble glittered silver in the summer sun. I spent my evenings playing capture the flag, an exhilarating game that requires fast feet and a bit of cunning.

Understandably, my parents thought it best to send me to a place where my energies could be shaped and expanded. I agreed. I thought I might be Olympic quality, like those skaters I'd seen, or the skiers hunched over their poles, ricocheting down mountains where ice hung from all the trees.

I remember the first night at the camp — but no, let me begin before then, at the bus stop, about to leave, and feeling, for the first time, a shudder of intense grief. My mother, an aloof woman whom I nonetheless adored, looked pale, her eyes foggy and distant. My father was a small man in the bakery business. Lately they'd been fighting. She wanted something grand out of life, something more than a muffin, whereas he was content to nozzle whipped cream on top of tarts. I loved my father, but I loved my mother more — more problematically is what I mean, in the crooked, hooked way only a daughter can love.

I hugged my parents goodbye, and when I hugged my mother I could feel a circle of sadness in her. By leaving I felt as if I were betraying her. I had heard their voices at night, his quiet, hers shrill — "you and you and you" — and I'd seen my mother sometimes sitting on the porch looking out at nothing. She was a severe and brittle woman, but even at that age I knew brittle was breakable. Sometimes, driving in the car, she crushed the accelerator to the floor, just for the feeling of speed, and other times she cried with her mouth closed. I had the feeling, there at the bus stop, that she wished she were me, about to board a bus heading for the horizon, a green-striped bus with Peter Pan dancing on its flank and girls unabashedly eating apples. And because I felt her longing, inchoate, certainly unspoken, my chest seemed to split with sadness, and also guilt. This was a new emotion, an emotion that sits in the throat, an emotion that is maybe more imagistic than all the others. Guilt made me imagine that while I was away, my mother would come undone: her arm would fall off; her hair would drift from her head. Guilt made me imagine that she would sit in the nights and cry, and what could I do about that? I wanted to say I'm sorry, but I didn't really know what for. I couldn't have said it then, what I've since felt my whole life, that separation is a sword, painful, to be avoided at all costs.

My first night at camp. I could hear the flagpole rope banging against its post; I could hear the cry of what were maybe coyotes in the woods and the susurration of thousands of tree frogs. I couldn't sleep, so I stepped outside, onto the damp dirt that surrounded the cabin, and in the single spotlight that shone down, I found a tiny toad, no bigger than a dime, with still tinier bumps on its taupe back. I lifted the amphibian up. I could not believe that God, or whoever, could make an animal so small, an animal that would have, if I cut it open, all the same organs as me, in miniature, the locket-size heart, bones like white wisps. How easy it is to break an animal. I could have crushed that frog with my fist — and part of me wanted to, while another part of me wanted to protect it, while still a third part of me wanted to let it go.

Before camp, I'd been a more or less happy girl, but that first night I couldn't sleep and by morning a wild sadness had settled in me. Where was I? Where was she? Someday I would die. Someone somewhere was sick. It was as if a curtain had been pulled back to reveal the true nature of the world, which was terror through and through.

That summer I became, for the first time in my life, truly afraid, and the fears took forms that were not good, that did not augur well for my later life, although I didn't know it then. That first day, sitting on the green lawn, watching a girl do a cartwheel and another girl mount the parallel bars, I developed an irrational fear that is still hard to explain: I became hyperaware of my own body, the swoosh of my blood and the paddling of my heart and the *huh huh huh*s of my breath, and it seemed amazing and tenuous to me that my body did all of this without any effort on my part. As soon as I became aware of this fact — almost as though I'd discovered my lower brain stem and how it was hitched to the spinal cord — as soon as I came to consciousness about this, I thought, *I can't breathe.* And truly it felt like I couldn't breathe. I thought, *I am thinking about my breathing, and if I think too hard about my breathing, which you're not supposed to think about, I will concentrate on it right away,* and I swallowed hard, and then I became aware of all the minute mechanisms that comprise a swallow, and so I felt I couldn't swallow anymore. It was like the lights were going out in my body, while girls in front of me did cartwheels on the green lawn, completely unaware that I was dying.

After that, the fears came fast and furious. I was afraid to think about walking, because then I would fall. Breathing, because then I would suffocate.

Swallowing was the worst of all, to suddenly feel you have no way of bringing the world down into your throat, of taking it in, no way. And I became afraid of the dining hall, with its vicious swordfish mounted on one wall, and its huge bear head with eyes like my mother's, dull, distant eyes, eyes at once wild and flat. I became afraid of pancakes, of toothbrushes, of cutlery, of water, of counselors urging me into the lake, where fronds fingered through the murk and scads of fish darted by, making a current cool against my legs.

That first week at camp, I fished a dime out of my uniform pocket (we wore only blue-and-white standard-issue uniforms) and called my mother. From far, far away I heard her voice. When had her sadness started? With my father, or before that, with her mother, who insisted that she, the oldest of three girls, do endless tasks and child care, so she was never able to shoot marbles, too busy shining the silver. My mother, I knew, had been a good girl, exceedingly good, and because of that, she hated my grand-mother. She called her Frances, and all holidays were barbed af-fairs, my mother sniping at her mother, making faces at the food because she, if only given the chance, could have done better.

My mother did not go to college despite the fact that she's bright. In my imagination, when I construct her history for her, be-cause she's so closed about her own, she wants to be a singer on a lit stage or she wants to be a painter with her canvas at a quiet lakeside. She wants something larger than her own life, larger than her husband's life, larger than the house and kids, where what she does all day is clean. Much, much later, when I was near grown, af-ter she and my father divorced, my mother would develop a pas-sion for Israel, its military might; she became fiercely, ragefully Zionistic, and, totally bursting the caul of her confinement, she smuggled Bibles into the USSR. But this was later, when she found an outlet for her energies, and if only I'd known that was going to happen, that she was going to get something good out of life — if only I'd known, maybe my fears would have been a little less.

From far away my mother answered the phone, and I said, "I want to come home," and she said, "Don't be a quitter, Lauren." She wanted for me a larger life, a life where girls stand on stages, take charge of a team, swim the length of a lake and back in a Speedo suit. But because she didn't have these things, I felt much too guilty to take them for myself. None of this did I say.

At camp, we were divided into teams, and every activity, from drama to Newcomb, was cast as a competition. It was a summer of color war. I watched the older girls run with their lacrosse sticks, cradling them close to their sides, the ball in the gut-string pocket a soft blur. I watched as we, the younger girls, were taught to drib-ble and to shoot. Part of me wanted fiercely to win these games, while a still larger part of me could not even allow myself to partici-pate, for somehow I would be betraying my mother if I did.

I was put on the Tigers team. Every morning after breakfast, standing at attention beneath that mounted swordfish, we would sing:

> Shielded by orange and black
> Tigers will attack
> Catching every cue
> Always coming through.

I remember in particular a game called bombardment, which we played in the gym on rainy days, Tigers versus Bears. In this game, each side is given a whole raft of basketballs, and the purpose is simply to hurl them at each other as hard as you can, and whoever gets hit is out. Before I'd left home, maybe I could have played this game, but certainly not now. Brown basketballs came whizzing through the air, smacked against the lacquered floor of the gym, ricocheted off a face or a flank, and one by one each girl got hit and so would sit out on the sidelines. I was so scared of bombardment that whenever we played it, I hung way in the back of the court, where the other team's balls could not reach me. And then one day, because of this, I lasted throughout the whole game; everyone on my team had been hit except me, and everyone on the other team had been hit except a senior girl named Nancy, a fourteen-year-old who had one leg longer than the other. She had custom-made shoes, her left heel stacked high enough to bring her up even so she didn't tilt. I'd watched Nancy walk out of the corners of my eyes; even with her shoes she was strangely clumsy, gangly, always giggling nervously just at the rim of a group of girls, her desire to be taken in palpable.

And now Nancy and I were the last two left in the game. Everyone on the sidelines was screaming *Go, go, go*. Nancy's skin was as pale as milk, the strands of veins visible in her neck. Her gimp foot, supported by the huge rubber heel of her sneaker, seemed to wobble. *Go, go, go*, but I couldn't do it, I couldn't hurl that ball at her; it seemed existentially horrible that we were called to do this sort of thing in the world, to live in a way where someone had to lose. I stood there, locked in place, mesmerized by her skin and her foot, while Nancy lifted the basketball high above her head and hurled it toward me with as much muster as she could muster, and I let the ball hit me on the hip. Nancy won. That was the only outcome I could tolerate.

It didn't take long for the counselors to realize something was wrong with me. I cried all the time. During free swim I retreated into the fringe of woods. The woods were next to a red barn, where horses hung their heads over stall doors and where there were golden squares of hay. Somehow, being near the horses calmed me. I liked their huge velvety lips, their thoughtful mastications. I liked the way they almost seemed to slurp up hay. I liked their rounded backsides, their plumed tails; I even liked their scat, flecked with grain and sweet-smelling. Today, whenever I enter a barn and smell that smell, I do a Proustian plunge back to that first barn, and to the chestnut ponies.

Riding was a camp activity reserved for the older girls. I began to watch those girls cantering around the ring, the horses seeping dark sweat on their muscular chests. The riding coach's name was Kim. She was a wisp of a woman in tan jodhpurs with suede patches at the knees. Once, when I was alone in the barn, I found her riding clothes hung up on a hook near the tack room. I tried on her green hunt jacket. It hung huge on me, but it felt cozy, and on its lapel there was a tiny brooch in the shape of a dragonfly.

"Would you like to try?" Kim asked me one day.

"I'm only ten," I said.

"Well," she said, "I have a horse who's only ten, too. Maybe you would make a good match."

"What's his name?" I asked.

"What's yours?" she said.

"Lauren," I said.

"Smokey Raindrops," she said. "But we call him Rain."

Rain, Rain — what a beautiful name. It was more a sound than a designation. "Yes," I said.

In fact, I didn't get to ride Rain that day. First, all the counselors, along with Auntie Ruth, the camp director, had to discuss it. Should I have lessons even though that was not part of my camp curriculum? Would that make me happy? They thought it might.

Riding is a sport that, like any other, requires more than just the circumscribed activity. There is the ritualistic preparation, the waxing of skis or the oiling of strings or, in this case, the grooming before the tack. A few days later Kim showed me how to do it, using a currying comb, picking a hoof, leaning down and cupping the hairy fetlock, lifting the leg, seeing the shine of the silver shoe with six nail heads in it. Time passed. Days passed. Caring for the horses was soothing, and I found when I was at the stable by these big breathing animals, I could forget about my own breath and just breathe.

All through the summer Kim taught me how to ride, alone, no other girl there. She taught me how to post, how to do dressage, how to jump. I learned to hoist myself up, foot in one stirrup, other leg flung over the broad rank back. "When you post," she said, "watch the left leg. As it extends, you rise."

The trot of a horse is like a metronome. It synchronizes you. It hypnotizes you. Left foot rise. Left foot rise. Your whole mind funnels down into this foot, the flash of hoof in the summer sun. And I'll never forget the day Kim taught me to canter, how she said, "Trot out, give him a kick with your inside foot," and suddenly the horse's tight trot broke into the rocking run, around and around the ring we went, so fast it seemed, the world blurring by in a beautiful way.

Riding is largely a singular sport; although there are shows and red ribbons, first places and sixth places, it can still be done, nevertheless, with no attention to the competition aspect. You cannot really play lacrosse or soccer unless you are playing against someone, and this againstness requires that you see yourself as separate, with all that that implies. But horseback riding is something you can do alone in the woods, or in a dusty riding rink, or even in your mind, in which you can canter, too. Riding is not about separation. It is not about dominance. The only person you might hurt is you. You are, at long last, without guilt.

Riding. It is about becoming one with the animal that bears you along. It is about learning to give and take, give the horse his head, take the rein and bring him up. It is about tack, the glorious leather saddles, and the foam-stained bits, which fascinated me, how Kim would roll them in sugar and slide them into a horse's mouth, its thick tongue clamped. It is, more than anything else, about relationship and balance, and as Kim taught me how to do these things — walk, trot, canter — a sort of peace settled in me, a working through my mother and me, a way of excelling at no one's cost.

And so the summer progressed. The only thing I could not do well was jump. Each time we approached the fence the horse seemed to sense my primordial fear, fear of the fence and fear of everything it contained, and it would bunch to a scuttering halt, or, more humiliating, the horse would stop, and then with me kicking, and kicking uselessly, it would simply walk over the bar. I watched Kim jump; she was amazing, fluid, holding on to her horse's hair as they entered the air, her face a mixture of terror and exhilaration, the balanced combination that means only one thing: mastery.

One month into the camp season was visiting day. My parents arrived carrying leathery fruit rolls and a new canteen. They seemed as separate as ever, not even looking at each other. My mother was appalled at the condition of my wardrobe. My clothes stank of sweat and fur. The soles of my boots were crammed with flaking manure. That was the summer, also, when I started to smell. "What's this?" she said, flicking through my steamer trunk. "Do you ever do your laundry?" She pulled out a white shirt with spatters of black mud on it, and stains at the armpits, slight stains, their rims barely visible.

"Lauren," she said.

"What?" I said.

She pursed her lips and shook her head. She held the shirt out as though to study it. And once again I saw that look of longing cross her face, but this time it was mixed with something else. I saw the briefest flicker of disgust.

A few minutes later, she went into our cabin bathroom, which we called the Greenie. She closed the door. I stalked up to it, pressed my ear against its wood. What did I do with my body? What did she do with hers? I heard the gush of water from the tap, the scrunch of something papery. The bathroom had a lock on my side only. Quietly, and for a reason I still cannot quite explain, I turned the lever and the lock slid quietly into its socket.

A few minutes later, when she tried to get out, she could not. She rattled the knob. We were alone in the cabin. I stood back and watched. "Lauren?" she said. "Lauren?" Her voice hurt me. It was curved into a question, and when I didn't answer, the question took on a kind of keening. "Lauren, are you there? Open the door." I stood absolutely still. I was mesmerized, horrified by the vulnerability in her voice, how small she suddenly seemed, and how I was growing in girth by the minute. For some reason I suddenly pictured her trapped in a tiny glass bottle, and I held the bottle in my hands. I could let her out or leave her.

I let her out.

"What are you doing?" she said. She stared at me. I stared back at her. I could see her sweat now; it ran in a trickle down the side of her brow. I wanted to wipe it away.

They left in the evening, when colored clouds were streaming across the sky. I stood in the parking lot and watched their station wagon rattle over the dirt road, raising clouds of dust. The next few days, I backslid. My fears returned. There was the problem with my breathing, but now accompanying this obsession was the need to walk backward while counting. I saw for sure that I was growing while she shrank. I saw for sure that I was growing because she shrank. I also saw something pointed in me, some real desire to win. Hearing that lock sink into its socket, I had felt glee and power.

I stopped riding then. I stopped going to the stables. I stayed in my bunk. I wrote letters and letters to my mother, the act somehow soothing my conscience. *Love, Lauren XXX. Kisses and hugs. I love you.*

At last, after four days had passed, Kim came to my cabin to get me. "You disappeared," she said.

"I'm sick," I said.

"You know," she said, "I never much liked my mother."

I stared at her. How had she known?

"What will you do?" she said.

"I don't know," I said.

"Are you going to sit on a cot for the rest of your life?"

"Maybe," I said.

"Just sit there and cry?" she said, and there was, suddenly, a slight sneer to her voice.

I looked away.

"I once knew a girl," said Kim, "who spent her whole life going from hospital to hospital because she loved being sick. She was too scared to face the world. Is that you?"

I have thought of her words often — a premonition, an augury, a warning, a simple perception.

I followed her back to the barn. It was noon. The sun was high and hot. She brought Rain out into the middle of the ring, tightened his saddle strap, and tapped on the deep seat. "All aboard," she said.

Sitting high on the horse, I could smell the leaves. I could smell my own sweat and all that it contained, so many contradictions.

"We're going to jump today," she said.

She went to the center of the ring, and this time she set the fence at four feet. "Now," she said, "cross your stirrups and knot your reins. A rider has to depend on her inner balance only."

I cantered toward the jump, hands on my hips, legs grasping. But each time, at the crucial moment of departure, Rain would screech to a halt and I'd topple into his mane.

"He senses your fear," Kim said.

At last, on the third or fourth try, she went into the barn and came back out with a long black crop. Standing in the center of the ring, right next to the jump, she swizzled the crop into the air, a snapping sound. The horse's ears flashed forward. "You have to get over it," she said. I centered myself in the saddle. I cantered twice around the rink and then turned in tight toward the bar. Kim cracked the whip, a crack I still hear today whenever I feel my fears — and I do, I often do — but I rose up, arms akimbo, in this leap merged with the mammal, its heart my heart, its hooves my feet, and we sailed into the excellent air. I did it. I found a way to move forward.

JOHN UPDIKE

Extreme Dinosaurs

FROM *National Geographic*

BEFORE THE NINETEENTH CENTURY, when dinosaur bones turned up they were taken as evidence of dragons, ogres, or giant victims of Noah's Flood. After two centuries of paleontological harvest, the evidence seems stranger than any fable, and continues to get stranger. Dozens of new species emerge each year; China and Argentina are hot spots lately for startling new finds. Contemplating the bizarre specimens recently come to light, one cannot but wonder what on earth Nature was thinking of. What advantage was conferred, say, by the ungainly eight-foot-long arms and huge triple claws of *Deinocheirus*? Or, speaking of arms, by *Mononykus*'s smug dependence on a single, stoutly clawed digit at the end of each minimal forearm? Guesses can be hazarded: the latter found a single stubby claw just the thing for probing after insects; the former stripped the leaves and bark from trees in awesome bulk. A carnivorous cousin, *Deinonychus*, about the size of a man, leaped on its prey, wrapped its long arms and three-fingered hands around it, and kicked it to the death with sickle-shaped toenails.

Tiny *Epidendrosaurus* boasted a hugely elongated third finger that served, presumably, a clinging, arboreal lifestyle, like that of today's aye-aye, a lemur that possesses the same curious trait. With the membrane they support, the elongated digits of bats and pterosaurs enable flight, and perhaps *Epidendrosaurus* was taking a skittery first step in that direction. But what do we make of such apparently inutile extremes of morphology as the elaborate skull frills of ceratopsians like *Styracosaurus* or the horizontally protruding front teeth of *Masiakasaurus knopfleri*, a late Cretaceous oddity recently uncovered in Madagascar by excavators who named the beast after Mark Knopfler, the lead singer of the group Dire Straits, their favorite music to dig by?

Masiakasaurus is an oddity, all right, its mouth bristling with those slightly hooked, forward-poking teeth; but, then, odd too are an elephant's trunk and tusks, and an elk's antler rack, and a peacock's tail. A difficulty with dinosaurs is that we can't see them in action and tame them, as it were, with visual (and auditory and olfactory) witness. How weird might a human body look to them? That thin and featherless skin, that dish-flat face, that flaccid erectitude, those feeble, clawless five digits at the end of each limb, that ghastly utter lack of a tail — *ugh*. Whatever did this creature *do* to earn its place in the sun, a well-armored, nicely specialized dino might ask.

Dinosaurs dominated the planet's land surface from some 200 million years ago until their abrupt disappearance 135 million years later. The vast span of time boggles the human mind, which took its present, *Homo sapiens* form less than 200,000 years ago and began to leave written records and organize cities less than 10,000 years in the past. When the first dinosaurs — small, lightweight, bipedal, and carnivorous — appeared in the Triassic, the first of three periods in the Mesozoic geologic era, the earth held one giant continent, Pangaea; during their Jurassic heyday Pangaea split into two parts, Laurasia and Gondwana; and by the late Cretaceous the continents had something like their present shapes, though all were reduced in size by the higher seas, and India was still an island heading for a Himalaya-producing crash with Asia. The world was becoming the one we know: the Andes and the Rockies were rising; flowering plants had appeared, and with them, bees. The Mesozoic climate, generally, was warmer than today's, and wetter, generating lush growths of ferns and cycads and forests of evergreens, ginkgoes, and tree ferns close to the poles; plant-eating dinosaurs grew huge, and carnivorous predators kept pace. It was a planetary summertime, and the living was easy.

Not *that* easy: throughout their long day on earth, there was an intensification of boniness and spikiness, as if the struggle for survival became grimmer. And yet the defensive or attacking advantage of skull frills and back plates is not self-evident. The solid-domed skull of *Pachycephalosaurus,* the largest of the bone-headed dinosaurs, seems made for butting — but for butting what? The skull would do little good against a big predator like *Tyrannosaurus rex*, which had the whole rest of *Pachycephalosaurus*'s unprotected body to bite down on. Butting matches amid males of the same species were unlikely, since the bone, though ten inches thick, was not shock-absorbent. The skulls of some pachycephalosaurs, moreover, were flat and thin, and some tall and ridged — bad designs for contact sport. Maybe they were just used for discreet pushing. Or to make a daunting impression.

An even more impractical design shaped the skull of the pachycephalosaurid *Dracorex hogwartsia* — an intricate sunburst of spiky horns and knobs, without a dome. Only one such skull has been unearthed; it is on display, with the playful name derived from Harry Potter's school of witchcraft and wizardry, in Indianapolis's Children's Museum. Duck-billed *Parasaurolophus walkeri*, another late Cretaceous plant-eater, sported a spectacular pipe-like structure, sweeping back from its skull, that was once theorized to act as a snorkel in swimming. But the tubular crest had no hole for gathering air. It may have served as a trumpeting noisemaker, for herd communication, or supported a bright flap of skin beguiling to a *Parasaurolophus* of the opposite gender. Sexual success and herd acceptance perpetuate genes as much as combative prowess and food-gathering ability.

Dinosaurs have always presented adaptive puzzles. How did huge herbivores like *Brachiosaurus, Apatosaurus,* and *Diplodocus* get enough daily food into their tiny mouths to fill their cavernous guts? Of the two familiar dinosaurs whose life-and-death struggle was memorably animated in Walt Disney's 1940 *Fantasia* (though in fact they never met in the corridors of time, failing to overlap by fully 75 million years), *T. rex* had puzzlingly tiny arms and *Stegosaurus* carried on its back a double row of huge bony plates negligible as defensive armor and problematic as heat controls. Not that biological features need to be efficient to be carried along. Some Darwinian purists don't even like the word "adaptive," as carrying a taint of implied teleology, of purposeful self-improvement. All that is certain is that dinosaur skeletons demonstrate the viability, for a time, of certain dimensions and conformations. Yet even Darwin, on the last page of *The Origin of Species,* in summing up his theory as "Natural Selection, entailing Divergence of Character and the

Extinction of less-improved forms," lets fall a shadow of value judgment with the "less-improved."

In what sense are living forms improvements over the dinosaurs? All life forms, even such long-lasting ones as blue-green algae and horseshoe crabs and crocodiles, will eventually flunk some test posed by environmental conditions and meet extinction. One can safely say that no dinosaur was as intelligent as *Homo sapiens,* or even as chimpanzees. And none that are known, not even a heavyweight champion like *Argentinosaurus,* was as big as a blue whale. One can believe that none was as beautiful in swift motion as a cheetah or an antelope, or as impressive to our mammalian aesthetic sense as a tiger. But beyond this it is hard to talk of improvement, especially since for all its fine qualities *Homo sapiens* is befouling the environment like no fauna before it.

The dinosaurs in their long reign filled every niche several times over, and the smallest of them — the little light-boned theropods scuttling for their lives underfoot — grew feathers and became birds, still singing and dipping all around us. It is an amazing end to an amazing evolutionary story — *Deinonychus* into dove. Other surprises certainly lurk within the still unfolding saga of the dinosaurs. In Inner Mongolia, so recently that the bones were revealed to the world just this past spring, a giant bird-like dinosaur, *Gigantoraptor,* has been discovered. It clearly belongs among the oviraptorosaurs of the late Cretaceous — ninety-pound weaklings with toothless beaks — but weighed in at one and a half tons and could have peered into a second-story window. While many of its fellow theropods — for example, six-foot, large-eyed, big-brained *Troodon* — were evolving toward nimbleness and intelligence, *Gigantoraptor* opted for brute size. But what did it eat, with its enormous toothless beak? Did its claw-tipped arms bear feathers, as did those of smaller oviraptorosaurs?

The new specimens that emerge as tangles of bones embedded in sedimentary rock are island peaks of a submerged continent where evolutionary currents surged back and forth. Our telescoped perspective gives an impression of a violent struggle as anatomical ploys, some of them seemingly grotesque, were desperately tried and eventually discarded. The dinosaurs as a group saw myriad extinctions, and the final extinction, at the end of the Mesozoic, looks to have been the work of an asteroid. They continue to live in the awareness of their human successors on the throne of earthly dominance. They fascinate children as well as paleontologists. My second son, I well remember, collected the plastic dinosaur miniatures that came in cereal boxes, and communed with them in his room. He loved them — their amiable grotesquerie, their guileless enormity, their unassuming small brains. They were eventual losers, in a game of survival our own species is still playing, but new varieties keep emerging from the rocks underfoot to amuse and amaze us.

JOE WENDEROTH

Where God Is Glad

FROM *Open City*

I HATE STRIP CLUBS. My new book has a picture of me on the cover in front of a strip club, and when I show it to people and say "This is me in front of my favorite strip club in Baltimore," I feel like I need to make all kinds of explanations. It isn't that I'm ashamed to be seen in front of a strip club, nor is it that I cherish the idea of being seen in front of a strip club. I guess when I step back and consider it, it seems childish to have one's picture taken there. What saves me, I hope, is the actual sign in the picture, which clearly distinguishes this particular strip club from most others. And then, too, the picture is good because the flash didn't work and you can just see my silhouette in the weird green-yellow light of the sign. That is, you can't see *me* so much as you can see *some guy*. The bar is called Tony's, and it's in Baltimore on Monument Avenue under an overpass on the outskirts of Highlandtown, not far from Route 40, which is an industrial-trucking-prostitution-and-strip-clubs area. I lived with my wife nearby (though she was not yet my wife at the time, and has, since becoming my wife, declared that she never wants to go to Tony's again), and we could walk to and from the place. Indeed, we *did* walk to and from the place. Those were the days. So in the picture, I'm standing in front of a filthy, dimly lit window with a painted sign in it. The sign reads:

ALL GIRL REVEIW
GO   GO

Between the GO and the other GO there is a faceless buxom woman — she sort of reminds me of the cover of one of the Cars' albums — you may know the one I mean. Sort of like a fifties pinup girl, very retro, very "stag." I guess what drew me to the sign at first was the misspelling of "review." The idea that, in the whole process of the making of the sign, there was no one capable of catching the mistake, or more likely no one who cared to make that kind of effort. This lack of concern for superficial matters quite faithfully conveys the essence of the place.

The first time I went to Tony's must have been in 1993 or 1994. As I said, it was a sort of neighborhood strip bar, and I recall we decided — my not-yet-wife and I — that we would walk over and check it out one evening. Inside, there was a U-shaped bar to the right; to the left there was an open room with two extremely beat-up pool tables. Directly to the left, essentially behind the sign window, was one booth, the only seating in the place, save the bar stools and a handful of tables set up on both ends of the pool tables. The restrooms were in the back, behind the pool table area and behind a variety of broken machines and chairs and such. It was your basic dive bar, but dirtier, and more possessed of an under-construction look. Well, that's not exactly right — it looked more like it *had been* under construction, but construction had been abandoned for some time. What was really unusual, though — what stood out, let's say — was the bevy of dancers.

It was a bevy of three or four that first evening, if I recall correctly, and my subsequent visits have verified that this is generally the rule: three or four dancers in constant rotation. When we first walked in, the young woman who gripped the pole was overweight; I had never seen an overweight stripper, and so I found her dance quite compelling. She weighed 270 if she weighed a pound. The men at the bar did not seem amused, did not seem to feel that anything unusual or ironic was taking place. The dancer herself did not seem to feel that she, as a stripper, was unusual; she moved in the usual stripper way, swaying and thrusting and all of that, but with an added trick: she was able to manipulate the folds in her flesh, allowing patrons a view into a great variety of cleavages. I recall that she was particularly adept with her ass cheeks; she achieved a kind of quivering and then a kind of optical illusion as she endeavored to allow viewers to believe in the possibility of seeing in to the core, the secret binding as it were. The next dancer to take the stage was not as big as the first — she was middle of the road, as far as weight goes, and did not have a pretty face. What distinguished her was her left arm, which was misshapen, and also considerably shorter than her right arm. Her choice in attire stood out, too: she wore a one-piece Minnie Mouse bathing suit. She, like her predecessor, was conspicuously comfortable with her vocation.

We sat at the bar and drank, my not-yet-wife and I. We marveled and we talked of whatever was on our minds — that is, aside from what we were seeing unfold in front of us. The other two dancers that evening were — let me think — one was probably a thin, middle-aged blond woman (thin save for a beer belly, that is) and one was probably an overweight black woman who shook her breasts violently. Tony's patrons that evening were white men and black men and us. Everyone was quite laid back. The bartender was Tony himself, and this has been the case almost every time I have been in; indeed, on the couple of occasions when Tony was not tending bar, he was seated at the bar. Tony is a small no-nonsense Greek man who, I later learned, went AWOL from the Greek navy in the seventies — somewhere in Central America — then drifted up to Baltimore and opened his bar soon after. It is a bar, he claims, that has from day one welcomed all races; in Baltimore this is not insignificant. But on this first visit I did not know about Tony's personal history yet. I knew what I have so far described. But then *knew* might be presumptuous; it's probably better to say that I *witnessed* what I have so far described — I did not *know* it.

The ladies — and they were clearly ladies — danced, and then they descended from the pole island and walked around the bar to ask for tips — a dollar, to be specific. Most strip clubs are constructed so that the strippers are able to approach, during their performance, the patrons seated at the bar, and to accumulate, thereby, their tips. This capacity to approach, mid-performance, in states of undress, is important, as it turns the front-row seating into a kind of challenge: to sit there is to confess, explicitly, your desire for that sort of intimacy. The capacity to approach also impacts, or challenges, the stripper; not only does it weave the achievement of intimacies into the dance — it at the same time marries the shedding of clothes with the accumulation of money. At Tony's, the dancer is not provided with the capacity to approach, during her performance, those who gaze upon her; there's just enough of a gap between the pole island and the bar to ensure that this is not possible. At Tony's, patrons seated at the bar are in some sense in the ideal spot; they're close enough to gawk, and yet not so close that they are made to pay for it. The main difference is really the way in which Tony's extracts the expected intimacy from public view and places it altogether outside the performance, where, should intimacy continue to exist at all, it must exist as something less heard-of. When finally the lovely tip-seeking lady arrives at your seat and asks you for a dollar — and by now she will usually have put her clothes back on — you feel more like you're tipping a pizza-delivery guy than a stripper. A dancer at Tony's makes her money when she's not dancing, and she makes her real money after she's combed the bar for tips. At that time, she will approach men in the bar, trying to find someone who would like to buy her a drink; the man who buys her a drink — and a drink for a dancer is steep — is entitled to sit close with her and talk as she drinks it. And then of course she might suggest taking him out into the parking lot. But what am I talking about here! — I am drifting away from the meaty crux, and I apologize for that. Let me get back to it: the living moment that is Tony's.

It seemed like every time I went back, something even more indescribable would occur. Soon after I introduced my brother and some friends to the place, we were over there on a Saturday night and there was a dwarf guy playing pool. This in itself would not be worth mentioning, but I managed to have a sort of run-in with the guy. He was playing pool, and he wasn't terribly good. I'm pretty good. But somehow he wins. My brother is, quite naturally, making fun of me, and so I say: "It's a fluke. I beat this guy eight times out of ten, easy." My rematch comes up and I miscue and scratch on an easy shot that would have gotten me to the eight ball. I am bitter, at this point, because the guy has been giving me advice all along — as if, because he beat me one time, he is some sort of pool shark. So he has this very easy shot that I have provided for him, and I am bitter, and so — well, you all know the rule about having to have one foot on the ground when you take a shot — of course, everyone knows this rule — well, the fact is, this rule would fairly disqualify my dwarf friend, so he ignores it. So as he leaps his torso up on to the table and arranges himself to take the easy shot to win the game, I say to him, from behind, and with just enough volume for him to hear: "One foot on the ground, pal." He ignores me and makes the shot. And the story has subsequently been etched into the weird crumbling tablet that is *our life at Tony's.*

The ladies have changed over the years, and continually, but the essence of the ladies has not. I recall one night I was in there with a friend, and mostly it was Eastern European young women dancing, but there was one straight-up Baltimore woman. So she dances and then descends and makes her way down to us to get her dollars. Wanting to make conversation, my friend says: "Hey, what's up with the patch on your arm — quitting smoking?"

"Oh, no," she says, "it's painkiller."

"Oh, man, what do you need that for?"

"Bone cancer," she says, and moves along to the next guy down the bar. Just when you think the pathos cannot be amped up, just when you think you have truly met with the bottom of the barrel, there comes a deeper blow, a deeper affirmation of mortality. That is Tony's.

I've actually been meaning to write about Tony's for a long time and have not been able to do it. I love *going* there — actually approaching the physical social space that Tony's is — but approaching it *in writing* has always seemed wrong to me, has always seemed fundamentally disrespectful, fundamentally destructive of the sublime foundation. Now that I have stopped to describe the place in more depth, it seems clear to me that Tony's is not really a strip club at all. I hate strip clubs, as I said, and people who like strip clubs hate Tony's. Folks who like strip clubs seek something that Tony's *decisively* does not offer. Tony's is not "nice," does not feel like a risqué Applebee's. It doesn't attempt to dignify the goings-on it shelters. Your typical "nice" strip club maintains itself as a safety zone; its atmosphere tells you that you are dignified. It says: poverty is far away from here, and so you are safe. That the atmosphere is this way is not a small point; safety is absolutely required in a strip club, and this because of the delicacy of the intended spectacle.

If we stop to break down that spectacle, we can begin to understand why it need occur in a safe space. In the typical "nice" strip club, a chasm is constructed and then placed between the subjects and the objects. People — men, mostly — come in to gaze upon the objects of their desire, and these objects learn how to move about so as to maintain and intensify this gaze. The gaze pays. The gaze takes and then the gaze pays. The space wherein this transaction takes place must be safe — and conspicuously so — because that transaction is so delicate. The gaze itself is delicate. Why? Well, the gazer must convince himself that the gaze, in these environs, is worth pursuing. This is tricky because he must accept at the very outset that he will not be allowed to take any kind of next step; he cannot touch the object, and he cannot touch himself — he is required to inhabit the gaze without hope for the transformation it is ceaselessly making thinkable. This inhabitation is not static, however; it's full of drawing-nears. The challenge, for a strip club, is to create a consistently titillating drawing-near . . . without evoking frustration at the decided lack of arrival. This is, as I said, not an easy thing to achieve and not an easy thing to maintain once it has been achieved. Clear rules — and numerous experienced bouncers — are needed. At Tony's, there are rules, but — and this is really the amazing thing if you have ever been there — there are no bouncers.

Tony's is more like a hospital, really, than a strip club. Or maybe it's better to say a hospice. The sort of place wherein no one thinks about the prospect of discharge. At Tony's, one thinks: *Life will never be other than this; I am sick, and this is a sickness that I will not outlive; this is the sickness that will take me all the way to where I have to go.* But there is something that's still missing in the analogy. *Think of Tony's as a hospice in which there is a celebration going on!* That's the great and mysterious leap. I've noticed a common reaction to Tony's — at least among the folks who are capable of loving the experience — and it goes something like: *How could this place exist?* Every time I go back to Baltimore, I fear that I will find that Tony's has ceased, and every time — knock on wood — my fears prove unfounded. Usually the existence of a public place is immediately understandable; one enters the place and feels how the place works, what the place is for, even how good it is at fulfilling that purpose. The longer one sits in Tony's, the more one wonders what it's for, how it works, even what its work could be. One wonders: *Whose idea was this, and how did that idea not get vetoed?* That is the nature of the celebratory leap at Tony's; its very existence seems inexplicable from so many angles. In this, I think of it as akin to life itself. Or rather, it is akin to what we, from our decidedly limited perspective, call life itself — that throng of specific species that has somehow, flukishly, gotten through into this moment.

The typical strip bar is not likely to produce this sense of the inexplicable; its designers never intended it to produce this sense. They designed it to produce a chasm and to be capable of making use of that chasm. At Tony's, the chasm does not exist — it has never been installed. The woman on the stage, the woman who walks over to you and asks you for a dollar when she is done with her dance — that woman is no different from the woman you pass in the supermarket. She is no different, no more an object, than you are. She is a patient and you are a patient; she is as much a patient as you are. Yes, it's true that you have not been asked to play her conspicuously difficult part, but you may as well have been. You are clearly, that is, *as qualified* as each and every dancer you encounter. The spirit of a hospice party is in this way de facto democratic. Each person is created equally flawed, equally mortal.

Another way to get at my point is to consider Narcissus — but not the whole of Narcissus, just Narcissus in his brief maturity, *before* death but *after* all the love drama, all the hope. The Tony's dancer is — or she and you, together, are — Narcissus in the calm blind pulse of inparticularity's most decisive triumph: facelessness. The beauty that got the ball rolling has not been lost, but it has been transformed by the naïve effort to take possession of it. Beauty, when at first it arose, caused breathlessness, in which the other was made conspicuous as an other, a substance powerfully distinct from the substance of the self. The very air — unbreathed — confirmed this distinction. But then the air was taken away, and your face became the face of an other, and again (and this time quite literally) you can't breathe. Breathlessness, which at first compelled you into a kind of anxious hope about the otherness of the other, turns back in on itself, back on *you*, the always already achieved face. My sense is that breathlessness, relieved of that anxious hope, feels something like a comfort. The dance, relieved of the I-you chasm, becomes the dance of this more mature kind of breathlessness. Such a dance is yours as much as it is the dancer's; she dances not *for* you — she dances *of* you, or of your potential, your grotesque and beautiful energy.

And as far as this energy goes — well, I drink diet soda and coffee all day, take whatever pills I can get my hands on, eat a bag of processed sugar every night, never exercise, never eat vegetables, drink too much, lie on the couch for hours and hours staring at the television. The Tony's dancer, well, I don't know how *she* gets from morning to night, but I do know that she *has* managed it, and that she has managed it only barely. And it's this *barely* that amazes — it's this barely that justifies the whole celebration. It's this barely that heartens me, forgives me, and makes me feel obligated to do my part, to be my region of the party. It's this barely that says: *Look at us — it is against all odds that we are upright and alive today!* And if the doctors have noticed that we are alive . . . and if the doctors — sensing the danger that exists for those who are alive — have proceeded to give orders *that we should not get out of this bed,* well, then we have disobeyed doctors' orders. We have gotten up from the bed and we are dancing. That's an interesting moment, if you've ever seen it, or if you've ever been it. More than interesting — it's the whole fucking ball of wax. It reminds me of an Aztec poem called "I Might Die in This Battle." This poem, to my mind, should be written in permanent marker on a stall at Tony's. Perhaps it will be.

> You are slow,
> my heart,
> afraid.
>
> Afraid to stand
> where God is glad.

LEE ZACHARIAS

Buzzards

FROM *Southern Humanities Review*

THEY WOOF. Though I have photographed them before, I have never heard them speak, for they are mostly silent birds. Lacking a syrinx, the avian equivalent of the human larynx, they are incapable of song. According to field guides the only sounds they make are grunts and hisses, though the Hawk Conservancy in the United Kingdom reports that adults may utter a croaking coo and that young black vultures, when annoyed, emit a kind of immature snarl. But to hear any of these sounds, you must be quite close. And I am quite close. Crouched over an unextended tripod at the edge of an empty parking lot in the Everglades, I am in the middle of a flock of black vultures, a vortex, maypole for this uneasy circle dance in which they weave and run at one another, raising their ragged wings and thrusting their gnarly gray heads. I would not call the sound they make a grunt or a hiss, nor a croaking coo, nor a snarl; it is more a low, embryonic woofing, a sound I know from my dog, who is also a black creature, not a bark or growl, not the voice itself, but the anticipation of one reverberating deep inside his throat. And though I keep shooting as they lurch at one another and dip their heads to peck at bottle caps and flattened pieces of tin, they creep me out. I have had the same sensation while snorkeling, an exhilaration in the magic of a world not mine that manifests itself in the same nauseous thrill of nerve as my dread. Buzzards. Carrion crows, Jim Crow, Charleston eagle. *Coragyps atratus.* From the Greek *korax,* meaning "raven," and *gyps,* meaning "vulture," Latin *atratus,* "clothed in black, as in mourning." The Grim Reaper's hooded cloak, wing-like sleeves, and protruding skeletal feet all come to us as a personification of the black vulture; Death's trademark scythe is the color and shape of the flight feathers, the long white primaries the bird displays as he hunches and spreads his wings. The Latin *vulturus* means "tearer." Give voice to the word and you cannot distinguish it from terror.

To photograph birds requires a great deal of equipment. I paid for most of mine — the carbon-steel tripod with its expensive ball head, the camera bodies and lenses, remote, filters, flash, reflectors, and specialized backpack — with money I inherited from my father. He would not have approved. He disapproved of most things. Though he could rage, he was a mostly silent man, skilled at mechanics and repair, who had no respect for impractical pursuits. He was not a bad man, though he was difficult, excitable, hard on others, obsessed with money. The first time I visited the Everglades he tried to talk me out of it — it was too far, he said, there was nothing there; instead he recommended that I visit Silver Springs, a nature theme park boasting glass-bottom-boat tours and a narrated jeep safari. He wasn't much for nature in the wild. He liked control. He was afraid of the unknown, not of death, but of life, which had too many variables. It was the unpredictable and irritating otherness of others that frightened him most.

What frightens me is the otherness of vultures. I am wondering whether they will tear at my flesh, raise their wings, and run at me. I should know, but I don't.

To photograph a wild creature, you must learn its habits.

The Bible does not differentiate between birds of prey and vultures, which are rarely predators, living instead as scavengers, consumers of carrion. One might even call them connoisseurs, for they prefer their meat fresh, and the turkey vulture favors the flesh of herbivores over that of carnivores. According to the Carolina Raptor Center, in captivity they won't eat possum, which is greasy, but happily chow down on rats. The black also feasts on fruit, though it has an unfortunate taste for turtle hatchlings, unlike the palm-nut vulture of Africa, a vegetarian that is surely the strangest of the twenty-three species that populate the world. But in biblical wisdom both predator and scavenger are unclean and hateful birds; if raptors are God's creatures, according to the Book of Leviticus, they are also an abomination: "And these are they which ye shall have in abomination among the fowls . . . the eagle, and the ossifrage, and the osprey, and the vulture." Ossifrage, from the Latin *ossifraga,* meaning "bone breaker," is an archaic name for the bearded vulture, an Old World species once plentiful in the Alps, Himalayas, and Pyrenees, the only vulture to consume bone as the primary part of its diet. Ornithologists no longer sanction use of the bird's other names, lamb vulture and lammergeyer, since it is incapable of killing lambs, let alone babies, despite the myths that have led to its near extinction. While some vultures prey on insects and small amphibians, and the black will steal young herons from the nest, they rarely attack live mammals, and their reputation for doing so is both exaggerated and largely a result of starvation. More than once I have gone out my back door to discover a puff of feathers light as dandelion fluff beneath the azaleas, signature of a hawk that has raided the feeder; thrice I have been startled by the sight of a great blue heron advancing across my small city yard toward the pond. Only recently scientists have confirmed that our ancestors, the ape-men, were not killed off by ferocious saber-toothed tigers but by eagles, which hunt primates larger than themselves by swooping down and piercing their skulls with their strong back talons. These are predators. "I hate vultures because they only frighten humans," says Mrs. Mackinnon in the *Book of Animals, Plants, Trees, Birds, Bugs, and Flowers* that informs Craig Nova's novel *The Good Son.* The titmice and chickadees, the thrashers and towhees, chipmunks, squirrels, fantails, koi, and Labrador retriever who share the space of my garden do not fear the vulture.

When Charles Darwin observed the "carrion-feeding hawks" of Uruguay in the summer of 1832, he lamented that although their structure placed them among the eagles, they ill became such a rank. Darwin was a self-taught observer rather than a trained scientist, but even the most learned scientists of the time mistakenly believed that the New World vultures were related to the eagles. While the Old World vultures that inhabit Africa, Asia, and parts of Europe did descend from the birds of prey classified as Falconiformes, the seven species that inhabit the Americas are classified as Ciconiiformes, related not to hawks but to storks. The similarities in appearance — the wattled necks, small naked heads, hooked beaks, weak though fearsome-looking talons, shaggy feathers, and pronounced hunch — are the result of convergent evolution, like but independent physical adaptations.

Yet so inevitable is the vulture's association with death, and so staunch our cultural will to deny it, that we persist in the biblical view of the vulture even as we tend to perceive those raptors from which the Old World vultures descended, the hawks and the eagles, as Darwin did: creatures of grace, nobility, and strength, equated with freedom instead of death. Darwin called the turkey buzzard a "disgusting bird" whose bald scarlet head is "formed to wallow in putridity." He was right about the head — bacteria die on the bare skin of the face, just as the bird's practice of defecating on its legs kills bacteria. But though their habits seem repulsive, vultures are among the cleanest of creatures. After feeding, adult condors wipe their heads and necks on grass or sand; though other carrion eaters spread disease, the acids in the vulture's digestive system are strong enough to destroy anthrax, botulin, cholera, and hantavirus — they can consume the most toxic corpses without getting sick or passing the germs along.

In *The Vulture,* novelist Catherine Heath describes a pet vulture that preys on its master's thoroughbred dogs as "a huddle of old rags thrown over a naked body, whose stringy neck and red head stuck out at the top as if surveying a hostile world from a safe shelter." The buzzards that perch on the light posts of Arrow Catcher, Mississippi, in Lewis Nordan's *Wolf Whistle* sit "with hunched shoulders and wattled necks like sad old men in dark coats." Ernest Hemingway calls them "huge, filthy birds sunk in hunched feathers." The villainous protagonist of "The Tell-Tale Heart" kills not out of passion or greed, but because his victim had the eye of a vulture. Pablo Neruda speaks not of the vulture's appearance but of his black habits. It is these habits that have made "vultures" into a favorite epithet for the media. We use it for politicians, lawyers, ambulance chasers, talk-show audiences, corporations, academics, and nosy neighbors. Celebrities detest the paparazzi as vulturous; in some circles all photographers are suspect. Writers too are characterized as vultures, feeding off others' lives. "Don't ever write about me," my mother said when I began penning stories. It's a rare family that cheers to learn one of its members is writing a memoir.

*

My father was ashamed of my writing. I know because he said as much to my mother, though they were already divorced. Otherwise I would not have known he read my books, for he never mentioned them to me, and after he died his companion of nearly twenty years told me, "Be sure to take your stories." I found the books I'd signed to both of them at the back of his closet. She didn't want them. Though there were a few books on a living room shelf, mine had never been among them. The language may have been occasionally cruder than my father thought it should be — "So that's what you sent her to college for," he said to my mother — but they were not autobiographical; he could not have felt betrayed or exposed. It was more that he didn't see the value of words. To spend one's time writing was to him as wasteful, as shiftless, as it would be to photograph birds. As he saw it, people who followed their dreams were idlers as well as fools. Repairing an engine, changing a tire — those were the sort of skills that, had I possessed them, would have seemed to him worthwhile.

On the ground a group of vultures is called a venue, but a group circling in the air is a kettle, as if they are swirling in a clear cauldron, a school of black fish swimming in a soup of pure air. Ungainly on the ground with their small heads, oversize wings, and heavy bodies, a gait that is at once a lurch and a run, vultures are astonishingly graceful in flight, a glide "in God's fingerprint," as George Garrett would have it. Darwin marveled at the sight of condors soaring in high, graceful circles. Even the turkey buzzard he found so abhorrent is transformed on the wing "by its lofty, soaring and most elegant flight"; Lewis Nordan's vultures sail "like hopeful prayers." Who has not watched them wheel overhead? Floating high above the landfills that punctuate the flatness of the interstate along the east coast of Florida, they undulate like kites tethered to the earth by invisible strings. In the mountains I thrill to discover how close I am to heaven by the arc of a turkey vulture swooping below. I am too dazzled by the wideness of the sky to follow the dots of the constellations, and I forget the names of all but the most basic forms of clouds; though I know the field markings of many birds, I cannot tell a vireo from a shrike in the air; but even at a distance far too great to note the shorter tail of the black or difference in coloration on the underside of the wings, I can easily distinguish between black and turkey vultures in flight. The turkey rarely beats its wings, holding them raised in a dihedral as it tilts from side to side, rocking as if buoyed by a gentle sea; the black holds its wings flat, beats more often, and does not tilt. Lacking a sense of smell, it flies higher than the turkey, whose olfactory sense is so keen engineers look for circling turkey vultures to locate gas line leaks and NASA used them to find remains of the ill-fated space shuttle *Columbia.* The magnifying center of the black vulture's eye is so powerful that it can locate food by sight from more than a mile above, though it often follows the turkey to a corpse. Indians of the South American highlands roast and consume condors' eyes in the belief that their own eyesight will be sharpened.

In the tropics the king vulture too flies higher than the turkey; in the dense rainforest both it and the black must depend upon the *Cathartes,* the turkeys and yellow-heads, to locate carrion by smell. With its gaudy wattled head of orange, red, yellow, purple, and black, the king is the most flamboyantly colored; in flight its white back and long ebony-tipped wings are spectacular. Rounding a curve of road in the Alajuela province of Costa Rica one Christmas, our van flushed a king vulture from his roost on the living fence, and I gasped as he spread his wings and slowly swept across the cassava field to the forest canopy beyond, so stunned by the sight that he was gone before I remembered the camera beside me on the seat.

Vultures soar. Unlike most birds, whose breast muscles power the beating of the wings, creating lift and propulsion, a vulture simply opens its wings to the air currents that lift and keep it aloft. Once in a storm so torrential I pulled to the side of the interstate, I watched a small bird flying in place, flapping its wings frenetically in an effort to battle the wind, which finally blew it backward, as if it were no more than a bit of ash. The vulture's flight is so beautiful because it appears effortless. And in fact it nearly is, for a vulture uses scarcely more energy in flight than it would in standing still. It's not surprising that the Wright brothers should have designed their first plane with the curved wingtips of the turkey vulture in mind. According to Michael Alford Andrews, Andean condors spread their wingtip primaries "like fingers feeling for life as they turn." David Houston's excellent *Condors and Vultures,* to which I owe most of what I know about the bird's flight, explains that once a vulture has gained altitude by circling inside a thermal, it can "glide away into still air, where it will slowly lose altitude" until it nears the ground, finds another thermal, and climbs again. They travel at remarkably high altitudes, as great as fifteen thousand feet for the vultures of Africa and the Andean condor; Houston reports a Ruppell's griffon alleged to have collided with a commercial aircraft at thirty-seven thousand feet. Imagine the alarm of passengers looking out a plane's window to see a vulture cruising just off the wing like a seagull following a boat's wake.

In youth my father was a handsome man, tall and broad-shouldered. On the street people sometimes mistook him for the rising film star John Wayne, though by the time I was old enough to remember he was already balding, no longer auburn but gray, with the same harried look on his face of other middle-aged men who worked whatever jobs they could find to pay the mortgage and support their wives and children. He would rather have sailed on the tankers he loaded with oil before punching a clock and then driving home. I don't think his work gave him pleasure, but nor do I think he thought it should.

Vultures are big birds. The largest bird that ever existed was a vulture of the Pleistocene epoch with a wingspan of sixteen to seventeen feet. Weighing up to thirty-three pounds, with a ten-and-a-half-foot wingspan that dwarfs a grand piano, the Andean condor is still the largest and heaviest bird that flies; climbers compare the sound of the wind rushing through its feathers to that of a jet plane. The largest of the Old World species, the Himalayan griffon, is only slightly smaller. Wingtip to wingtip the turkey vulture measures seventy-nine inches, and is larger than the American black, which has the shortest wingspan of all, a mere fifty-four inches. But to crouch in the shadow of the black's scythe-tipped wings and feel the sweep of their breath as they open is to lose all sense of inches. This smallest emissary of death has an embrace of four and a half feet. When they are even partially unfolded, the bird must hunch to keep its wings from dragging on the ground. This is no bluebird.

It is said that vultures circled above Romulus and Remus. Over and over they appear in literature and film as a dark omen. In Alain

Robbe-Grillet's *Jealousy* the portentous nature of the vulture pictured atop a mast on a calendar seems to confirm in the husband's mind his wife's infidelity. The protagonist of Ernest Hemingway's "The Snows of Kilimanjaro" knows that he is going to die when the buzzards move in, three "squatting obscenely" on the ground while a dozen swirl overhead "making quick-moving shadows." In Zora Neale Hurston's *Their Eyes Were Watching God* a thousand buzzards precede the deadly hurricane. In William Faulkner's *As I Lay Dying* it is the sight of vultures in the distance that tell Darl his mother has died. And whenever we see them in a cartoon or Hollywood western, we know another outlaw is expiring just over the next hill. *Patton* opens with an African white-backed vulture sitting on the mountain over the film's title; in the first scene soldiers shoot two vultures to keep them from the battlefield corpses, denying them the cherished memories of Lewis Nordan's ancient Mississippi buzzards, who endure the lean twentieth century of roadkill by feasting on their recollection of "the glorious Festival of Dead Rebels."

My father died shortly after noon. He shot himself in the treeless backyard of the Florida house he shared with his companion, which backed on the open fairway of the community golf course, though he did not play. She had gone to the beauty parlor; it was her habit to shop afterward, to "go bumming" as she called it. When she returned a few hours later, she went through the house calling his name. She saw him through the window. I don't know if she stepped outside. In any case I'm sure she wouldn't have looked up. And perhaps there wasn't time for the buzzards to have gathered.

Though from the vulture's point of view it would hardly seem to matter which side prevails, many nations have used vultures as symbols of victory. In Samuel Johnson's fable "The Vulture," a female is overheard instructing her young in the arts of a vulture's life — the easiest way to find food, she tells them, is to look for the place where enemies wage war. In his eclectic *Vulture: Nature's Ghastly Gourmet*, a book to which I am as indebted as I am to Houston's, Wayne Grady lists a number of ancient monuments decorated with gruesome depictions of vultures devouring or hovering over the slain enemy.

But as the turkey vulture has extended its range northward,

some see the bird not as the harbinger of death but the harbinger of spring. Bruce Ehresman, a biologist with the Iowa Department of Natural Resources, calls turkey vultures "much more reliable than robins." Scott Weidensaul, whose observations contest the notion that turkey vultures are nonmigratory, maintains that they are the real sign of spring in the central Appalachians, reappearing "most often around the first week of February," followed by common grackles, then the red-winged blackbirds, until finally the robin returns at the end of February or early March, though only if the snow has melted. Here, on the Piedmont Plateau of North Carolina, I see no such sign, and so I wait for the Bradford pears and poke around the ivy for crocus.

My father was from Wisconsin. He grew tired of waiting for spring, and when he retired he moved to Florida. He might have moved to El Paso, but he didn't like the radio station. In Florida, he reported proudly, it was summer nearly all year round, which is why the black vulture, which does not tolerate cooler temperatures as well as the turkey, is so common there. Vultures used to drink from the bucket beneath his downspout.

I have often observed black vultures at Florida's Myakka River State Park. There they flock in great numbers, trolling the air above the lake, roosting on railings and roofs as if they are basking — and perhaps they are — the russet winter afternoon sun warming their dull black feathers and lending a subtle lavender to the wrinkled gray skin of their heads. One year when they seemed particularly active, I spotted half a dozen standing on a car parked beside the lake, where they appeared to be gorging on bloody bits of flesh, though the grisly morsels turned out to be only shreds of the car's red upholstery. The windows were closed, and in my ignorance, assuming their olfactory organ to be as keen as a bear's, I supposed the owner had left lunch meat in a back-seat cooler, astonished that they could have pecked through the roof as easily as a chick liberates itself from the egg. On the lake a boat was gliding toward shore, and as I watched, the occupant leaped to his feet, screaming, "My car! My car! Get off my car, you damn buzzards!"

But in my photographs the unbroken shell of blue-gray metal reflects their silvery talons like water. A few years later a chatty ranger at the Everglades Anhinga Trail told me that Ford had used fish oil in the sealants on the 1999 Taurus. The occasion for our conversation was the unusual number of black vultures on the trail, brought to the ground by the cool weather. He had just come from the parking lot, where on such days he had seen flocks of black vultures attack the sealant so vigorously that tourists returned to their cars to find the windshields popped out. It's true that the black, which prefers coastal areas, often dines on fish. At the Wild Bird Center on Key Largo I have watched it eat its sardine more delicately than my dog eats his meat and kibble. Once at the Anhinga Trail my husband, son, and I all observed a black vulture attending a great blue heron that had caught a fish too large for it to swallow. The heron tried it head-first, then tail-first, and sideways, dropping the fish to the ground after each attempt and walking a few steps away as if to consider another approach, but the vulture moved in to feed only after the heron gave up and departed. Perhaps its patience was only caution, for the same ranger regaled me with the tale of a researcher who got too close to a great blue, which drove its beak into the man's skull and killed him — most aggressive bird there is, he confided. Who can say whether a vulture is fearful or forbearing? In Darwin's era vultures liked to tear the leather from ships' rigging, though the leather would have borne no more visual resemblance to a cow than Ford's sealant to a gar. They may be prudent, but if it's true they have no sense of smell, they are not just scavengers, but vandals.

Properly speaking, we should not call them buzzards, buzzard being a British designation for a large hawk. The word comes from the French *busard*, which means hawk, and in the Old World *busard* refers to the genus of soaring hawks called *Buteo*, the most common of which in North America is the familiar red-tailed hawk; in Australia the bird called a black-breasted buzzard is a hawk of the genus *Hamirostra*. But we do not speak properly; in common American usage a buzzard is the same thing as a vulture; it is a contemptible, cantankerous old person; it is a greedy and ruthless person who preys upon others. As an adjective, in the past it was used to mean senseless or stupid. A search of books on Amazon.com brings up 342 results for vultures and 363 for buzzards, including one titled *The Old Buzzard Had It Coming*.

*

My father loved cars, though he never drove anything fancier than a Ford Crown Victoria. He never kept a journal, but he kept a log of his gas mileage. Mechanical though he was, a noise beneath the hood sent him into a panic. A dent or a scratch drove him wild. Though we were in an empty parking lot, he was so afraid I would hit something in the single driving lesson he agreed to give me that I didn't learn to drive for another ten years. My husband taught me. Many years after that, when I had failed to sell a new novel and had to think about buying a used car instead of a new one, I asked my father's advice. To my astonishment he sent me a check for five thousand dollars. I think all he ever really wanted was for me to ask his opinion on something that mattered to him. He didn't care if I told him I loved him, but he wanted that token of respect.

Once I came across a lone black vulture feeding at the side of the road from Florida City to Key Biscayne. When I slowed the car to watch, it paused and looked up, standing over the carcass and watching me until I drove on. An hour or so later, when I drove back the same way, there was no evidence that it had ever been there. Perhaps it dragged the skeleton into the brush the moment I was out of sight. Like a dog, it would have carried the corpse in its mouth, for though the vulture's talons are as fearsome as an eagle's in appearance, their grasp is weak. Only the bearded vulture uses its talons to grip.

Generally the black is a communal feeder. Though in the rain-forest the turkey vulture is most likely to locate a kill, at a larger carcass it yields to the black, and both yield to the king. Even among its own ranks the turkey is a hierarchical diner, but feeding is less a competition than a collaboration, with each species dining on a different part of the animal. When larger vultures tear into mammals the size of horses or cows, they make the flesh available to the turkey, which has the weakest beak and on its own must content itself with animals the size of chipmunks and squirrels. The long necks of the largest vultures allow them to reach into the organs, while others feast on skin, tendons, and the tougher meat; the turkey, black, and hooded species take the scraps and pick the bones clean. In its habitat the bearded, the only vulture to have a feathered head, is the last to feed, for its specialty is bones, which it picks up with its feet, swooping down to crack them against a rock.

It is reputed to prepare tortoises the same way; the ancient Greeks blamed it for the death of Aeschylus. As Wayne Grady retells the story, a bearded vulture with a tortoise in its talons mistook his bald head for a rock and dropped the tortoise to crack its shell, instead cracking the poet's. I like the irony, but the image that enchants me is that of the feeding chimango, the caracara that Darwin observed to be the last to leave the table, lingering at the carcass so long that it might often be "seen within the ribs of a cow or a horse like a bird in a cage." I picture the cathedral arch of those bleached white ribs, inside it a dark canary without song.

At the table my parents, my brother, and I often sat with our heads bowed. It was not to pray. We were trying not to talk. My parents didn't seem to remember how to have a conversation, though once, surely, they had been able to talk without erupting, had been able to speak without a fight. My father had so many allergies he didn't enjoy eating anyway. We picked at our food and waited for the meal to be over.

The turkey vulture is more solitary and less aggressive than the black. While the black defends itself by vomiting, as a friend who shot one with an air rifle as a child learned firsthand, the turkey more often plays dead. At the Carolina Raptor Center, which stages a photo shoot every spring, I have been close enough to touch it, though I would not. The bird's very solitariness precludes it.

To see a turkey vulture up close is to know the bird's tragic beauty, for there is a majesty to the crimson head, bare save for a sparse black stubble; the bird looks less bald than vulnerable and shorn, a Nazi collaborator exposed before a French village. The raised nostrils have no internal division; they are like the space left by a handle, the eye of a thick red needle; one looks not into but through them. All the vilification and fear the vulture inspires seem contained in the sidelong wary sadness of the eye, not the sharp black stare of an eagle or a heron's mean pupil in its fixed yellow ring, but a doleful attention that is the same soft shade of brown as my dog's. The bird's muteness sits upon its shoulders. It knows what death tastes like, but cannot speak of the flavor. To see a turkey vulture up close is to be reminded of death not as portent but as the weight of an unbearable witness. Would he rather have been a nightingale? He cannot say. His dirge has no throat, his wisdom no voice. Two million years of silence haunt his expression. To see a turkey vulture up close is to know what loneliness looks like.

When my father was young he did some hunting. When I was young he liked to fish. But he was not the kind of man who took up hobbies. He was a loner. He had friends, but no close ones. I don't think he ever had a pet. He filled his time by fixing things, so many things it seems now as if everything we owned must have broken. He gave to objects the kind of attention he could not deliver to people; yet I have no recollection of his hands, no memory of the texture of the skin or the shape of his nails. He had beautiful handwriting, but no inclination for words. His name and "Love, Dad" beneath the printed verse of a birthday card are the only words I can see in the clean, graceful loops of his script.

In the United States it is illegal both to shoot a vulture and to keep one as a pet. I would think that few desire to, though the sister of a former president of Ecuador kept a condor, and wildlife rehabilitators report that vultures are intelligent, more so than other raptors, as well as mischievous and inquisitive. Darwin claimed that they stole a pocket compass in a red morocco case and carried off a big black hat. At the Carolina Raptor Center one developed a habit of untying the staff members' shoestrings; when they tried to trick it by wearing shoes with Velcro tabs, the bird learned to undo those too. I think of George the Goose, who used to unlace my boots at the train station in Princeton Junction the year I lived in New Jersey. Or my dog, who loved to steal socks and make us chase him through the house when he was a pup, who now greets me every morning by dropping a tennis ball on my face. Like crows, which I have often observed skating across the frozen surface of my backyard pond, vultures frolic. Young blacks toss rocks like balls. They play tag and follow-the-leader. According to the Turkey Vulture Society, some of the soaring and circling they do may be for fun, just as Darwin suspected. Their lives seemed so pleasurable to Edward Abbey — "floating among the clouds all day, seldom stirring a feather" — that he insisted he wanted to be reincarnated as one. They're not just personable birds, they're sweet, insists the society's president. Vultures raised by humans love and trust them; even after rejoining their natural communities they continue to respond to human attention. One is reported to have followed a boy to his school bus each day, flying off to forage only after the bus was gone, and returning in the afternoon to accompany the boy home. Only my dog comes close to being that loyal.

My father was a misogynist, a deeply conservative man who felt women should be seen and not heard. The whole problem with his marriage, as he saw it, was that my mother didn't want to follow; a marriage, he said, can't have two leaders. Still, he always claimed that he would not be there for her if she ever got sick — in that case, he seemed to believe, it was everyone for herself. He detested women drivers and did not see the point of sending me to college. When my son, his only grandchild, was born, he said he guessed now I was fulfilled and wouldn't need to write.

Though we think of the Grim Reaper as male, in most vultures it is not possible to tell the difference between male and female by appearance, and in Federico Garcia Lorca's *Blood Wedding*, the figure of Death is not a vulture itself but a beggar woman in a vulture costume. The ancient Egyptians believed that only female vultures existed; they were able to perpetuate the species because they were impregnated by the south and southeast winds. The Egyptian goddesses Nekhbet and Mut wore vulture headdresses. Nekhbet, goddess of Upper Egypt, often portrayed as a vulture hovering at the pharaoh's head, was also the goddess of childbirth; the hieroglyph for Mut, whom the Greeks associated with Hera, meant mother. The crown of Upper Egypt bore the image of a vulture, and the gold facemask of King Tut has a vulture over the right eye and a cobra, symbol of Lower Egypt, over the left. So sacred was the bird to the Egyptians that "pharaoh's chicken" is the first wild animal known to have been given legal protection.

In some versions of Mayan legend the vulture is the mother and protector of the Serpent Priestess, who lived among jaguars, though in other versions the bird is male, perhaps in reference to the king vulture, whose scientific name, *Sarcorhamphus papa*, means the pope's fleshy beak, and refers to the bulb of bright orange skin above the orange-and-black beak. The common name predates the Spanish conquest of South America. A royal tomb dating from A.D. 450 in the pre-Columbian city of La Milpa in Belize contains the remains of a ruler known as Bird Jaguar whose adornments include a large pendant of a king vulture's head carved from jade. Wayne Grady reports that in Mayan legend humans descended from jaguars; the vulture, who was personified as a lord or king, was the messenger who mediated between humans and the gods, "'the conduit to the gods and the afterworld . . . deified and venerated as an ancestor and god after his death'" (quoted without attribution).

Some Indian villages in Peru have annual ceremonies involving the condor. One reenacts the Spanish conquest and Quechua myth by pairing a bull, introduced to Peru by the Spanish, with a native condor, whose feet are sewn to the back of the bull with strips of leather. In a frenzy the two creatures buck, pitch, and lurch around the plaza together. If the condor survives, it is released, a victory that symbolizes successful Indian resistance, though I can't help wondering how the Indians overcome the resistance of bird and beast to the process of the sewing.

The Andean condor, which appeared on the pottery and textiles of cultures that predate the Incas, is still a symbol of strength and endurance in South America, figuring on the national crests of Bolivia, Chile, Colombia, and Ecuador. In Chile the condor is a coin featuring the bird's image. The name of Chile's capital province, Cundinamarca, comes from the native word for condor, and in Bolivia the Order of the Condor is the highest award of merit.

In North America we know the California condor as the Thunderbird through the legends of the Tlingit, who believed the flapping of its wings caused thunder and lightning to flash from its eyes. In many West Coast native communities shamans were believed to receive their powers from the condor. The Costanoans raised raptors to be sacrificed at funerals, eagles to Venus and condors to Mars. In Iroquois legend the Golden Eagle, Head Chief of all the birds, chose vultures as his faithful servants, for it was his law that the earth be kept clean.

In African folklore the bird's ability to show up wherever there is a carcass is a sign of extrasensory powers; many Africans believe they dream the location of food.

Not all myths venerate vultures. In Hindu belief, though vultures are carriers of the human spirit, they are also the gatekeepers of hell. In European folklore the bearded vulture is reputed to be as predatory as the wolf, though its otherworldliness makes it more frightening. In North American Tsimshian legends the condor abducts young women and destroys its rivals with a great wind. And in ancient Greek myth, it was not two eagles but two bearded vultures that flew down to tear out Prometheus's liver every day.

My father was not a religious man. As a child he was sent to Catholic schools, where a nun rapped his hand with a metal-edged ruler and split his knuckles. Did he look up, I wonder, when he felt the chill of her shadow, or did he just hear the sweeping wing of the nun's black habit as she brought the blade of the ruler down? I don't know if he had any faith before. He never did after. His view of death was practical, his view of life dark. He threatened to die so often it was a shock when he did.

Both Tibetans and the Parsees of India dispose of their dead by feeding them to vultures. According to myth, Sakyamuni Buddha gave himself to feed a hungry tiger; in another version he fed his own flesh to a hawk in order to spare a pigeon — thus sky burial is regarded as a final act of charity in which the deceased provides food to sustain living things, and the Tibetan name for the practice, *jhator*, means giving alms to the birds. Interference with *jhator* is a serious breach of Tibetan religion, in which the vultures, sacred messengers called *dakinis*, the Tibetan equivalent of angels, are believed to carry the soul up to heaven, where it will await reincarnation; Tibetans fear they will not return if driven away. In Xue Xinran's nonfiction account of a Chinese woman's search for her soldier husband in Tibet, the Tibetans were so angry at the Chinese soldier, who accidentally disrupted a wartime sky burial by shooting one of the vultures, that he could placate them only by killing himself, allowing the Tibetans to call back the sacred birds by feeding his body to them.

Although *jhator* is embedded in Tibetan Buddhism, its origins predate the religion in Tibet. The kings of the Yalung Dynasty were entombed and the remains of Dalai Lamas and other high Buddhist figures are preserved in stupas or encased in gold, but neither burial nor cremation is practical in a country with so little fuel and such hard ground. Until Buddhism was introduced in the ninth century, water burial was the most common method of disposal — poor people simply dropped the bodies of their dead into a river, though in more elaborate forms of water burial the corpse was cut into small pieces to be consumed by fish, just as it is dismembered and hacked into pieces for the vultures in *jhator,* which is now chosen by more than three-quarters of Tibetans; those who cannot afford the *o-yogin* butcher simply place their dead on high rocks for the birds and wild dogs.

At the Drigung Monastery in central Tibet, the best known of the three major sites, as many as ten sky burials are conducted a day. Here the vultures are so sated they must be coaxed to eat, but at many of the more remote sites the birds are so ravenous they must be fended off with sticks while the body is prepared. Though it is considered a bad omen if they do not consume the entire corpse, a sign that demons have taken over the spirit, some remote sites are strewn with tufts of hair and bones, as well as scraps of clothing, beer bottles, broken ax handles, and rusty blades. At Langmusi on the Sichuan border, where tickets to the *jhator* illustrated with a flock of vultures devouring a human body are sold despite the efforts of the Chinese to restrict attendance, one witness reports seeing a headless, armless skeleton.

At such remote sites the ceremony may be no more than a prayer uttered by the single butcher, but at Drigung preparations begin the day before, when the body is washed, shaved, placed in a fetal position, and wrapped in a white shroud. Lamas chanting prayers to release the soul from purgatory lead the procession to the charnel ground, a large fenced meadow with a circle of stones surrounded by prayer flags hanging from chortens. At dawn the sky-burial master blows a horn and lights a fire of juniper or mulberry branches to summon the vultures to roll out a five-colored road between heaven and earth, though surely the incense also helps purify the foul air. While the mourners watch, the *o-yogin* butcher or *tomden* rips off the shroud and begins the dismemberment, cajoling the vultures as he hacks off limbs, removes the flesh, and smashes the bones. Often he and his assistants laugh and chat as they work, mixing the pulverized bones with a *tsampa* of roasted barley flour, yak butter, and tea to make them more palatable to the birds. All the while they speak to the vultures, coaxing, inviting. "Come eat," they say in Tibetan. "Birdies," they call, in a language that seems less their own than the birds'.

In India, where the actual consumption of the body is hidden from view, sky burials are required by orthodox Parsee doctrine, which holds that corpses contaminate anything they touch and therefore cannot be buried, cremated, or thrown in the river. Here the body is placed in a closed granite structure with one-hundred-foot towers known as the *dakhma*. Once all clothing and adornment have been removed with hooked rods and the body has been washed, perfumed with myrrh, and blessed by the officiating priest, it is placed on one of the three-tiered stones atop the towers, open at the top to the vultures. When the body is ready, a signal is given, and male mourners in a nearby prayer pavilion begin praying. It is the voice of their prayers that summons the birds.

There was no service for my father; he wanted none. No prayers, no eulogies. He would have liked a brief notice of his death in the newsletter put out by Texaco, the company for which he had worked for forty years, but his companion was afraid for strangers to know she was alone, and so he had no obituary either. Only a death certificate marked his passing. His body was cremated, his ashes scattered from a plane over the Gulf of Mexico. He made the arrangements himself. Years later, in a restaurant where I had taken her to lunch, my mother said, out of the blue, "I think it's good what your father did. Potassium for the fish." I was so upset — we were *eating;* we hadn't been talking about my father, except for the running conversation in her head — I dropped my fork and went to the ladies' room and wept.

My father was who he was. He died how he died. But because he was my father I loved him.

Though it seems as if the symbol of death ought to be eternal, in Asia vultures have been dying off. What would we fear if the buzzard were gone? In the United States, though populations of black and turkey vultures are increasing, thanks to our bounty of roadkill, a captive breeding program was necessary to save the California condor, which came so close to extinction that by 1987 there were only three birds left in the wild. It will take more than that to save the Old World long-billed griffon and the slender-billed and Indian white-backed vultures, all listed as Critically Endangered, the highest level of risk for extinction, by the World Conservation Union. So radically has the vulture population of South Asia declined that in 2001 the Parsee Council of India installed solar reflectors to speed decomposition in the *dakhma,* where more than a hundred vultures are needed to keep up with the three or four corpses a day. In Europe the vulture population is one percent of what it was in the nineteenth century. Because they are slow breeders and eat at the top of the food chain, vultures are more vulnerable than most birds to environmental threats. We may have learned the lesson of DDT, but only recently has the effect of diclofenac been recognized. This nonsteroidal anti-inflammatory used to treat sick cattle in South Asia causes renal failure in vultures; what is good for the cow is fatal to the bird, so lethal that contamination of less than one percent of livestock carcasses created the most rapid decline in population ever recorded for a wild bird. In 2006 Pakistan became the last country in South Asia to ban its use; had it not, the vultures of South Asia would have gone the way of the dinosaurs and woolly mammoths.

Who would miss them? It is not just the Parsees who are affected by their disappearance. Carcasses of animals that the vultures are no longer numerous enough to consume have created public health problems in Pakistan, India, and Nepal. Besides the diseases spread by the carcasses themselves, rotting carrion has resulted in a booming population of feral dogs and outbreaks of rabies. We may loathe vultures, but we need them.

My father left no note, of course. I wouldn't have expected one, though I looked.

When vultures woo they seem to summon all the voice their unequipped throats can muster. The New World black spreads his wings, lowers his head, and emits a puffing sound; the turkey groans. It is as close to a serenade as these creatures without song can come. When they warn they grunt or hiss; they may even snarl. But what I hear does not sound like a grunt or a hiss, neither a snarl nor a groan, not a puffing or even a croaking coo; it is more a low, embryonic woofing, not the voice itself but the anticipation of one reverberating deep inside the throat. I cannot tell whether they are warning me or wooing, though here in their midst, surrounded by a flock of them at the edge of an empty parking lot in the Everglades, it would seem important to know.

In the end they ignore me. They wander off; I pack up my camera and tripod and go. I will learn their habits and more, but I will never speak their language.

Yet some of the happiest hours of my life have been spent in the open air of a salt marsh in the company of birds. It is an acquired taste, for I grew up in the Midwest, where farmland falls away from the road like a low tide and the highway seems an endless bridge over nothing, the horizon so treeless and vast that if someone beside a farmhouse a mile away lifted a hand to wave I would see it. The Midwest affords everyone a vulture's view. Perhaps that is why it has always seemed such a lonely place to me. Even in the safety of my car I feel dwarfed and exposed.

If I ever saw vultures wheeling in the sky over the midwestern cornfields, I don't remember. The first time I saw one on the ground was at Merritt Island National Wildlife Refuge in Florida. My father had died less than two months before, and I was on my way home from his house, the house that I now owned, where I had spent the past week working on his estate. I knew of the refuge only from a picture on a calendar; it was not a place I had always longed to see, but a place that was on my way home. Stopping was an attempt to give that dark errand some small facet of pleasure.

Driving the highway through the Everglades to Flamingo, I always feel on the edge of openness in the way I am on the edge of it as I pass over the midwestern farmland, a traveler, an observer, a person apart. It is different at Merritt Island, where an unpaved road winds along dikes once used for mosquito control, a sandy seven-mile lane through 140,000 acres of saltwater estuaries, brackish marsh, and freshwater lagoons. I rarely saw another car in the two days I spent cruising the wildlife drive and paved back road, the radio off, windows and sunroof open, eating peanut butter crackers for lunch and peeing in a Dixie cup I dumped out the window. In the afternoon I walked the trails through the hammocks of oak and palm, listening to the drill of a pileated woodpecker whose bright red crest I could just spot through the trees. At dawn I parked beside the small swales where egrets, ibises, and wood storks fed and squabbled. Each time I opened my door they flushed upward with a great whooshing of wings, then settled again like parachutes, pecking and squawking. On the ponds there were great black formations of coots, and in the distance a streamer of dazzling white pelicans. In the clarity of the weak winter light the mudflats glittered, quivering with sandpipers and tiny crustaceans, while an osprey sailed the far sky. A rail skittered into the brush at the start of the Cruickshank Trail, the five-mile loop I hiked around a shallow lagoon and through the marsh while a balmy breeze wisped at my collar and fingered my hair. The only sound was the whistling *kik-kik-kik* of the terns that swooped and dipped and flashed their forked white origami tails against the bright blue heaven. I had not spoken a word for two days. The landscape was as wide, exposed, and dwarfing as the Midwest, but I had disappeared inside it. When I got back to my car, four turkey vultures blocked the narrow road. They were huge, rough-feathered, dark, a color I would describe as more a dirty chocolate than black; the sun shone off the red heads and ivory hooks of their beaks. Though I confess to superstition — I will back away from a black cat and circle an open ladder — they did not strike me as an omen. Despite the recentness of my grief, they did not remind me of death or its tedious business. They were simply there, as I was, in a kind of matter-of-factness so profound we can know it only in nature. It may have been a minute or ten that we regarded one another. Then they waddled to the side and let me pass. That evening, driving the back road, I came upon a vulture tree. It was dusk, and the hunkering vultures and bare black bones of the branches were silhouetted against the faded dust-blue sky in a way that seemed incredibly beautiful to me. It is in such confrontations with the eternal shape of death that we know most fully we're alive.

In "The Snows of Kilimanjaro" the dying writer dreams that he is saved, carried by a small silver plane up over the wildebeest and zebras, the forests and bamboo slopes, only to understand that where he is going is into the unbelievable whiteness of death. He is borne on the buzzard's wing, like a Buddhist carried up to heaven by the *dakhini*.

I do not dream of vultures. I have never dreamed of flying, though as a child, lying in the dark, awake, voiceless, listening to my parents fight, I used to dream of escape. Perhaps that's why I grew up to be a writer. In bed at night now my dog nests against my thigh. Sometimes in his sleep he twitches and yips, chasing squirrels, tasting the hunt. Africans believe that vultures dream the location of their food. But who really knows where the dog and vulture soar while they sleep? Why would we dream, if never to leave the domain of our waking world? I don't know where I go as I sink into the blackness of that temporary death, only that in the morning I wake with a low woofing in my throat that, if I'm lucky, will turn into song.

Contributors' Notes

PATRICIA BRIESCHKE's work can be found in *Rainbow Curve, Appalachee Review, Karamu, PMS, The Rambler, Sou'wester, The MacGuffin, New Millennium Writings, Prism International,* and in the second edition of *The Best Creative Nonfiction* (2008). In addition to teaching creative writing, she has a Ph.D. in public policy and has worked as a professor in Ohio and New York. She lives in Waccabuc, New York.

RICH COHEN is the author of *Tough Jews, The Avengers, Machers and Rockers, Lake Effect,* and *Sweet and Low.* His work has appeared in *The New Yorker* and *Rolling Stone,* among many other publications, and he is a contributing editor to *Vanity Fair.* He lives in Connecticut.

BERNARD COOPER's most recent book is *The Bill from My Father* (2006), a memoir about his relationship with a father who once sent the author an itemized bill for the cost of his upbringing. Cooper is the recipient of a PEN/Hemingway Award, an O. Henry Prize, and fellowships in literature from the Guggenheim Foundation and the National Endowment for the Arts. This is his fourth appearance in *The Best American Essays.*

ATUL GAWANDE, a 2006 MacArthur fellow, is a general surgeon at the Brigham and Women's Hospital in Boston and an associate professor at Harvard Medical School and the Harvard School of Public Health. He has been a staff writer for *The New Yorker* since 1998. His first book, *Complications: A Surgeon's Notes on an Imperfect Science,* was a *New York Times* bestseller and a finalist for the 2002 National Book Award. His most recent book, also a *Times* bestseller, is *Better: A Surgeon's Notes on Performance* (2007). Gawande lives with his wife and three children in Newton, Massachusetts.

ALBERT GOLDBARTH, who was born in Chicago in 1948, is the Adele V. Davis Distinguished Professor of Humanities at Wichita State University. He is the author of many volumes of poetry (two of which have received the National Book Critics Circle Award) and five collections of essays (of which *Many Circles: New and Selected Essays* received the PEN/West Award in creative nonfiction). His forthcoming book is a collection of poetry, *To Be Read in 500 Years.*

EMILY R. GROSHOLZ is the author of five books of poetry, most recently *Feuilles/Leaves,* a suite of poems with French translations by Alain Madeleine-Perdrillat, illustrated with studies for Bach's *Goldberg Variations* by Farhad Ostovani. She is also the author of three books of philosophy, including *Representation and Productive Ambiguity in Mathematics and the Sciences,* and has edited collections of essays on Simone de Beauvoir, W.E.B. Du Bois, Maxine Kumin, and the philosophy of mathematics. She is a professor of philosophy, African-American studies, and English at Pennsylvania State University and a member of the research group REHSEIS/CNRS/University of Paris-Diderot; since 1984 she has served as an advisory editor for the *Hudson Review.* She lives with her husband, Robert Edwards, and their four children in State College, Pennsylvania.

ANTHONY LANE was born in 1962 and educated at Cambridge. Since 1993 he has been a film critic for *The New Yorker.* A collection of his writings for the magazine, *Nobody's Perfect,* was published in 2002. In 2001 he received a National Magazine Award for reviews and criticism.

JONATHAN LETHEM is the author of seven novels, including *Girl in Landscape* and *You Don't Love Me Yet.* His fifth, *Motherless Brooklyn,* won the National Book Critics Circle Award and has been translated into more than twenty languages. In 2005 he was named a fellow of the MacArthur Foundation. He lives with his family in Brooklyn, New York, and Maine.

ARIEL LEVY is a staff writer at *The New Yorker* and the author of *Female Chauvinist Pigs: Women and the Rise of Raunch Culture.* She lives on Shelter Island with her spouse and their gay wedding china.

JAMAL MAHJOUB is a British-Sudanese novelist who has lived in Khartoum, the United Kingdom, and Denmark, and now lives in Barcelona. He writes in English and has published seven novels, several of which have been translated into a number of languages, including French, German, Spanish, Italian, and Turkish. His writing has won many prizes, including the Guardian/Heinemann African Short Story Prize and the Prix de l'Astrolabe in France. He is working on a novel and nonfiction book on Sudan.

LOUIS MENAND is the author of *The Metaphysical Club*, which won the 2002 Pulitzer Prize in history, and *American Studies*, a collection of essays. He is the Anne T. and Robert M. Bass Professor of English at Harvard. He was a contributing editor at the *New York Review of Books* from 1994 to 2001. Since 2001 he has been a staff writer for *The New Yorker.*

ANDER MONSON lives in Tucson, where he teaches at the University of Arizona. He is the author of three books: *Neck Deep and Other Predicaments* (essays, 2007), *Other Electricities* (fiction, 2005), and *Vacationland* (poems, 2005). "Solipsism" was written for his website, otherelectricities.com, using Adobe's Dreamweaver software, to accompany and expand the artifact of the *Neck Deep* book, and was subsequently reprinted in, and redesigned for, *Pinch*. He edits the magazine *Diagram* (thediagram.com) and the New Michigan Press.

RICK MOODY is the author of four novels, three collections of stories, and a memoir, *The Black Veil*. His most recent publication is *Right Livelihoods: Three Novellas*.

HUGH RAFFLES is the author of *In Amazonia: A Natural History*, which won the Victor Turner Prize for ethnographic writing and was named as an American Library Association Outstanding Academic Title. His work has appeared in *Granta*, *Natural History*, and *Public Culture*, among other publications. His latest book, to be published next year, is an exploration of encounters between humans and insects in a wide range of times and places. He is a professor of anthropology at the New School, in New York.

DAVID SEDARIS is the author of the books *Dress Your Family in Corduroy and Denim*, *Me Talk Pretty One Day*, *Naked*, *Holidays on Ice*, and *Barrel Fever.* He is a regular contributor to *The New Yorker* and National Public Radio's *This American Life*. "This Old House" is published in his latest collection of essays, *When You Are Engulfed in Flames*.

SAM SHAW's writing has appeared in numerous magazines and anthologies, including *The Best American Mystery Stories*, *The Best American Nonrequired Reading*, and *The Best American Sports Writing*. He also writes for television and has contributed to NPR's *This American Life*. He lives in Brooklyn, New York.

CHARLES SIMIC is a poet, essayist, and translator. He was born in Yugoslavia in 1938 and immigrated to the United States in 1954. His first poems were published in 1959, when he was twenty-one. In 1961 he was drafted into the U.S. Army, and in 1966 he earned his bachelor's degree from New York University while working at night. Since 1967 he has published twenty books of poetry, seven books of essays, a memoir, and numerous books of translations of French, Serbian, Croatian, Macedonian, and Slovenian poetry, for which he has received many awards, including the Pulitzer Prize, the Griffin Prize, a MacArthur fellowship, and a Wallace Stevens Award. *The Voice at 3:00 A.M.*, a volume of selected and new poems, was published in 2003, and a new book of poems, *That Little Something*, appeared in the spring of 2008. Simic is a frequent contributor to the *New York Review of Books* and the poetry editor of the *Paris Review*. He is an emeritus professor at the University of New Hampshire, where he has taught since 1973, and the poet laureate of the United States.

LAUREN SLATER is the author of five books of nonfiction and one collection of short stories. *Opening Skinner's Box: Great Psychological Experiments of the Twentieth Century* was nominated for a Los Angeles Times Book Prize in science writing and won the Bild der Wissenschaft Award in Germany for the groundbreaking science book of the year. Slater has received many other awards — including, recently, from the National Endowment for the Arts — and her work has been translated into eighteen languages. Her essays and articles appear frequently in *National Geographic, Elle,* and the *New York Times*. This is her third appearance in *The Best American Essays*, and she served as guest editor of the 2006 volume. Slater is at work on a book tentatively titled *Zoophilia: My Life with Animals*.

JOHN UPDIKE was born in 1932 in Shillington, Pennsylvania. After graduation from Harvard in 1954 and a year at an English art school, he worked for two years for *The New Yorker's* "Talk of the Town" department. Since 1957 he has lived in Massachusetts as a freelance writer. His most recent books include a novel, *Terrorist,* and *Due Considerations: Essays and Criticism. The Widows of Eastwick,* his twenty-third novel, will be published in 2008.

JOE WENDEROTH has written three books of poetry — *Disfortune, It Is If I Speak,* and *No Real Light* — the novel *Letters to Wendy's,* and *The Holy Spirit of Life: Essays Written for John Ashcroft's Secret Self.* His films can be seen on YouTube. Wenderoth is an associate professor of English and teaches in the graduate creative writing program at the University of California, Davis.

LEE ZACHARIAS has published essays in *Shenandoah, Gettysburg Review, Five Points, Prairie Schooner, Michigan Quarterly Review, Crab Orchard Review,* and other journals, including *Southern Humanities Review,* where "Buzzards" won the 2008 Hoepfner Award. The author of *Helping Muriel Make It Through the Night* (short stories) and the novel *Lessons,* she teaches at the University of North Carolina, Greensboro.

Notable Essays of 2007

SELECTED BY ROBERT ATWAN

Notable Special Issues of 2007

Portland, The Difficulty of Saints, ed. Brian Doyle, Winter.

Sewanee Review, Literary Peregrinations, ed. George Core, Summer.

Shenandoah, Essays on Tom Wolfe, ed. R. T. Smith, Spring.

Tampa Review, Mary McCarthy: A Creative Nonfiction Appreciation, ed. Richard Mathews, 33/34.

Tin House, Evil, ed. Rob Spillman, 31.

Virginia Quarterly Review, South America in the 21st Century, ed. Daniel Alarcón and Ted Genoways, Fall.

Washington Post Magazine, The Things That Matter, ed. Tom Shroder, December 2.

Wilson Quarterly, Overdrive: Competition in American Life, ed. Steven Lagerfeld, Autumn.

THE BEST AMERICAN SERIES®

THE BEST AMERICAN SHORT STORIES® 2008
Salman Rushdie, editor, Heidi Pitlor, series editor
ISBN: 978-0-618-78876-7 $28.00 CL
ISBN: 978-0-618-78877-4 $14.00 PA

THE BEST AMERICAN NONREQUIRED READING™ 2008
Edited by Dave Eggers, introduction by Judy Blume
ISBN: 978-0-618-90282-8 $28.00 CL
ISBN: 978-0-618-90283-5 $14.00 PA

THE BEST AMERICAN COMICS™ 2008
Lynda Barry, editor, Jessica Abel and Matt Madden, series editors
ISBN: 978-0-618-98976-8 $22.00 POB

THE BEST AMERICAN ESSAYS® 2008
Adam Gopnik, editor, Robert Atwan, series editor
ISBN: 978-0-618-98331-5 $28.00 CL
ISBN: 978-0-618-98322-3 $14.00 PA

THE BEST AMERICAN MYSTERY STORIES™ 2008
George Pelecanos, editor, Otto Penzler, series editor
ISBN: 978-0-618-81266-0 $28.00 CL
ISBN: 978-0-618-81267-7 $14.00 PA

THE BEST AMERICAN SPORTS WRITING™ 2008
William Nack, editor, Glenn Stout, series editor
ISBN: 978-0-618-75117-4 $28.00 CL
ISBN: 978-0-618-75118-1 $14.00 PA

THE BEST AMERICAN TRAVEL WRITING™ 2008
Anthony Bourdain, editor, Jason Wilson, series editor
ISBN: 978-0-618-85863-7 $28.00 CL
ISBN: 978-0-618-85864-4 $14.00 PA

THE BEST AMERICAN SCIENCE AND NATURE WRITING™ 2008
Jerome Groopman, editor, Tim Folger, series editor
ISBN: 978-0-618-83446-4 $28.00 CL
ISBN: 978-0-618-83447-1 $14.00 PA

THE BEST AMERICAN SPIRITUAL WRITING™ 2008
Edited by Philip Zaleski, introduction by Jimmy Carter
ISBN: 978-0-618-83374-0 $28.00 CL
ISBN: 978-0-618-83375-7 $14.00 PA